Quilter's Complete Guide

Marianne Fons & Liz Porter

Library of Congress Catalog Number: 92-060992
Hardcover ISBN: 0-8487-1099-1
Softcover ISBN: 0-8487-1152-1
Manufactured in the United States of America
Ninth Printing   1996

Published by Oxmoor House, Inc., and Leisure Arts, Inc.

Oxmoor House, Inc.
Book Division of Southern Progress Corporation
P.O. Box 2463, Birmingham, AL 35201

Editor-in-Chief: Nancy J. Fitzpatrick
Senior Crafts Editor: Susan Ramey Wright
Senior Editor, Editorial Services: Olivia Wells
Director of Manufacturing: Jerry Higdon
Art Director: James Boone

Quilter's Complete Guide

Editor: Sandra L. O'Brien
Editorial Assistant: Shannon Leigh Sexton
Designer: Melissa Jones Clark
Copy Chief: Mary Jean Haddin
Copy Editor: Susan Smith Cheatham
Assistant Copy Editor: L. Amanda Owens
Production Manager: Rick Litton
Associate Production Manager: Theresa L. Beste
Production Assistant: Pam Beasley Bullock
Patterns and Illustrations: Melinda Johansson, Karen T. Tillery
Senior Photographer: John O'Hagan
Photostylist: Katie Stoddard
Senior Production Designer: Larry Hunter

Contents

Introduction

When we met in a basic quilting class in 1976, we were not aware that we were part of a renewed interest in American quilts and quiltmaking. Folk art historians and collectors were rediscovering the quilt, and the Bicentennial encouraged a positive reassessment of national crafts in which the American quilt was to take a star position. Both of us had learned sewing from our mothers, but those sewing skills had not included quiltmaking. We had pursued our personal interests in knitting and embroidery. We both came to our first quilting class ripe for a hobby that, as it turned out, has kept us busy for many years. Our children were babies and toddlers then, and we were much in need of a pastime that could satisfy the young mother's yearning for something in her daily round of work that would STAY done. Our early projects in patchwork, appliqué, and quilting immediately satisfied that need.

Soon, we were team-teaching beginners' classes. Boosting each other's confidence by working together, we collaborated on course plans, class handout sheets and projects, and refined our skills. We were hungry for literature on quilting and eagerly consumed the few magazines available and each new quilting book that was published. We began writing quilting books ourselves, learning—through the processes of writing, re-writing, and editing—how to make instructions clear and easy to follow.

This book is designed to be a valuable reference for quilters of all levels. The first section, the Quiltmaking Primer, covers not only quilting basics, patchwork, and appliqué, but also the principles of simple pattern drafting, quilt planning, settings, and edge finishes, plus current quick-cutting and quick-piecing methods. By using the skills in the Quiltmaking Primer, you can make scores of quilting projects. Instructions for projects found in the Primer are written in a clear, precise style with the beginning quilter in mind. In the Primer, you'll also find a brief history of

quiltmaking, a description of tools and supplies, and a discussion of fabric and color.

Chapters in the second section, Beyond Basic Quiltmaking, build on the basic skills from the first section. Instructions for projects are written with the assumption that the quilter has a good working knowledge of basic quiltmaking techniques. Included are chapters on patchwork and appliqué that are filled with special techniques and approaches to more challenging patterns. A chapter on borders, settings, and sashing treatments teaches methods that can transform a simple pattern into an out-of-the-ordinary quilt. The chapter "Etcetera Quilts" provides how-to information on novelty techniques such as crazy patchwork, Seminole piecing, and sashiko quilting. We'll also give you advice and guidelines on evaluating your own workmanship and entering competitions. The final chapters of the book provide information on the display, care, and collecting of quilts, and a glossary of quilting terms defines the vocabulary of quiltmaking and describes types of quilts you should know.

We meet hundreds of quilters every year in our travels around the country to present classes, and we are always impressed by the excitement and joy quiltmaking and the love of quilts give our students. Some of them are individuals in their retirement years, some are professionals who work under constant pressure, and others are young mothers, as we were when we started quilting.

We believe *Quilter's Complete Guide* is a book that will not only give you valuable instruction in the art of quiltmaking, but will also introduce you to a hobby that will bring you pleasure for many years.

Happy Quilting!
Marianne and Liz

Americana Sampler

The sampler quilt on these pages was inspired by several we have seen in picture books of old quilts and on our travels as quilting teachers.

In the nineteenth century, a quilter often kept a record of the patterns she had made in the form of individual blocks, or tried out new designs by making sample blocks. At some point in her career, she sewed her collection of blocks together. The resulting quilt was like a photo album, full of memories and her own history.

As we created blocks and projects for the teaching sequences in our book, we made extra blocks from each pattern, with an eye toward sewing a sampler quilt, like those of old, for the cover of our book. We soon realized that it is a visual table of contents for the *Quilter's Complete Guide*.

Sampler Quilt

Size: 94" x 70"

1. Road to Paradise
2. St. Louis
3. Spiral Diamonds
4. Country Angel
5. Grandmother's Fan
6. Windblown Square
7. Royal Cross
8. Ohio Star
9. Strip
10. Toad in the Puddle
11. Memory
12. Checkerboard
13. Posy
14. Nine Patch in Hourglass Set
15. Nine Patch
16. Shoo Fly
17. Sweetheart Block
18. Homespun Block
19. Sawtooth Strip
20. Jacob's Ladder
21. Heart and Hand
22. Bow Tie
23. Celtic True Lover's Knot
24. Big Dipper
25. Wheels
26. Goose Chase Strip
27. Strip
28. LeMoyne Star
29. Dresden Plate
30. Lone Star
31. Baby Blocks
32. Hole in the Barn Door
33. Checkerboard
34. Broderie Perse *Butterfly*
35. Sawtooth Star
36. Gentleman's Fancy
37. Rail Fence Strip
38. Rambler
39. Log Cabin
40. Floral Wreath
41. Spiral Diamonds
42. North Carolina Lily
43. Criss-Cross
44. Schoolhouse
45. Goose Chase Strip
46. Cross and Crown
47. Bear's Paw
48. Hawaiian Breadfruit
49. Heart Basket

Setting Diagram

What Is a Quilt?

A quilt is a bedcover made of two pieces of fabric with some kind of filler between. Simply speaking, the function of a quilt is to provide warmth. Its filler, or batting, may be wool, cotton, or synthetic fibers. The quilt top is the area of creativity, and it can be constructed in many different ways. The quilt backing, or bottom layer, is generally one piece or several pieces sewn together with purely functional intent. Uniformly spaced stitches hold the three layers together. Top, batting, backing—these are the raw elements of a quilt.

Quilt History

Although the basic needlework skills required for making quilts have existed for centuries, these skills were brought together in a unique way by settlers in eighteenth- and nineteenth-century America. Colonial women used their knowledge of sewing techniques to create bold and beautiful bedcovers. Indeed, the American quilt is a combination of several needlearts, all of which have histories that predate the written word.

Quilting itself has been traced to ancient Egypt and China. The concept is simple: An inner layer of fiber provides warmth, just like insulation between the inner and outer walls of a house. Quilting or stitching through the layers was necessary to prevent shifting and clumping of the insulating fibers when garments or bedcovers were used or washed.

Primarily in cold-weather England, but in other European countries as well, quilting was used as early as the eleventh century to hold together the layers of fabric for the padded garments worn under armor. Various references in literature confirm that quilting was a common form of needlework from that time on. Historical accounts prove that quilted petticoats or underskirts for women and quilted waistcoats for

men, as well as quilted bedding, were stylish in England in the middle of the eighteenth century and probably crossed the Atlantic with the colonists.

Patchwork and appliqué, the chief types of needlework used to construct quilt tops, also have long histories. Patchwork, produced by sewing small bits of material together to make a large piece, may be the oldest form of needlework, since man's first clothing was probably made of animal skins sewn together. Early examples of patchwork have been found in India, Persia, and other countries. Appliqué, which consists of a background fabric with smaller pieces stitched onto it to form a design, also has examples from antiquity. Egyptian and Peruvian appliqué artifacts have been described by historians, and the use of fabric appliqué in England dates back to the Middle Ages, when it was employed in making heraldic banners.

Seventeenth-century European trade with India resulted in the huge popularity of Indian textiles. The exotic Eastern designs were gradually toned down to better suit English tastes. But when protective laws were pushed into effect by outraged English and French manufacturers of silk and wool, Indian chintzes and calicos, favored for their colorfastness, became scarce. This scarcity led the English needlewoman to cut up her small supplies of printed chintz to piece with plain fabric or to appliqué the floral motifs onto plain background fabric to make the prints go as far as possible. This type of appliqué was called *broderie perse* from the French, which means to embroider chintz.

The English men and women who came to the New World in the early seventeenth century brought European traditions with them, and quilts were probably among their transported household furnishings. Finished quilts and fabric for making quilts were definitely among the goods imported for sale to colonists.

The first quilts made in America were undoubtedly very English in style. Quite possibly they were whole cloth—quilts that involved no patchwork or appliqué, only the quilting stitches to secure the filler. However, no known examples remain from the seventeenth century. Historians have unearthed written references to quilts in wills, inventories, and newspaper notices of eighteenth-century America, enough to suggest that quilted bedding of various types was somewhat common, at least among those affluent enough to list their belongings.

The great flourishing of American quiltmaking began in the nineteenth century, when the thousands of patchwork and appliqué block designs, so common to quiltmaking today, were created by American needlewomen. The quilts made during that hundred-year period became distinctly American. Many writers on American history, art, and feminism have commented on the remarkable display of creative variety shown in nineteenth-century quilts. Women with virtually no training in art or mathematics (for the intricate computations involved), but with abundant sewing skills and a hunger for beauty, produced millions of quilts both for utility and pleasure. Some were worn out, but many remain as treasured family heirlooms or collectors' prized possessions. These quilts provide seemingly endless inspiration for quiltmakers of today.

Although 1976, the year of the American Bicentennial, is commonly viewed as the beginning of the current quiltmaking revival, it is important to realize that the making of quilts in America is an unbroken tradition. Color schemes, patterns, overall styles, and standards of workmanship have come in and out of popularity, but some form of quiltmaking has been practiced throughout our history. Many of the patterns of the 1920s and 1930s quiltmaking fad are the ones people recognize most readily today—the Grandmother's Fans and Flower Gardens made by relatives they remember. The only period in which quilts seem to have been largely forgotten was from the 1940s to the early 1970s. Even before 1976, several art historians and collectors were beginning to think that the quilt might be the single most significant artifact in the study of American folk art.

The revival that began in the 1970s has continued energetically into the 1980s and the beginning of the 1990s, with many thousands of women, and some men too, making a whole new generation of remarkable quilts. Today's quilters enjoy the abundant creative aspects of their quiltmaking pursuits, as well as an added bonus of satisfying social interaction with other quilt lovers through quilters' guilds, quilt shows, and conferences all over the country. Currently, quilters employ today's tools and equipment to explore and update traditional patterns and techniques of the past. Some textile artists use quiltmaking elements to create beautiful contemporary art pieces that seem to depart widely from tradition but, at the same time, carry it on.

Now, American-style quilting is gaining international interest. In the United States, large-scale quilters' conferences draw participants from Europe, Japan, Australia, New Zealand, and other parts of the world, and American quilt teachers are being invited abroad to share their skills. The first worldwide quilt competition was held in Salzburg, Austria, in 1988.

Here at home, many states have conducted research projects to seek out and document the known history of quilts within their geographical boundaries. Art museum schedules increasingly include quilt displays, and prices paid by collectors for outstanding antique examples have risen steadily.

Quilts attract historians, collectors, families, and needleworkers, each for different reasons. Historians study quilts for clues to the past. Collectors enjoy quilts for their beauty and value. Families treasure quilts as part of their heritage, because they represent works of their ancestors. Quilters love quilts for all of these reasons, as well as for the pure joy of working with pattern, color, and texture. Though the popularity of quilts may increase or diminish with the fashions of the times, the special satisfaction of making a quilt will always be available to anyone who takes the time to learn how.

Tools, Fabrics, and Colors for Quilts

Like every hobby or craft, quiltmaking requires some basic equipment. If you do other types of sewing, you probably already have many of the supplies you will need to make quilts. We advise you to purchase good-quality supplies, because they will last a long time. Basic quilting supplies are available in quilt shops, fabric stores, or from mail-order sources.

Knowledge of some basic color terms can guide you in making successful quilts and help you understand what is happening with colors in quilts you view.

Tools, Fabrics, and Colors for Quilts

Our list of Basic Tools and Supplies includes the things you will need to practice most of the skills covered in this book. The second list, Additional Tools and Supplies, includes more specialized tools and equipment that are fun to have but not necessary to get you started making quilts. At the end of the chapter we'll discuss some fabric terms, how much fabric to purchase, and how to prepare your fabric for quiltmaking. We'll also share some thoughts on color and on combining fabrics for quilts.

Basic Tools and Supplies

Batting. For each project in this book, we'll tell you how large the batt needs to be. Begin by purchasing either a crib-sized batt, large enough for one small project, or a full-sized batt, large enough for several small projects. Choose a high-quality polyester batt recommended for hand quilting. Information on batting is in the chapter "Get Ready To Quilt."

Box for Supplies or Sewing Kit. You'll need some kind of container to transport and store your supplies. Quilters employ everything from simple cardboard boxes to elaborate tool and tackle boxes, baskets, and handmade carrying cases for holding their gear.

Colored Pencils, Markers, or Crayons. These are used in the designing and drafting stages of quiltmaking.

Compass. An inexpensive school-supply compass will work to draw small circles and curves, but you may eventually need a ruler compass or yardstick compass attachment to draw larger circles.

Darning Foot. You will need this sewing machine accessory if you want to try free-motion machine quilting.

Dressmaker's Measuring Tape

Eraser. A separate eraser is a must and will be available long after the eraser on your pencil has worn down.

Graph Paper. Begin by purchasing either a pad of four- or eight-squares-to-the-inch graph paper and a pad of either five- or ten-squares-to-the-inch graph paper. We prefer graph paper with heavier lines every inch.

Later you may want some of the many specialized graph papers ruled in hexagons or assorted types of triangles and diamonds.

Iron and Ironing Board. Choose an iron that you can use on either steam or dry setting.

Masking Tape. You will need a roll of ¼"-wide masking tape and a roll of wider tape.

Needles. Hand-sewing needles are sized by number in two different ranges: numbers 1 through 12, and numbers 13 through 26; the higher the number in each range, the finer and shorter the needle. For quiltmaking, purchase an assorted package of quality sharps needles and a package of betweens or quilting needles, ranging in size from 7 to 12. **Sharps** are general, all purpose sewing needles that are best used for appliquéing and patchwork. **Betweens** are used for quilting. As you sew, you'll discover what size needle works best for you to do various tasks on different kinds of fabrics.

For hand sewing and appliqué, we use a number 11 or 12 sharp; for basting quilt layers together, we use a size 7 or 8 sharp. Marianne likes to use a size 10 between needle to hand quilt; Liz prefers a size 12.

Pencils. Use pencils to mark fabric shapes for patchwork and appliqué and to mark quilting designs.

Keep pencils sharp and mark thin lines. Below, we list some basic markers; other specialized fabric markers are discussed in the chapter "Get Ready to Quilt."

🏠 #2 lead pencil to mark fabrics and to draw on paper.

🏠 mechanical pencil that holds 0.5 mm (thin) lead. Use leads labeled B (medium) or HB (medium hard) to mark fabrics and to draw on paper.

🏠 washable graphite pencil

🏠 silver drawing pencil. Silvery metallic gray shows well on light and dark fabrics and washes out easily.

🏠 white pencil. Either an artist's-type or chalk pencil works well to mark dark fabrics. But use a chalk pencil only to mark projects as-you-go since the markings will disappear or rub off quickly.

Caution: We do not recommend using the blue, felt-tipped, wash-out markers on quilts. Chemicals sometimes remain in the fabric even after washing in cold water, causing permanent discoloration and damage.

Pencil Sharpener

Permanent Markers. Use permanent markers only where you want the marks to remain forever.

You will need:

🏠 black broad-tip permanent marker to darken lines on paper patterns.

🏠 fine-point brown or black permanent pen to sign and date your quilts and to label templates.

Pins and Pincushion. Choose long, thin, sharp (dressmaker's) pins for piecing and appliquéing. They should also be rustproof. We both prefer pins with small glass heads.

Either a simple stuffed pincushion or magnetic pin catcher will do, but a magnetic pin catcher is sure handy when you drop all your pins on the floor!

Plastic-Coated Freezer Paper (plain or gridded). Plain freezer paper can be found at your local grocery store. Gridded freezer paper, especially made for quilt-making, can be found at quilt shops or from mail-order supply companies. We use freezer paper for certain types of templates.

Quilting Hoop. We believe that a 14" circular wooden quilting hoop is all you'll ever need to quilt even the largest quilts. Some quilters prefer square or rectangular plastic-tubing hoops.

Other hoops that you may find useful are a 10" circular wooden hoop, used when quilting small projects, and a semi-circle hoop, used when quilting borders. More information on hoops is on page 74 in "Get Ready to Quilt."

Rotary Cutter, Extra Blades, and 18" x 24" Cutting Mat. Choose a heavy-duty cutter, rather than the standard size. We both prefer cutting mats ruled with a grid of either 1" or 2" squares.

Rulers. You will need a variety of rulers:

🏠 either a 2" x 12" or 2" x 18" clear plastic ruler marked in a grid of ⅛" squares for drawing patterns and adding seam allowances to patterns or fabric pieces.

🏠 6" x 24" heavy plastic ruler designed to use with a rotary cutter. Choose a ruler with ⅛" markings, numerous horizontal and vertical lines, and guidelines for making 30°, 45°, and 60° cuts.

🏠 12" or larger ruled square to use with a rotary cutter. Choose a square with ⅛" markings and numerous horizontal and vertical guidelines.

Safety Pins. If you plan to machine-quilt a large quilt, you will need approximately 350—500 1"-long brass safety pins.

Scissors. You will need the following scissors:

🏠 8" good-quality dressmaker's fabric shears. Use them only to cut fabric. They should be sharp enough to easily cut through several layers of fabric.

🏠 utility scissors for cutting paper and template plastic.

🏠 Optional: Either a pair of thread nippers or embroidery scissors for clipping threads.

Seam Ripper

Sewing Machine. A simple straight-stitch machine will be sufficient for most tasks, but you will need a zigzag stitch for machine appliqué.

Template Vinyl or Plastic. Purchase one or two 11" x 17" sheets of frosted vinyl in a thickness that can be cut with scissors. We prefer inexpensive, ungridded template vinyl. Some quilters like to make

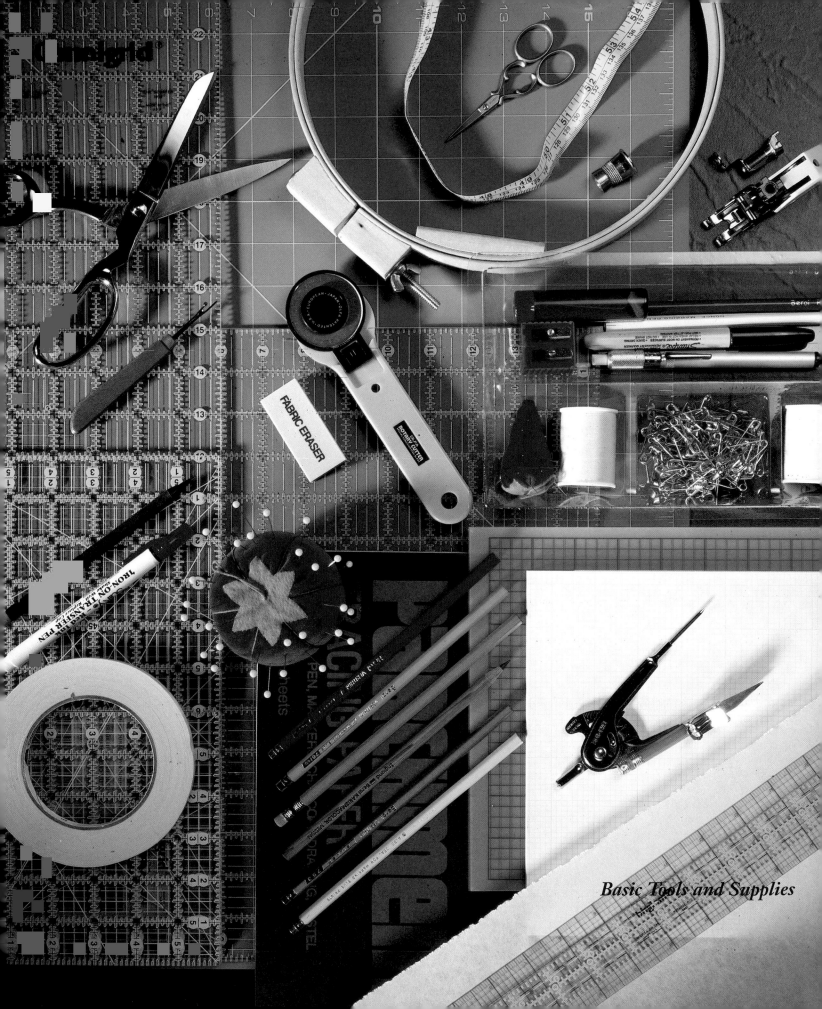

Basic Tools and Supplies

templates from discarded X-ray film, miscellaneous plastic, posterboard, or fine-grade sandpaper.

Thimble. Choose a thimble to fit the middle finger of your sewing hand. It should fit snugly but not tightly on your finger. If you are purchasing a metal thimble, look for one with a flat end and tiny, deep dimples or grooves to hold the end of a needle securely as you quilt. Some quilters prefer leather thimbles; others treat themselves to a silver or gold one.

Thread. For starters, you'll need:

🏠 white, tan, or medium gray cotton or cotton-covered polyester sewing thread. Polyester threads can cut cotton fibers.

🏠 natural or off-white cotton or cotton-covered polyester quilting thread to use for hand quilting.

🏠 clear, transparent nylon thread for machine quilting. The thread should be thin and soft, not stiff and wiry like fishing line.

Tracing Paper. Purchase a 12" x 18" or a 19" x 24" pad.

Walking or Even-Feed Presser Foot. This is a handy sewing machine accessory for machine quilting and for sewing on binding.

Additional Tools and Supplies

Quilters today are blessed with an array of tools to make quiltmaking quicker, easier, and even more fun than in the past. Sometimes the continuous supply of new tools and supplies is confusing, and it is difficult to know which items you need and which are only the latest gimmick. The list below includes some nonessential specialized items we enjoy using to make quilts.

Appliqué or Bandage Scissors. Because of the protruding lip, either of these scissors helps prevent accidentally cutting the wrong fabric when trimming fabric from behind appliqué pieces.

Beeswax. Rub beeswax along the thread to stiffen it, strengthen it, and reduce tangling when quilting.

Draftsman's Circle Template, 45° Triangle, and Flexible Curve. If you can't find these handy tools in your local quilt shop, try an art supply store.

Dressmaker's Cutting Board. A large, fold-out, corrugated cardboard cutting board, printed with a 1" grid, is convenient for enlarging patterns presented on grids, cutting fabrics, and marking background grids on quilts.

Light Box. Homemade or purchased, a light box consists of a sheet of glass or clear plastic placed over the open end of a box with a light in it. The light enables you to see through dark fabrics so that you can trace designs from a paper pattern.

Needle Threader. Since the eyes of hand sewing needles seem to be getting smaller as we get older, we find a needle threader relieves a lot of frustration.

Opaque Projector. This piece of equipment may be borrowed from your local library or rented from a photocopy center. It is used to enlarge patterns.

Quilt Design Stencils

Quilting Frame. Since a good frame is a big investment, evaluate the features of various models before purchasing one. More information about quilting frames is in "Get Ready to Quilt."

Quilting Thread Holder. Deluxe models have a magnetic strip for holding needles and a slot for holding your thimble.

Quiltmaking Books. Start with a small selection of basic books and add others as your interests grow.

Reducing Lens. The opposite of a magnifying glass, a reducing lens makes objects appear smaller and farther away. Use it to "give yourself some distance" from your quilt in order to study the developing pattern or fabric contrast. (You can also get the same effect by looking at your work through the lens of a camera.)

Rulers to Use with a Rotary Cutter. Between the two of us, we have tried almost every ruler manufactured. Two of our favorite extra rulers are:

🏠 6" x 12" ruler to make cross cuts and to pack along in a suitcase when we travel.

🏠 6"-square ruler to measure and cut small pieces.

Sequin Pins. You may like to try using sequin pins to hold fabric pieces in place for hand appliqué; the thread is less likely to catch on them than on long pins.

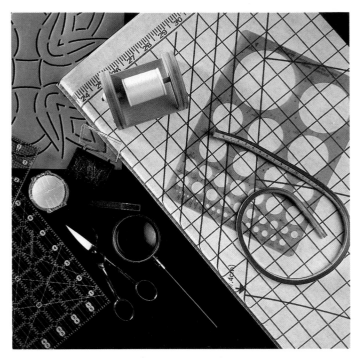

Additional Tools and Supplies

Tote Bags to Transport and Store Supplies. Besides tote bags, we enjoy the customized quiltmaker's totes that have pockets and zippered compartments for your quilting supplies.

Triangle-Marking Template. When you need to cut many triangles and squares, this handy tool decreases your preparation time by helping you cut them from the same fabric strip.

Fabrics for Quilts

Most quiltmakers prefer 100%-cotton broadcloth-weight fabric for quilts. It's easy to sew, neither too stretchy nor too tightly woven, doesn't ravel easily, washes well, and is relatively colorfast. Cotton also takes a crease well so patchwork seams are easy to press, and seam allowances folded under for appliqué stay put.

Always purchase good-quality fabric. Train your eyes and your fingers to recognize quality yard goods. Avoid fabrics that feel stiff, are loosely woven and stretchy, or are misprinted. Fabrics that would make a comfortable, durable blouse or man's shirt are the right texture, weave, and weight.

Fabric Terms

Throughout this book and other sewing books, you will encounter these common fabric terms:

Bias. The diagonal of a woven fabric is the bias. The true bias is at a 45° angle to the selvages. The bias has the most stretch or give.

Grain. The lengthwise and crosswise threads in woven fabric are the grain. The lengthwise grain (warp) is parallel to the selvages. Fabrics are most stable and have the least give on the lengthwise grain, since the warp threads are held taut in the loom during the weaving process. The crosswise grain (weft) is perpendicular to the selvages and has a little more stretch than the lengthwise grain. Arrows on patchwork pattern pieces indicate how the pieces should be placed on the fabric. When using fabric without a nap or sheen, align the arrows with either the lengthwise or crosswise fabric grain. This is called cutting pieces on the straight of grain.

Right Side and Wrong Side. Printed fabrics and fabrics with a finish, such as chintz, have a definite right side and wrong side. Template tracings are made on the wrong side of the fabric for patchwork and the right side for appliqué.

Selvage. The lengthwise finished edges of the fabric are the selvages. Since these edges do not have the same give as the rest of the fabric and are sometimes unprinted, avoid including them in the cut pieces. Instead, use the edge as a guideline and place the template at least ½" from it.

Fabric Finishes

Some fabrics are chemically or heat-treated to create certain effects or add desirable properties. Below are some common finishes on cotton fabrics.

Permanent Press. This finish helps reduce wrinkling by building a memory into the fiber. Permanent press fabrics can't be permanently straightened by pulling them on the bias; after washing and drying, they return to the way they were before they were washed.

Polished Finish. The polished, shiny finish will dull or disappear on most 100%-cotton fabrics after they have been washed. Washing the fabric without soap or detergent will help retain the finish. If a polished look is important for your quilt, consider using polyester/cotton fabrics that retain their sheen after washing.

Soil- and Stain-Resistant Finishes. These chemical finishes help prevent stains from setting into the fabric. Unless the finish makes the fabric stiff or difficult to sew, fabrics with these finishes can be used in quilts.

How Much to Buy

The amount of fabric, or yardage, needed to make the projects in this book is listed along with the instructions. Although you can go to the store and buy the required amount of fabric for a particular project, most quilters eventually get the "fabric-buying bug" and buy fabrics for the sheer pleasure of doing so, even if they have no idea where the fabrics will eventually wind up. They enjoy having a fabric collection they can draw upon as project ideas arise.

If you want to stockpile some fabrics, two obvious things to consider are your budget and the storage space you have available. Here are a few guidelines we follow when deciding how much of a particular fabric to buy.

We generally buy fabric in ¼-yard, 1-yard, 3-yard, or 6-yard increments. We buy ¼-yard pieces if we have no plan for the fabric but just want to own some, or if we are gathering fabrics for a scrap quilt. Quilt shops sell conventional ¼-yard cuts and also special quilter's quarters or fat quarters. These pieces are approximately 18" x 22", which is often a more useful size than a conventional 9" x 44" piece. Some shops also sell 9" x 18" pieces called fat eighths.

We buy 1 yard if we really like the fabric but aren't sure how we will use it. If we are considering using a fabric for a border on a full-size quilt, we purchase at least 3 yards. We buy at least 6 yards if the fabric is on sale, and if it would make a wonderful quilt backing.

Fabric Preparation

We recommend that you wash, dry, and iron fabrics before using them in quilts. Washing removes excess dye and sizing from the fabric and may shrink it also. You can throw like colors in with the family's laundry. We wash fabrics in warm water and detergent or Orvus Paste soap (a mild soap designed for washing livestock and available in quilt shops or at livestock supply stores) and dry them at a medium or permanent-press setting in the dryer.

Some dark fabrics, especially reds, purples, and blues, tend to bleed or release dye during washing. To test a fabric for colorfastness and to see if it has quit bleeding, stop your washing machine during the final rinse. Scoop out some rinse water into a clear glass and look for color. If the fabric is still bleeding, wash it again. If it continues to bleed, don't use it in a quilt, or use it only with fabrics of similar color that won't be affected if it does bleed.

After washing, checking for colorfastness, and drying your fabrics, iron them with a steam iron set at the appropriate setting for the fabric. (You may prefer to save this step until you are ready to cut the fabric.)

Some Thoughts on Color

Color is the dimension of fabric that strikes us first, grabs our attention, and beckons us to take a closer look. Perhaps more than any other single element, color influences how we react to a particular fabric or quilt.

Many quilters in the past accomplished stunning color effects in their quilts by instinct, imitation, experimentation, and by accident. Many quilters today begin with some basic understanding of color terms, color schemes, and how some visual illusions are created with color, but they still have to rely on instinct and experimentation to translate theory into reality in their quilts.

Knowledge of basic color terms and effects can guide you in making successful quilts and help you understand what is happening with colors in quilts you view.

Terms That Describe Colors

Hue: the name of the color, what distinguishes one color from another. Red, blue, green, and yellow are color hues.

Value: the lightness or darkness of a hue or color. Pastel colors, such as pink and lavender, are light in value; colors such as navy blue and maroon are dark in value. We often refer to three shades of a color when we are really referring to three values.

Tint: lighter values of a hue, such as clear pastels, made by adding white to the color. Pink is a tint of red, peach a tint of orange, and lavender a tint of purple or violet.

Tone: a dulled, grayed value of a hue formed by mixing pure colors with gray. Tan, beige, taupe, and dusty rose are examples of tones.

Shade: darker values of a hue, made by adding black to a pure color. Navy is a shade of blue, and maroon is a shade of red.

Chroma or intensity: the relative purity of a color. Orange has high chroma or intensity; peach has low chroma. The more intense or pure a color is, the less space it needs to occupy in your design to be noticed.

Warm colors: yellows, oranges, and reds. Warm colors are visually stimulating and exciting and tend to advance in relation to other colors.

Cool colors: violet (purple), blue, and green. Cool colors are calming and soothing and tend to recede in relation to other colors.

Color wheel: a circular arrangement of the twelve basic colors. Conventionally, yellow is positioned at the top of the color wheel, red at right, and blue at left.

Primary colors: the three basic colors that can be combined to create the other colors on a twelve-part color wheel. Most color wheels describe the primary colors as yellow, red, and blue.

Secondary colors: colors created by mixing equal amounts of the primary colors. Yellow and red combine to make the secondary color orange, red and blue to make violet or purple, and blue and yellow to make green.

Intermediate or tertiary colors: colors created by mixing primary and secondary colors. The secondary colors are yellow-orange, red-orange, red-violet, blue-violet, blue-green, and yellow-green.

Terms That Describe Color Schemes or Harmonies

Each of us has a private or subjective concept of color harmony — in other words, the colors we feel go together. Over the years, color theorists have proposed some formal color harmonies based on the relationships of colors. The list below includes simple descriptions of some of these technical terms for color relationships.

Achromatic: without color. An achromatic color scheme consists of the interplay of black, white, and shades of gray.

Monochromatic: a combination of various values, shades, tints, or tones of a color. A quilt with various blue fabrics has a monochromatic color scheme. Sometimes the color is also combined with white or black.

Polychromatic: containing several colors.

Analogous: a combination of two or more colors located next to each other on the color wheel. Blue, blue-violet, and violet are analogous colors. The combined colors can all be pure and intense, dulled and of low intensity, or any combination of shade, tone, or tint that is visually pleasing. Most people find that they can easily create a successful combination of analogous colors.

Complementary: a combination of two colors that are opposite each other on the color wheel. The colors can be combined as pure hues or as tints, tones, and shades. Red and green, yellow and purple, and blue and orange are the three complementary color schemes that include the primary and secondary colors. Intermediate colors can also be organized in complementary color schemes. For example, red-orange and blue-green are complementary colors. The *Floral Wreath* wall quilt on page 136 and the *Pa ndau* piece on page 175 are examples of a red-and-green complementary color scheme.

Combining Fabrics in Quilts

As much as quilters love purchasing fabric, they are frequently confused when deciding how to use their fabrics to make a successful project. Some seem to have a knack for combining fabrics and colors to create interesting or unusual combinations that really work. Others struggle and struggle and never seem pleased with their efforts and, in some cases, use their uncertainty as an excuse for never getting any projects made. While we don't pretend to have all the answers, here are a few ideas about fabric and color that we have found useful.

Two main factors determine which fabrics to combine: the characteristics of the prints (creating visual texture and creating character or a mood) and color of the fabric (creating a color scheme and contrast in hue or value).

We like to combine small-, medium-, and large-design prints. Using prints of various design scales adds to the visual texture of a quilt. We include light-, medium-, and dark-value fabrics so our quilts have contrast and designs read clearly.

A simple approach to combining fabric is to choose one fabric that contains several colors. Then select other coordinating fabrics.

Using formal color relationships, such as a monochromatic, analogous, or complementary color scheme, is another approach. Work within a specific color scheme, or use color to create an illusion such as depth, transparency, or illumination. Choose a particular mood or character you want your quilt to have and select prints and colors that contribute to the mood. Make a red-white-and-blue patriotic quilt, a red-and-green Christmas quilt with seasonal prints, a child's quilt based around a character print, an Amish-style quilt of subdued solid-color fabrics combined with black, or a quilt with an antique look made from new fabrics that are reproductions of fabrics from another era.

The color scheme and decorating style of the room where you intend to use or display the quilt may suggest certain colors or types of fabrics. Perhaps you'll choose a bold floral chintz for a Victorian or English Country look, or graphic black-and-white geometric prints combined with primary solids for an ultra-modern office.

You can look to the colors in nature for inspiration to capture a sunset, the desert, the mountains, or the seashore in a quilt.

Study how other quiltmakers combine colors and fabrics. Attend quilt shows and think about what is happening in the quilts you see, or study antique quilts to determine why they have a certain look. Quilt books and magazines provide a wealth of old and new quilts to inspire you.

One school of art encourages artists to begin by imitating various schools of painting and then to go on to develop their own style. This approach works for quiltmaking, too.

Color and texture constantly surround us; trust your senses to guide you wisely. As you experiment with fabrics and colors, you'll undoubtedly have both successes and failures. Remember, even experienced quiltmakers have varying degrees of success; sometimes even the best plans simply don't work for one reason or another. Although practice doesn't necessarily make perfect, it certainly helps!

Basic Skills
Reference Guide

In quiltmaking, as in any other craft, there are certain basic skills used in many phases of the craft.

Basic Skills Reference Guide

This chapter is designed to serve as a quick reference guide and to acquaint you with the fundamentals of hand sewing, machine sewing, and pressing.

Hand-Sewing Skills

Threading a Sewing Needle. To reduce thread tangling, thread a needle with the end of the thread coming off the spool. First, trim the end of the thread on the diagonal so that it is freshly cut and not frayed. Insert the thread end through the eye of the needle. If you have difficulty, try moistening the eye of the needle so that it will attract and grab the end of the thread.

A needle threader is a helpful tool for threading a needle with a small eye. Insert the wire loop of the needle threader through the eye of the needle. With the needle threader in place, insert the end of the thread through the loop. Draw the needle threader loop back out, pulling the thread through the eye of the needle.

After the needle is threaded, measure and cut the desired length of thread; use approximately 27" of thread for hand sewing. An easy way to quickly measure the correct length of thread to use is to cut a length of thread equal to the distance from your elbow to your hand and half way back. Longer lengths of thread tangle more easily, wear thin where they are bent at the eye of the needle, and fray from being repeatedly pulled through the fabric.

To prevent thread from kinking and knotting as you sew, try running it over a cake of beeswax several times to strengthen and slightly stiffen it before sewing. Quilting threads are treated with silicone or other chemicals to prevent tangling. If the thread does kink and twist as you stitch, occasionally let the needle and thread hang down to untwist.

Hand-Sewing Knots

Backstitch Loop Knot. Use a backstitch loop knot to end the thread for most hand sewing, except hand quilting. To tie a backstitch loop knot, follow the instructions as illustrated.

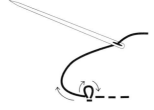

1. When last stitch is completed, backstitch by inserting needle approximately ⅛" behind last stitch, bringing needle back up at end of seam and forming loop on top of previous stitch. Pull backstitch up, leaving loop on top of work.

2. Run needle through loop. Pull thread tightly to close loop and form knot. Repeat knot if desired. Clip excess thread.

Ending Knot for Hand Quilting. Instructions for ending the thread when hand quilting are on page 80.

Quilter's Knot. A good beginning knot for most hand-sewing tasks, including quilting, appliqué, and piecing, is a quilter's knot. Knot the end of the thread that you cut last, rather than the end you threaded through the needle. To tie a quilter's knot, follow the steps as illustrated.

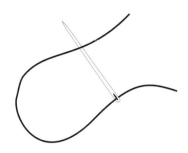

1. Hold threaded needle between thumb and forefinger about midway along needle shaft. With other hand, pick up long end of thread and place tail on top of needle, allowing end to extend approximately ½" beyond needle. While holding needle, pinch thread that is on top of needle between thumb and forefinger.

2. With other hand, wrap main part of thread around needle three times. Number of wraps determines size of knot; wrap more times for larger knot. Pinch wraps between thumb and finger.

3. While pinching wraps and needle with one hand, let go of long thread with other hand. Grasp needle near point and pull needle through wraps. While pulling needle, keep gently pinching wraps with fingers until all thread is pulled through wraps, forming nice, firm knot. (If you failed to form knot, you probably wrapped with thread tail rather than main part of thread.) Clip tail near knot for sewing, but leave ½" tail when quilting to help secure thread in batting.

Square Knot. To form a square knot, hold a thread end in each hand. Wrap right thread around left thread around right thread. Pull tight to form a knot. The chapter "The Ins and Outs of Quilting" explains how a square knot is used to tie a quilt.

Hand-Sewing Stitches

Appliqué Stitch, Blindstitch, or Slipstitch. Use the appliqué stitch, also called blindstitch or slipstitch, to secure a folded edge of fabric to a base fabric. Use this almost invisible stitch for hand-appliqué and to hand-finish quilt binding.

1. Pull needle and knotted thread up through base fabric and folded edge of top fabric (appliqué piece), barely catching edge of fold.

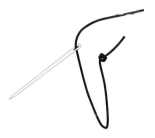

2. Re-insert needle into base fabric immediately next to where thread comes through fold. Run needle behind base fabric approximately ⅛". Bring needle up through base fabric and folded edge, barely catching folded edge. Pull up stitch so that it is snug against fabrics but does not distort base fabric. Stitches on top should be almost invisible.

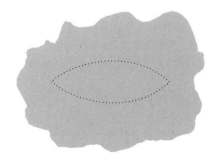

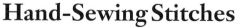

3. Stitches on back side of base fabric should be basically straight and approximately ⅛" long.

Buttonhole Stitch. Use this decorative stitch to secure appliqué pieces in decorative hand appliqué, some *broderie perse* appliqué, and to embellish the folded edges of fabric pieces in crazy quilting. Thread the sewing needle with embroidery floss, pearl cotton, or other decorative thread. The thread color may either match or contrast with the piece you are stitching.

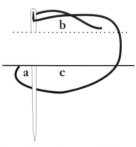

1. Pull needle and knotted thread up through base fabric (a). Insert needle through appliqué piece (b), approximately ⅛" to ¼" from folded edge.

Bring needle back up through base fabric just beyond folded edge and through thread loop being created by the stitch (c). Pull up stitch.

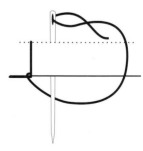

2. Continue in same manner to create line of stitching.

Diagonal Basting Stitch or Tailor's Padding Stitch. This stitch is used in quiltmaking to baste together the layers of a quilt.

The large stitches on the top slant, and the smaller stitches on the back are straight. The chapter "Get Ready to Quilt" explains how this stitch is used.

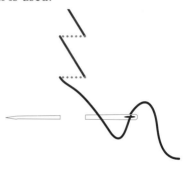

Running Stitch. Use a running stitch to temporarily sew pieces together and to baste turned-under seam allowances for hand-appliqué. Use white or light-colored thread because these will not discolor or leave dark lint on the fabric.

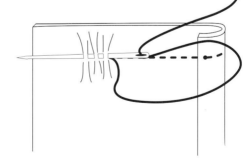

Weave the tip of the needle through the fabric, grouping three to five stitches on the needle, depending on stitch length. Pull the needle and thread through the fabric. Stitches should look the same on front and back.

Piecing Stitch. Use this sturdy stitch to hand-piece patchwork seams. The piecing stitch is similar to a running stitch, except that each series of stitches begins with a backstitch.

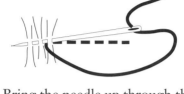

Bring the needle up through the fabric. Insert the needle into fabric one stitch length behind where the thread came through the fabric. Take several short running stitches on the needle; then pull the thread through. Begin each new series of stitches with a backstitch.

Whipstitch. Use the whipstitch, also called the overcasting stitch, to join pieces in the English-piecing method. (This patchwork technique is explained in "Beyond Basic Patchwork.")

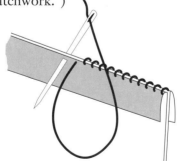

With right sides of folded fabric edges together, insert the needle through both folds, barely catching the edges. Insert the needle close to the previous stitch through both folds and gently pull the thread through to hold pieces together. Do not pull tight or the stitches will distort the fabrics.

Machine-Sewing Skills

A sewing machine that makes an even, straight stitch is all you need to machine-piece or machine-quilt your projects. For machine appliqué, you will need a machine that makes a basic zigzag stitch.

Become familiar with your sewing machine instruction manual and refer to it to choose the recommended presser foot and throat plate for the job at hand. Unfortunately, many of us open our manual only when desperate or when faced with an unfamiliar sewing situation.

Machine Needles. Use the needle size recommended for the fabric you are sewing. Needles in the size range of 10 to 14 or 70 to 90 are appropriate for sewing most quilt fabrics. The higher the number, the larger the needle. Use universal needles or sharp-point needles recommended for woven fabrics; ballpoint needles are for sewing knit fabrics.

Skipped stitches, irregular stitches, and uneven tensions are frequently caused by stitching with a dull, bent, or barbed needle. Replace sewing machine needles frequently and make sure they are inserted properly. If you can't remember when you last changed the needle, it is definitely time to replace it.

Stitch Length. Set the stitch length at 10 to 15 stitches per inch or between 2 and 3 for most seams. Use a reasonably short stitch that holds the fabrics together securely but is not impossible to remove in case you make a mistake.

Gauging a ¼"-Wide Seam. The standard width for patchwork seams is ¼". If your seam width varies from this, the corners and points on your patchwork pieces may not match, and your projects will turn out the wrong size.

It is best to make a final stitching test to double-check your seam width. To do this, cut two 3" squares of fabric. Sew them together along one side and press seam allowances to one side. Measure across the squares.

The seamed squares should measure 5½" across because you have taken ¼" off each square. If your measurement is not 5½", re-adjust the seam guide.

Gauging. On many machines, the distance from the needle to the edge of the presser foot is exactly ¼". Sew a test seam, aligning the presser foot edge with fabric edge, and measure the distance from the stitching to the fabric edge. If the needle position cannot be adjusted, purchase a presser foot that will give you ¼" seams, or place a strip of masking tape on the throat plate ¼" to the right of the needle to serve as a seam guide. Test the seam guide by sewing and measuring a sample seam.

Pinning. Pin the fabric pieces together with right sides facing. For easy removal, place pins perpendicular to the seam with pin heads toward the fabric edge. Pin at the ends, then the center, and along the length of the seam as needed. If one piece is slightly longer than the other, distribute fullness evenly along length of seam. Sew with the longer piece on bottom; the feed dogs will ease in the excess fullness.

Starting a Seam. Two common problems that develop at the beginning of a seam are having a tangled mass of beginning threads on the back and having fabric pull down into the throat plate opening. To eliminate these problems, hold the thread tails with your left hand as you begin stitching. If this does not solve the problem, hold the thread tails with your left hand while turning the hand wheel with your right hand to lower the needle into the fabric. Using a straightstitch throat plate, with a tiny needle hole, also prevents fabric from being pulled down into the throat plate.

Starting a seam with a fabric scrap. Another way to hold loose threads at the beginning of a seam is with a scrap of fabric. Sew on the fabric scrap first, then sew a few stitches with no fabric under the needle, and then feed in your fabrics. When the seam is completed, sew onto the fabric scrap again.

Sewing a seam. Guide the fabric by placing your right hand on the fabric in front of the presser foot and your left hand on the fabric to the left of the presser foot. Don't be tempted to pull or push the fabric through the machine; just steer the fabric through, letting the machine do the work.

Sewing with Pinned Fabrics. When you reach a pin, either remove it or slowly sew over it. Hitting pins dulls the needle and can break the pin or needle.

Ending Seams. When sewing patchwork, it is not necessary to secure the ends of seams that will be crossed by successive seams. Simply sew from one fabric edge to the other. If the seam will not be crossed by a later seam or if you are not stitching to the edge of the fabric, secure the ends of your seams by backstitching.

Backstitching at the Beginning and End of a Seam. Sew forward a few stitches, stitch in reverse a few stitches on top of the previous stitching, and sew forward over backstitching to the end of the seam. At the end of the seam, sew a few stitches in reverse on top of the previous stitching; then sew to the fabric edge.

Pivoting at the Beginning of a Seam. If you have problems sewing straight when sewing in reverse or if you must begin and end your stitching in an exact spot, such as when setting in pieces for some patchwork designs, pivot and turn your work rather than stitching in reverse.

At the beginning of a seam, turn your work so that you can stitch approximately ¼" forward to the beginning point, stopping with the needle in the fabric. Raise the presser foot and pivot the fabric so that you can sew forward over the first stitches and then to the end of the seam.

Pivoting at the End of a Seam. At the end of a seam, sew up to the ending point, pivot the fabric, and sew forward a few stitches over the previous stitching.

Pressing Patchwork

Pressing is not the same as ironing. When ironing, the iron is moved back and forth across the fabric to remove wrinkles. The goal of pressing is to set seams and remove wrinkles without stretching or distorting the fabric. Always lift the iron to move it from one position to another. Use an up-and-down motion, rather than a sliding motion. Press, rather than iron, all seams and completed projects.

Develop the habit of pressing as you go when sewing. Press a seam before crossing it with another seam or joining seamed pieces. Press a seam first with right sides of fabric facing to embed stitches. Then press seam allowances to one side.

Seam allowances pressed to one side form a barrier to prevent batting fibers from migrating out between stitches and are stronger than seams that have been pressed opened. In addition, you only have to deal with them on one side of the seam when you quilt. Whenever possible, press patchwork seam allowances toward the darker of the two fabrics so that seam allowances will not show through the lighter fabric.

Some patchwork seams have minds of their own and clearly indicate the direction they need to be pressed to make the block lie flat. When pressing these blocks, it may not be possible or advisable to press toward the darker fabric. Instead, press toward the lighter fabric and trim the darker seam allowance slightly narrower than the lighter one, if necessary.

Preliminary **finger pressing** helps eliminate small folds or tucks along seams. Also, because the seam allowances are not firmly creased to one side, you can easily finger-press them in the opposite direction if you decide to change your pressing strategy. It is also a convenient way to press seams when you are away from home and do not have access to an iron.

To finger-press, place the seam on a firm surface with the darker fabric on top and right sides facing. Pull the top fabric (the darker fabric) over the seam allowance to reveal the right sides of the fabrics. Run your fingernail along the top of the seam. This temporarily presses the seam allowances toward the darker fabric.

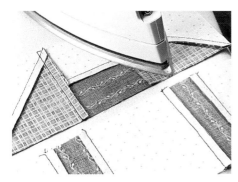

Pressing seams that abut. For seams that meet and for true corners or points, press seam allowances in opposite directions. Ideally, seam allowances that will be on top when you join units should be pressed away from you and toward the sewing machine for easier matching.

Pressing long seams. 1. To press long seams, lay strips or rows across width of ironing board. Have darker fabric, or fabric you want to press seam allowances toward, on top as you work and press.

2. Open out darker top fabric to reveal right side of seam. Finger-press along length of seam. Next, carefully press along right side of seam, pressing seam allowances to one side.

First Steps in Traditional Patchwork

Patchwork quilts, also called pieced quilts, are made by sewing small pieces of fabric together to form a larger piece. The small pieces are usually geometric shapes such as squares, rectangles, or triangles, joined in a set order to create a design.

The earliest American patchwork quilts from the 1700s were often pieced in a medallion format, which consisted of a central motif surrounded by patchwork borders. During the mid-1800s, the patchwork block, a single design unit repeated over the surface of the quilt top, began gradually to replace the earlier medallion format. Many historians believe the quilt block evolved because lap-sized patchwork units were easier to work on than larger pieces.

First Steps in Traditional Patchwork

In this chapter you will learn how to understand and work with patchwork patterns, to make templates, to cut out fabric pieces, and to hand- and machine-piece patchwork blocks. If you've purchased a rotary cutter and mat for your first quilt project, thoroughly read this chapter and the chapter on quick-cutting and -piecing before proceeding with your quilt.

Patchwork Patterns

Patchwork patterns in books and magazines are presented in various ways. Many current publications, including this book, present as many full-size patchwork patterns as possible. These patterns are ready to use for making templates; no enlargement or drafting by the reader is necessary.

Single-line Pattern. When full-size patterns are printed with a single outline, the patterns are usually finished size and do not include seam allowances. **Finished size** is the size the piece will be after it is sewn to other pieces. Check the pattern page or the project instructions to confirm that the patterns are finished size. If so, you will need to add seam allowances either to the templates or to the fabric pieces before they are cut out.

Double-line Pattern. When full-size patterns are printed with two pattern outlines, an outer solid line and an inner dashed line, the patterns include ¼" seam allowances. The inner dashed line is the sewing line and indicates the finished size of the pattern piece. The outer solid line is the cutting line. A **matching point** (a dot on pattern) indicates where seam lines meet and is used as a guide for pin-matching seam lines on fabric pieces.

Helpful information is often printed within the pattern outline on full-size patterns. When making templates, transfer all information from the pattern onto your templates. Often patterns are identified by a letter and the name of the block. The letter corresponds to a piece in either a drawing of the block or a piecing diagram that shows how to assemble the block. The number of pieces to cut for one block is often printed on the pattern. The arrow indicates how to position the template on the fabric. Place the arrow on the straight of the fabric grain. In other words, position the template so that the arrow runs parallel to either the lengthwise or crosswise threads of the fabric.

To conserve space, many publications will **stack patterns** and list the number to cut elsewhere. Pay close attention to cutting lines and review piecing diagrams before making templates. (This is very worthwhile when making a complicated quilt with many pieces.)

Patterns with Dimensions. Sometimes, if a pattern piece is too large to fit on the page or if space is at a premium, project instructions will either list the dimensions of a particular piece or include a small diagram with dimensions. Dimensions are often listed for setting pieces, borders, large triangles, squares, or rectangles.

The dimensions for a piece usually include seam allowances, but check the instructions to make sure before cutting pieces from fabric. To make a template, first use a ruler and pencil to draw the shape full-size on graph paper. If the shape is large and you need only a few pieces, measure and draw the shape onto the fabric.

Pattern Drafting. To save space, some patchwork books include only small drawings of individual blocks. Since the drawings usually range from 1" to 2" square, many patterns can be presented in very little space. To use the patterns, you must enlarge them to the desired size before making templates. The enlarging process is a part of pattern drafting.

Enlarging Grid. Occasionally, patchwork patterns are presented with an enlarging grid superimposed over a small-block drawing. To use this type of pattern, first enlarge it to full-size. If the drawing is labeled "1 square = 1"," use graph paper and draw a grid of 1" squares. Then, transfer each square of the small diagram to the corresponding square on the grid you have drawn.

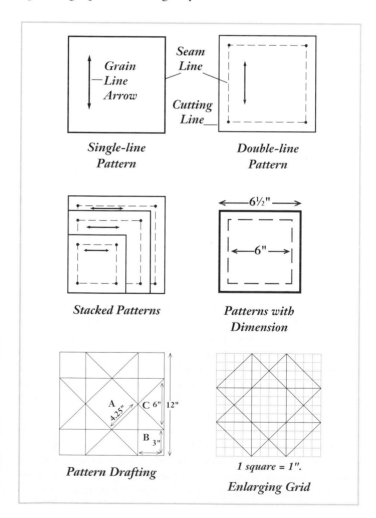

Single-line Pattern

Double-line Pattern

Stacked Patterns

Patterns with Dimension

Pattern Drafting

Enlarging Grid

1 square = 1".

Templates

Templates are firm patterns, usually made from vinyl (plastic) or posterboard, that you mark around to transfer shapes onto fabric. Templates must be sturdy to hold up under repeated markings; replace templates as they become worn. Vinyl templates are more durable than posterboard ones. Make a template for each different pattern piece or shape in your design. Label each template with the pattern letter, grain line, right or wrong side, and name of the quilt design. Labeling for the number to cut and the fabric is optional.

There are two basic types of templates: finished-size templates and templates with ¼" seam allowances. Use **finished-size templates** to mark pieces for hand piecing and for appliqué. When fabric is marked with finished-size templates, the fabric pieces will have sewing lines marked but not seam allowances. Add seam allowances directly on the fabric before cutting out pieces.

To make a finished-size template from a single-line pattern, trace the pattern outline. To make a finished-size template from a double-line pattern, trace the inner dashed line.

Use **templates that include ¼" seam allowances** to mark fabric for most machine piecing. Mark around the template edge, which is the cutting line. The fabric pieces will not have seam lines marked on them. The fabric edges, aligned with the sewing machine presser foot and throat plate, will serve as a guide for sewing an accurate ¼"-wide seam.

To make a template that includes seam allowances from a double-line pattern, trace the outer solid line, the inner dashed line, and the matching points. Cut out the template on the outer solid line. Having both lines marked on templates serves as a reminder that the templates include seam allowances, and the inner dashed lines and matching points aid in aligning pieces.

To make a template that includes seam allowances from a single-line pattern, first make your own double-line pattern. Trace the pattern on tracing paper or draw it on graph paper using a dashed line. Add ¼"-wide seam allowances all around pattern and mark matching points.

Making Templates and Checking Templates for Accuracy

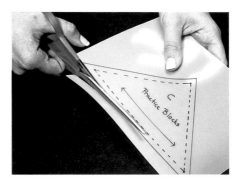

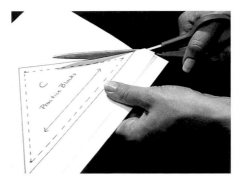

Vinyl templates. To make template from durable frosted vinyl, place vinyl over full-size pattern and trace pattern outline with pencil, ballpoint pen, or felt-tip pen. Add all information printed on pattern. Make lines thin and accurate. Using utility scissors, cut out template along inner edge of drawn line.

Posterboard templates. To make template from posterboard or other opaque material, first trace pattern outline and all information printed on pattern onto tracing paper. Roughly cut out traced pattern and glue it onto posterboard. Carefully cut out template, cutting through both paper and posterboard.

Check the accuracy of templates by comparing them to original patterns. Accurate templates are crucial to the success of patchwork projects. If templates are not accurate, fabric pieces will not fit together properly, and block will not be correct size.

Fabric-Marking Strategies

An ideal fabric-marking surface prevents the fabric from slipping and sliding as you mark. The surface should be slightly rough to help hold the fabric in place. A rotary cutting mat, a table covered with a smooth tablecloth, or a 12"-square board covered with fine-grit sandpaper are good marking surfaces.

Choosing a Fabric Marker

A well-sharpened lead pencil is the best all-round marker for most fabrics. Use a silver artist's pencil or light-colored tailor's chalk pencil to mark dark fabrics. Always use non-permanent markers such as these to mark sewing lines. To mark cutting lines, use a fine-tip pen if other markers don't show up well on the fabric. Avoid using a ballpoint pen or any other marker that may smear, bleed, leave a residue, or discolor fabric.

To prevent dragging and stretching the fabric as you mark around a template, hold the pencil or marker at an angle, rather than straight up, and "stroke" the point along the edge of the template. Take special care not to stretch the fabric as you mark the corners of pieces.

Marking with the Fabric Grain

Full-size patchwork patterns usually have a grain line arrow printed on them, which indicates correct template placement on the fabric. Align the arrow with the straight of the fabric grain. The arrow should run parallel to the fabric threads. Most pieces can be positioned on the lengthwise or crosswise grain, but long pieces should be marked and cut only on the lengthwise grain to control stretch.

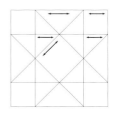

If grain line arrows are not marked on patterns, you will need to determine them. As a general rule, the longest side of a piece should be on the straight of grain. Plan your marking so that the edges of the pieces along the outside of a patchwork block are on the straight of grain. Bias edges to the outside of a block often result in distorted blocks.

Determining the Order to Mark and Cut

Mark and cut the largest pieces, such as borders and setting pieces, from your fabric before cutting the smaller pieces for the patchwork. (See diagram below for suggestion of fabric layout.) Following this cutting order ensures that you will have enough length to cut borders in one continuous piece and quickly reduces a very large fabric piece to a workable size.

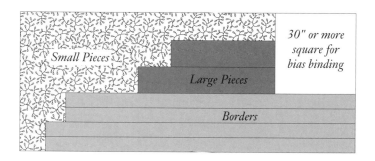

Marking Special Fabrics

Some fabrics require special approaches when marking them. Dark-colored solid fabrics and polished or glazed fabrics may have directional shading or sheen, depending on how the fabric is turned. This effect is similar to the nap on corduroy or velvet. Directional fabrics are those that are printed with designs that have a definite top and bottom. If you want all the trees, houses, or other printed motifs to be upright, take extra care when marking and sewing.

Striped fabrics are also directional fabrics. To take advantage of the sense of movement they will give your work, do some planning before cutting these fabrics.

The designs on many printed fabrics may seem to be printed in a random manner, but the motifs are usually arranged in a regular sequence, often diagonal rows. Unfortunately, the design is often not printed on the

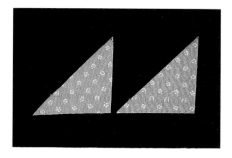

true fabric grain or on the true bias. Therefore, when marking certain shapes, the motifs will appear to fall off the edge of the piece if the edge does not line up with the arrangement of the motifs. The fabric on the left shows the printed motif falling off the diagonal side of a triangle. To avoid this problem, position the template so that it is aligned with the printed design but only approximately on grain. The triangle on the right is cut to compensate for the printed design.

Marking Reverse Pieces

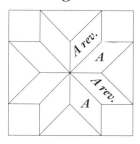

Many patchwork designs include reversed shapes. In other words, both the shape and its mirror image are part of the design. Parallelograms and other asymmetrical shapes are often reversed. In the star block diagram, four of the parallelograms that create the star points are reverse pieces.

Cutting instructions and template patterns indicate reverse pieces by rev., r, or R following the number to cut.

To mark fabric for original pieces, place the template wrong side up on the wrong side of the fabric (with the writing on the template facing the fabric). To mark fabric for reverse pieces, turn the template over so that the right side (with the writing and other markings) is facing up. You may find it helpful to label one side of the template "up for original" and the other "up for reverse."

Basics of Hand Piecing

Before the invention of the sewing machine, all patch-work blocks were hand-stitched. Today, hand piecing is still a valuable skill. Sewing by hand allows you more control than machine sewing, making it easier to achieve accurate results. Sewing curved seams, setting pieces into an opening, and sewing short, non-continuous seams are all easy to manage by hand. Hand-piecing produces seams with "soft-edges," and because you never stitch into the seam allowances, you can press the seam allowance in any direction.

Learn These Hand-Piecing Skills While Making a Shoo Fly Block

- *using finished-size templates*
- *pin-matching*
- *making triangle-square units*
- *free-floating seam allowances*
- *following a piecing diagram*
- *hand-piecing seams*
- *unit-row construction method*
- *pressing hand-pieced blocks*

Materials:

¼ yard each of 2 fabrics
Basic sewing supplies (see page 12)

Finished Block Size: *9" square*

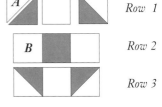

Row 1

Row 2

Row 3

Shoo Fly Block Piecing Diagram

1. Make finished-size templates for triangle A and square B from patterns on page 41. Position template on **wrong** side of fabric at least ½" from fabric edge. Align grain line arrow with lengthwise or crosswise grain; mark around template. Leave at least ½" between all pieces to allow for seam allowances. Mark four triangles and four squares on first fabric (red). Mark four triangles and one square on second fabric (blue).

2. Before cutting out pieces, add ¼" seam allowances around marked shapes for cutting lines. Lay ruler along one side, allowing ¼" of ruler to extend beyond marked line, and draw line. Repeat for each side. Cut out pieces.

3. Refer to Shoo Fly Block Piecing Diagram and lay out fabric pieces right side up to form block. At first glance, you may think pieces will not fit together. Seam allowances make pieces such as triangles seem larger than the squares they must match. When sewn together, they will fit.

Unit-Row Construction Method

The basic principle for assembling most patchwork is to begin by joining smaller pieces into bigger units, such as sewing together right triangles to form squares, called **triangle-square units.**

Units are joined into rows, and the rows are joined to complete the block. This method is called the **unit-row construction method**.

Making Triangle-Square Units

1. Pin two adjacent triangles (A) along long sides (hypotenuse) with **right sides** facing and raw edges aligned. Insert pin through corner of sewing line (matching point) on top triangle; then insert pin at corresponding corner of bottom triangle. Secure pin, positioning shaft of pin perpendicular to seam. Repeat for other corner. Use additional pins along length of seam as needed. Using pins to align sewing lines is called **pin matching**. Pin four triangle-square units.

2. Remove pin at corner, insert threaded needle into pin hole, and take small stitch forward. Make a backstitch over first stitch and run five or six stitches onto needle, stitching along marked sewing line. Pull stitches up and continue sewing seam in this manner. Try to make each stitch approximately ⅛". Turn work over to check that you are stitching along sewing line on both top and bottom pieces. End seam with **backstitch loop knot.** (See "Basic Skills Reference Guide," page 22.)

3. Finger-press seam allowance toward darker triangle. Trim triangle tips even with edges.

Assembling Units into Rows

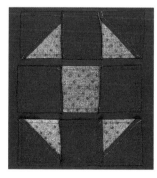

All units within row should be same size. Compare triangle-square units to square B. They should each measure 3½" square, including seam allowances. Refer to Shoo Fly Block Piecing Diagram on page 34 and sew units into three rows; finger-press.

Free-Floating Seam Allowances

1. Stitch rows together. Stitch up to point where seams meet. Remove pin that matches seams, make stitch through pin hole; backstitch to reinforce.

2. Slip needle through top seam allowance to reach other side of seams. Flip seam allowances toward seam you have just sewn. Take one stitch forward; then backstitch to reinforce corner.

Pressing Hand-Pieced Blocks

Press seam allowances toward darker fabric so that they radiate at seam junctions and corners to eliminate bulk. The block should measure 9½" square, including seam allowances. A variance of ⅛" is acceptable, but if your block is much smaller or larger, remake it.

Basics of Machine Piecing

Although some quiltmaking purists feel that quilts should be entirely hand sewn, there is little or no difference between the finished appearance of a hand-pieced quilt and that of a machine-pieced quilt. Most patchworkers today piece their blocks on a sewing machine. With practice, you will probably find that you can piece most blocks, especially those assembled by the unit-row construction method, as accurately and precisely on the sewing machine as you can by hand. Even if you never plan to machine-piece a quilt, you may find a knowledge of machine-piecing techniques quite helpful.

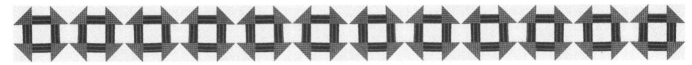

Learn These Machine-Piecing Skills While Making a Hole in the Barn Door Block

- *using templates with seam allowances*
- *chain-piecing two-bar units and triangle-squares*
- *unit-row construction method*
- *maintaining sharp points on outside of block*
- *machine-piecing rows to rows*
- *pressing machine-pieced blocks*

Materials:

¼ yard each of 3 fabrics
Sewing machine and basic sewing supplies

Finished Block Size: *9" square*

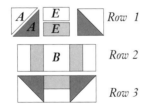

Row 1
Row 2
Row 3

Hole in the Barn Door
Block Piecing Diagram

1. Make templates with seam allowances for triangle A, square B, and rectangle E from patterns on page 41.

2. Position template on **wrong side** of fabric at least ½" from fabric edge. Align grain line arrow with lengthwise or crosswise grain. Mark fine line around template, which is your cutting line.

Because templates include seam allowances, successive pieces can be placed against cutting line of another piece to save marking and cutting time and to allow the maximum number of pieces on your fabric.

Mark four triangle As on first fabric (blue plaid), four rectangle Es on second fabric (red stripe), and four triangle As, four rectangle Es, and one square B on third fabric (white print). Carefully cut them out on drawn lines. Stacking fabric and cutting through several layers at once will speed up this step.

3. Because fabric pieces marked with templates that include seam allowances do not have sewing lines marked on them, you must be able to gauge and sew an accurate ¼"-wide seam on your machine. Practice sewing accurate ¼" seams on scraps of fabric until you are confident that you can sew straight, precise seams.

Refer to Block Piecing Diagram and lay out pieces right side up to form block.

Chain Piecing Two-Bar Units

This block contains a central square with **triangle-squares** at the corners, and outer squares made with joined pairs of rectangles, called a **two-bar unit**.

When several small pieces need to be joined, chain piecing helps prevent small pieces from being dragged down into machine throat plate at the beginning of seams. It also saves time because you repeat the same process over and over and do not have to stop as often to clip threads.

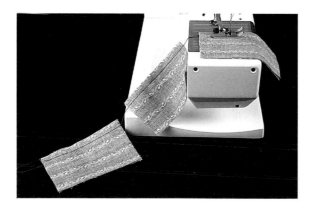

To chain-piece four two-bar units, pair rectangles, one from each fabric, with right sides facing and raw edges aligned. (You don't need to pin these or most other pairs of individual pieces unless seam will be longer than approximately 6".)

Take a precise ¼" seam on long edge of each pair, stitching from raw edge to raw edge. (Backstitching is not necessary at the end of the seam since it will subsequently be crossed by another seam that will secure the stitching.) Without cutting the threads at the end of the seam, take a few stitches without any fabric under the needle, creating a short thread chain that is approximately ⅛" long. Then, feed through the next pair of rectangles. Continue to feed through pairs of rectangles until you have sewn all of them. After all rectangles have been joined, clip threads between the two-bar units. Finger-press seam allowances toward the darker fabric.

Unit-Row Construction Method

Compare all units to see that they are the same size; adjust any seams as needed. All units for this block should measure 3½" square, including seam allowances. Refer to Hole in the Barn Door Block Piecing Diagram on page 36 and join units into three rows.

Finger-press seam allowances away from the center unit in rows 1 and 3 and toward the center square in row 2. Pressing seams in opposite directions reduces bulk and aids in matching pieces.

Maintaining Sharp Points on Triangles

After rows have been sewn and pressed, measure to make sure triangle tips along the top of row 1 and bottom of row 3 are ¼" from the raw outer edge of the block to allow for seam allowances. With experience you will be able to judge your workmanship without having to measure. If the triangle tips are too close to the raw edge, they will be blunted or chopped off when the block is joined to other blocks or pieces. If the tips are too far from the raw edge, they will float.

Joining Rows

Place first two rows of blocks together with right sides facing. Seams that joined units into rows should butt up tightly to each other with seam allowances pressed in opposite directions. Pin-match ends of rows and points where seams on one row meet seams from another row. Insert pins perpendicular to fabric ¼" from raw edge (along seam line). Raw edges of rows may or may not match exactly. Sew rows together from raw edge to raw edge. Stitching should go through places where pins align pieces. (If necessary, take a slightly wider or narrower seam to sew through matching points. Do this with caution.) Then gradually return to an exact ¼" seam. Either remove pins just before reaching them or sew slowly and carefully over them. Sew row 3 to other side of row 2 to complete block. Triangle tips at ends of rows should be ¼" from the raw edge to allow for seam allowances around the block.

It is easiest to match seams when top seam allowances are facing away from you (toward sewing machine) and

bottom (underneath) seam allowances are facing toward you (away from sewing machine). (See seam allowance (a) on photo.) The machine pushes the top seam against the opposing bottom seam and almost automatically matches them. With practice, you will probably find that you do not need to pin-match seams that are butted in this way but can merely hold them in place as you sew.

When top seam allowances are facing toward you and bottom (underneath) seam allowances are facing away from you, matching seams is slightly more difficult. (See seam allowance (b) on photo.) Some machines tend to

Easing Pieces to Fit

When confronted with two pieces or rows that should be the same size but are not, ease the slightly longer piece to fit the shorter piece, pin-matching points. Add pins to distribute fullness evenly along seam; then stitch with the shorter piece on top. The sewing machine feed dogs will ease in the fullness on the bottom piece. In other words, sew with a "baggy bottom."

If pieces or rows are too dissimilar in size to ease without puckering, check to be sure that you cut the pieces the correct size and that your seams are ¼" wide.

push top seams forward and out of alignment with bottom seams. To "out-think your sewing machine" and counteract this tendency to mismatch seams, try pin-matching the top seam approximately a pin width ahead of the bottom seam; then let the machine push the top seam forward into alignment with the bottom seam.

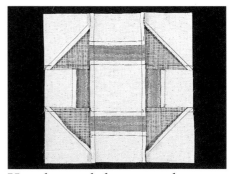

Lightly and carefully press block from wrong side to set direction of seams. Turn block over and touch up any seams that are not fully open. Use a large ruled square and measure block. It should measure 9½" square, including seam allowances. A variance of approximately ⅛" from this is acceptable, but if your block is much smaller or larger, you will have to remake it.

Learn to Maintain Sharp Points on Triangles While Machine-Piecing the Ribbon Star Block

In a Shoo Fly block, all triangle points or tips fall to the outside, but on many other blocks, such as the Ribbon Star, triangles are positioned so that their tips must form sharp points within the block.

Materials:

¼ yard each of 3 fabrics

Finished Block Size: *9" square*

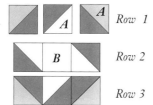

Ribbon Star Block
Piecing Diagram

1. Make templates with seam allowances for triangle A and square B from patterns on page 41. From fabric for star pieces (pink), cut one square B and four triangle As. From fabric for ribbon pieces (navy), cut eight triangle As. From background fabric (pink and blue print), cut four triangle As. Refer to block piecing diagram and lay out pieces. Piece triangle-squares and join units into three rows. Check position of triangle tips in each row; they should be ¼" from raw edge to allow for seam allowances.

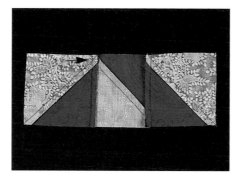

2. On wrong side of unit, find stitched X at place where seam that joins two triangles meets seam that joins two block units. This X determines location of finished triangle tips and is the matching point for pinning and stitching rows together. To join rows, pin-match seams of rows 1 and 2, using stitched X points. Sew rows together, stitching through center of the X. (If any seams that join pieces into rows are off slightly, take slightly narrower or wider seam in some places in order to sew through X.)

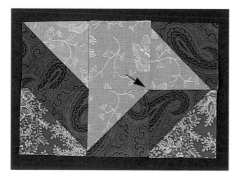

3. Stitching through center of X ensures crisp triangle points. (See arrow.) If seam is too narrow, triangle points will float. If seam is too wide, they will be blunted or chopped off.

Assembly-Line Methods for Machine Piecing

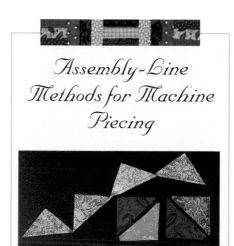

Many patchwork projects use multiples of the same patchwork block. Using assembly line methods will allow you to piece several identical blocks more quickly than if you piece them individually. Stack pieces right side up. Chain-piece each stack to form units. Press units and return each stack of units to their position in the laid-out blocks. Chain-piece units into rows. Chain-piece rows to complete blocks.

Goose-Chase Units

A Goose-Chase unit is a pieced rectangle that is formed by sewing two smaller right triangles to the short sides of another right triangle that is twice the size of the smaller ones. These units are combined with other shapes into patchwork blocks, such as Sawtooth Star, or you can join the units into long strips for a Goose Chase Border or Flying Geese Quilt. The photo below shows a single unit and a strip of joined units.

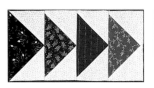

Learn These Machine-Piecing Skills While Making a Sawtooth Star Block

🏠 *making a template from a diagram with dimensions* 🏠 *joining Goose-Chase units to other pieces*
🏠 *making Goose-Chase units* 🏠 *machine-piecing rows of different widths*

Materials:

¼ yard each of 2 fabrics
Graph paper

Finished Block Size: *12" square*

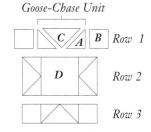

Goose-Chase Unit

	C/A	B	Row 1
D			Row 2
			Row 3

Sawtooth Star Block Piecing Diagram

1. Using diagram on page 41, draw pattern for square D on graph paper. Make templates for patterns A, B, C, and D. Use a sewing machine needle or other large needle to pierce holes at corners of sewing lines so that you can mark matching points. On fabric for star, mark one square D and eight triangle As. After marking around triangle template, insert pencil through corner holes in template to mark matching points. (Matching points can be marked before or after cutting, but they are easier to mark before cutting.) On background fabric, mark and cut four triangle Cs and four square Bs.

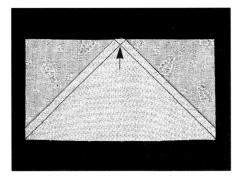

2. Refer to block piecing diagram and lay out pieces for block. Make four Goose-Chase units. Pin-match long side of triangle A to one short side of triangle C. Insert pin through each matching point on triangle A; then insert same pin through corresponding point on triangle C. Stitch seam and finger-press seam allowances. Repeat on other short side of triangle C. Trim triangle tips even with raw edges of Goose-Chase unit.

Stitching of Goose-Chase unit forms X on wrong side of unit, ¼" from raw edge. Center of X is matching point for pinning and stitching these units to other units or pieces.

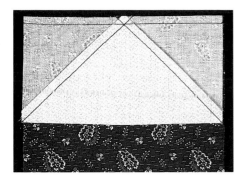

3. Use center of X as matching point when Goose-Chase units are pin-matched to another piece or unit. Pin Goose-Chase unit to one side of square D. Stitch exactly through center of X to maintain a crisp triangle corner. Sew with Goose-Chase unit on top. Sew second Goose-Chase unit to opposite side of square D to complete row 2 of block.

4. Refer to block piecing diagram on page 40 and assemble rows 1 and 3. Because Goose-Chase units are rectangular, rows for blocks with Goose-Chase units are often of uneven widths. Notice that row 2 of Sawtooth Star is wider than outer rows. To complete Sawtooth Star, join rows, taking care to maintain crisp corners on Goose-Chase units.

Aligning Patchwork Pieces

With practice, you will develop an eye for a ¼" seam and will be able to visualize matching points. One trick is to pair templates and align sewing lines. Pin fabric pieces before sewing so that they are aligned in same way as templates. Another method is to trim off excess fabric at an angle that matches angle of piece to which it will be sewn. To do this, trim excess template that extends beyond edge of other template as shown (see arrow).

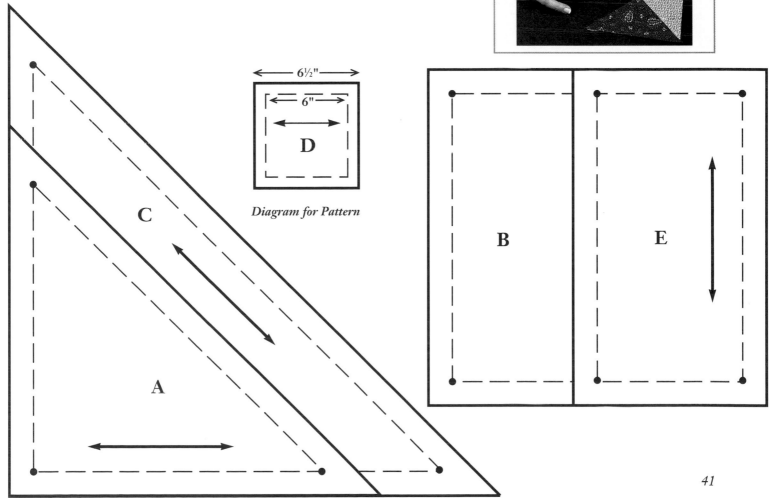

6½"

6"

D

Diagram for Pattern

C

A

B

E

Drafting Patchwork Blocks and Adding to Patchwork Skills

*P*attern drafting is the process of drawing a pattern to a desired size. If you want to reproduce an antique quilt, enlarge a small block drawing from a book or magazine, make a block in a size different from the pattern you have, or design your own block, you will need to know how to draft a pattern.

Drafting Patchwork Blocks and Adding to Patchwork Skills

Basic Grids

Most patchwork blocks can be divided into a grid of equal-sized squares, also called **block units** or **units**. Visualize a grid of squares superimposed over the block. The block may divide into rows of two, three, four, five, six, seven, or more square units in each row. In some cases, seams will fall along the grid divisions; in other cases, the grid divisions will differ from the actual seam lines. Transferring blocks onto grids is the **grid method** of drafting. Most patchwork blocks can be drafted onto one of the basic grids.

Some patterns, however, do not divide evenly into the squares of a grid. Designs based on eight-pointed stars, on hexagons, or on equilateral triangles are examples of patterns that will not draft onto a grid of equal squares. The chapter "Beyond Basic Patchwork" explains how to draft some common non-grid patterns.

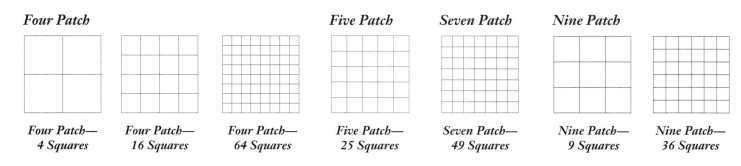

Four Patch   *Five Patch*   *Seven Patch*   *Nine Patch*

Four Patch—   *Four Patch—*   *Four Patch—*   *Five Patch—*   *Seven Patch—*   *Nine Patch—*   *Nine Patch—*
4 Squares   *16 Squares*   *64 Squares*   *25 Squares*   *49 Squares*   *9 Squares*   *36 Squares*

Block Units

In the chapter "First Steps in Traditional Patchwork," you learned how to work with simple block units, as shown in diagrams 1 through 4 below. Other common patchwork block units are shown in diagrams 5 through 11 with corresponding piecing diagrams.

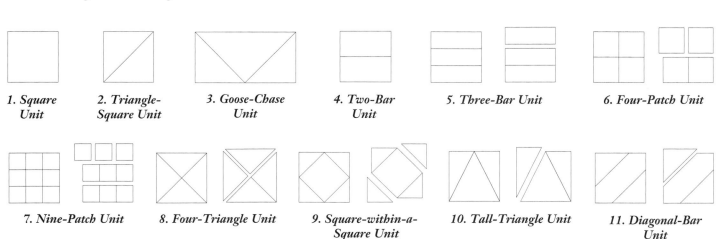

1. Square Unit   *2. Triangle-Square Unit*   *3. Goose-Chase Unit*   *4. Two-Bar Unit*   *5. Three-Bar Unit*   *6. Four-Patch Unit*

7. Nine-Patch Unit   *8. Four-Triangle Unit*   *9. Square-within-a-Square Unit*   *10. Tall-Triangle Unit*   *11. Diagonal-Bar Unit*

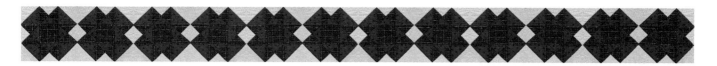

Learn to Draft Three Different Sizes of the Swamp Patch Block

Materials:

The only supplies you need to draft most blocks by the grid method are a ruler, pencil, and graph paper. Four-, five-, eight-, or ten-squares-per-inch graph paper will handle most blocks. (Always check graph paper for accuracy before using.) In some instances, you will also need sheets of plain paper that are larger than the size you want to draw the block, and draftsman's tools—a 45° triangle or a large ruled square.

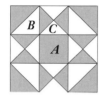

Swamp Patch Block

Method 1: Use this method when desired block size can be drawn on a sheet of graph paper. (Large sheets of graph paper can be purchased at an art supply store.)

Examine the original block drawing. If shapes are not identified, label each different shape with a letter. Determine the finished size for your block. The easiest method is to choose a block size that can be divided easily by the number of square units in the block. For example, 3", 6", 9", and 12" are convenient sizes for drafting a nine-patch block. Each unit for a 6" block would be 2" square (6" ÷ 3 = 2"). If the unit size is in halves, fourths, or eighths of an inch, use four- or eight-squares-per-inch graph paper. If unit size is in fifths or tenths of an inch, use five- or ten-squares-per-inch graph paper.

1. Using sharp pencil, draw square on graph paper equal to your block size. (This drawing will be used later to make templates.) Divide square into grid that corresponds to number of units in block.

To draft 6"-square Swamp Patch block, draw 6" square. This is a nine-patch block, so draw 3 x 3 grid of 9 units. (Each unit is 2" square.)

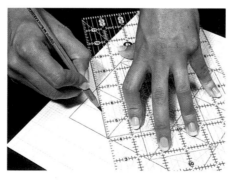

2. Divide units as corresponding squares in original block are divided. For example, draw diagonal lines across squares to make triangles. Label shapes to correspond with original block drawing.

Method 2: Use this method when desired block size is large, and therefore, it would be easier to draft the block units.

When determining the finished size of your block, choose a block size that can be divided easily by the number of square units in the block. For example, each unit for a 9" Swamp Patch block would be 3" square; for a 15" block, each unit would be 5" square.

1. Since square A is size of unit, draw square the size of unit onto graph paper and label it A to correspond to block drawing. To draft 9" Swamp Patch block, draw 3" square.

2. The B triangles are created by dividing unit diagonally. Draw another unit (3" square) and divide it in half to form two triangles. Label triangle B.

3. Smaller C triangles are created by dividing unit into four triangles. Draw unit and divide it diagonally both ways to make four triangles. Label triangle C.

Method 3: Use this method when the size of block units is in thirds or sevenths of an inch. Because the unit lines do not fall on the lines of readily available graph paper, a grid is drawn on a plain sheet of paper, instead of graph paper.

1. Determine finished size for block and unit size. For example, each unit for 7" nine-patch block, such as Swamp Patch, would be 2⅓" (7" ÷ 3 divisions = 2⅓" unit size), not convenient size for most types of graph paper or to measure with most rulers. To draft 7" Swamp Patch block

accurately, draw 7" square onto plain sheet of paper. Divide square into grid by choosing number slightly larger than block size that is multiple of number of divisions in block. For this example, 9 would be such a number since it is divided evenly by 3 and is larger than 7. Place ruler end at upper left corner of 7" square. Slant ruler diagonally until 9" mark intersects lower right side of square. Since 9" divided by 3 equals 3", make dot every 3" along ruler. (Mark dots at 3" and 6".)

2. Draw lines through dots, from top to bottom of square, dividing square into three equal parts.

3. Repeat to mark horizontal divisions.

4. Divide units to correspond with units in original block and label.

Using Units to Design Blocks

Begin by choosing a grid, such as a nine-patch grid. Draw a grid of nine squares; then, divide some or all of the units into more complex units. For example, draw a triangle-square unit in each corner to create the Shoo Fly block. Experiment by dividing other solid units into more complex ones. Try dividing solid units into triangle-square units. Or, divide them into four-triangle units

to form a Swamp Patch block. Using two-bar units in this position instead makes the Hole in the Barn Door. And using four-patch units instead makes a Prairie Queen block. These are all well-known patchwork patterns.

Keep trying until you come up with something new. Replacing side units with tall-triangle units results in an original design. We named our block Shoo Fly Star.

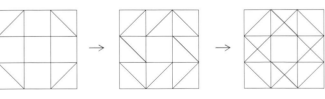

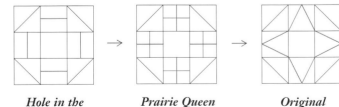

Shoo Fly   *Ribbon Star*   *Swamp Patch*   *Hole in the Barn Door*   *Prairie Queen*   *Original Block— Shoo Fly Star*

Adding to Patchwork Skills

Some straight-seam blocks do not break down into rows for the unit-row construction method. These blocks are usually constructed by using one of three other basic construction methods—the **four-triangle method**, the **diagonal-bar method,** or the **center-outward method**.

Four-Triangle Construction Method

Blocks constructed with this method have seams that run diagonally from corner to corner in both directions, dividing the blocks into four triangular units.

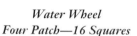

Water Wheel
Four Patch—16 Squares   *Piecing Diagram*

Triangle Unit

Center-Outward Construction Method

Blocks constructed with this method begin with a center unit. Other pieces or units are added either alternately to opposite sides, or clockwise or counter-clockwise around the center unit.

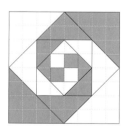

Snail Trail Four Patch—
64 Squares

1.   *2.*   *3.*   *4.*

Diagonal-Bar Construction Method

Blocks constructed using this method have a diagonal-bar unit that runs from corner to corner with large triangular units on both sides of the bar. They are essentially larger, more complex versions of the basic diagonal-bar unit. Two blocks that fit into this category are Friendship Name Chain and Chicago Pavements.

Diagonal-Bar Unit

Triangle Unit

Friendship Name Chain
Nine Patch—9 Squares   *Piecing Diagram*

Diagonal-Bar Unit

Triangle Unit

Chicago Pavements
Four Patch—64 Squares   *Piecing Diagram*

Learn These Drafting and Piecing Skills
While Making a Criss-Cross Block

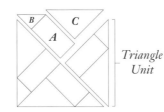

🏠 *drafting a block using Drafting Method 1*   🏠 *piecing a block using four-triangle construction method*

Materials:

¼ yard each of 3 different fabrics

Graph paper

Pencil

Ruler

Finished Block Size: *6" square*

Piecing Diagram

**Criss-Cross
Nine Patch—
36 Squares**

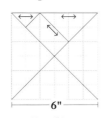

**Drafting
Diagram**

1. Draft Criss-Cross block to 6" finished size by drawing 6" square. Divide square into a 36-square grid and then draw lines diagonally from corner to corner to make four triangles. Use grid lines as guides and subdivide each triangle into three pieces: triangle C, triangle B, and rectangle A, as shown. Make templates.

2. From first fabric (white), cut four triangle Cs. From second fabric (red), cut four triangle Bs. (Note grain line arrows.) From third fabric (blue), cut four rectangle As.

3. Join pieces in sequence shown to form four triangle units. Pair units and join. Complete block with long diagonal seam.

Learn These Drafting and Piecing Skills While
Making a Windblown Square Block

🏠 *drafting a block using Drafting Method 2*   🏠 *piecing a block using center-outward construction*

Materials:

¼ yard each of 3 different fabrics

Graph paper

Pencil

Ruler

Finished Block Size: *12" square*

Windblown Square

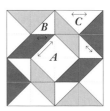

**Windblown Square
Four Patch—
16 Squares**

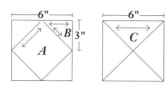

Drafting Diagrams

1. Draft block to 12" finished size. Since block is 16-square four-patch, each grid square or unit equals 3" (12" ÷ 4 grid squares on a side = 3"). Long side or hypotenuse of triangle C equals two grid squares. Draw 6" square and divide it diagonally into four triangles. Label triangle C. Draft patterns for square A and triangle B by drawing square-within-a-square unit in 6" square.

2. Make templates for three pattern pieces. (Recommended grain lines are indicated on block drawing and drafting diagrams.)

From background fabric (large print), cut one square A, four triangle Cs, and four triangle Bs. From second fabric (blue) and third fabric (red), cut two triangle Cs and four triangle Bs each.

3. Piece Windblown Square block by making increasingly larger square-within-in-a-square units, as shown.

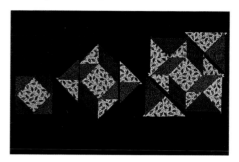

Learn These Drafting and Piecing Skills While Making a Gentleman's Fancy Block

drafting a block using Drafting Method 2   *piecing a block using diagonal-bar construction method*

Materials:

¼ yard each of 4 different fabrics
Pencil
Graph paper
Ruler

Finished Block Size: *12" square*

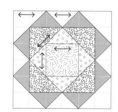

Gentleman's Fancy
Nine Patch—36 Squares

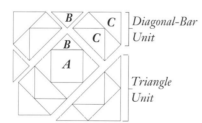

Piecing Diagram

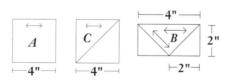

Drafting Diagrams

1. Draft Gentleman's Fancy block to 12" finished size. Since block is 36-square nine-patch, each grid square or unit equals 2" (12" ÷ 6 grid squares on a side = 2"). Since square A is size of two grid squares, draw 4" square on graph paper for A. Triangle C is ½ of square A; draw another 4" square, divide it into two triangles, and label one triangle C. Longest side or hypotenuse of triangle B equals two grid squares. The triangle is one grid square high. Draw 2" x 4" rectangle; draw triangle B within rectangle for Goose-Chase unit.

2. Make templates for three pattern pieces. (Recommended grain lines are indicated on block drawing.) From background fabric (cream print), cut four triangle Cs and four triangle Bs. From second fabric (red plaid), cut one square A and eight triangle Bs. From third fabric (brown print), cut four triangle Cs. From fourth fabric (teal), cut four triangle Bs.

3. Join pieces, as shown.

Basic Settings and Borders for Quilts

Having a working knowledge of basic straight and diagonal sets is vital, since the majority of quilts are made using these sets. Borders are added to a quilt setting to enhance the beauty of a quilt. Choose fabrics and colors for borders that are either the same as those in the center of the quilt or of similar color value or design.

Basic Settings and Borders for Quilts

This chapter defines terms that apply to most quilt settings and to basic borders and describes sewing techniques for joining blocks and adding borders. You'll also learn how to plan simple quilts and how to make a quilt the size you want by altering block size, settings, and borders. Also included are guidelines for estimating yardage for quilts you plan yourself.

Basic Settings Terminology

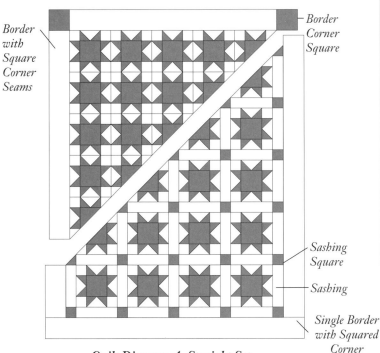

Quilt Diagram A, Straight Set
Top Portion–Block-to-Block Set
Lower Portion–Sashing with Squares Set

Quilt Diagram B, Diagonal Set
Top Portion–Alternate Plain Block Set
Lower Portion–Continuous Sashing Set

Straight Set. In a straight-set quilt, the sides of the blocks run parallel to the sides of the quilt, as shown in Quilt Diagram A. Some block designs are directional, such as House on a Hill, and are set straight.

Diagonal Set. In a diagonally set quilt, blocks are set on point with the sides of the blocks running diagonally at a 45° angle to the sides of the quilt, as shown in Quilt Diagram B. Many blocks, such as Grape Basket, are intended to be set on point. Large setting triangles along the sides of the quilt and corner fill in around the blocks to complete the quilt.

Block-to-Block. A straight- or diagonal-set quilt may be set block-to-block, without sashing, as illustrated by the top portion of Quilt Diagram A. Blocks may be of identical or varied design.

Alternate Plain Block. The alternate plain block set is a variation of a basic straight or diagonal block-to-block set. Plain blocks, also called setting squares, alternate with pieced or appliquéd blocks. Alternate plain blocks are usually not used in quilts with sashing. The top portion of Quilt Diagram B shows an alternate plain block diagonal set.

Sashing or Lattice Strips. Sashing is the fabric that separates blocks, framing them and making the quilt larger. There are two kinds of sashing: continuous and sashing with sashing squares. The lower portion of Quilt Diagram B shows a quilt set with continuous sashing. One piece of fabric runs the full diagonal length of the quilt one way with short sashing inserted between blocks, perpendicular to the continuous sashing. The lower portion of Quilt Diagram A shows a quilt set with sashing and sashing squares.

Assembling a Quilt Top
Straight Set, Block-to-Block

1. Lay blocks in vertical rows to make sure every block is positioned correctly. After arranging and positioning blocks, with right sides facing and raw edges aligned, pin-match blocks together for each row. After a row is pinned, match corners of blocks and secure with additional pins before stitching.

Sew blocks together to form rows. Press seam allowances to darker fabric or to one side to reduce bulk and to aid in matching seam lines of next row.

2. Lay completed rows on floor before joining to make sure blocks and rows are positioned correctly.

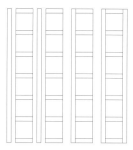

Straight Set

With right sides facing, join rows in sets of two. Pin-match ends of rows and points where seams of one row meet seams of another row. Raw edges of rows may or may not match exactly, but seam lines should be pin-matched. Seams should abut tightly with seam allowances pressed in opposite directions. If any seams do not match because of sewing errors, remove stitching and resew seam or seams. Trim any tails (or points) and dangling threads. After all rows have been paired and stitched, join pairs to complete quilt top. Press top after borders have been added.

Straight Set with Continuous Sashing

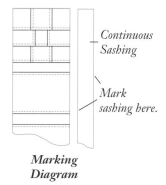

Continuous Sashing, Straight Set

1. Short sashing is needed for top of each block in this setting plus one for bottom of each vertical row. Length of short sashing equals width of each block (with seam allowances). Sashing width is given in quilt pattern or determined by quilter.

Lay blocks and short sashing on floor in vertical rows, making sure that every block is positioned correctly. With right sides facing and raw edges aligned, pin-match short sashing to top of each block and sew. Then join blocks with sashing in rows. Add sashing to bottom of each row. Press seam allowances to one side.

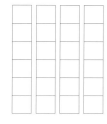

Continuous Sashing

Mark sashing here.

Marking Diagram

2. Continuous sashing piece is equal to length of a row plus seam allowances. Mark each continuous sashing piece on wrong side at seam intersections of each row before joining to ensure that blocks will be aligned across quilt. (See diagram at left.) For example, if length of each block is 12" with 3"-wide sashing, mark continuous sashing piece at 12" and 3" intervals.

Straight Set with Sashing and Sashing Squares

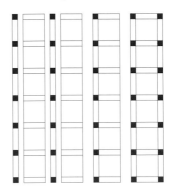

Sashing with Sashing Squares Straight Set

1. Lay out and assemble rows in manner described for continuous sashing. To make sashing with sashing squares, cut sashing pieces equal to length of each block plus seam allowances and equal to width of sashing attached to blocks plus seam allowances. Sashing square dimensions are equal to width of sashing plus seam allowances. Alternate sashing squares with sashing to form one long sashing piece.

2. With right sides facing and raw edges aligned, pin-match sashing seams to seams of rows and sew. Join sashing to one side of each row. Join row sets and sashing to each other. Add sashing to last row to complete top. Press seams to one side.

Diagonal Set

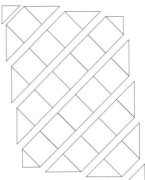

Block-to-Block Diagonal Set

The method for assembling a diagonal set, with or without sashing, is basically the same as that for a straight set. The major difference is the necessity of setting and corner triangles and, in some sets, plain setting squares. After setting triangles and squares have been cut, lay blocks in diagonal rows on the floor. (See next section to learn how to make setting triangles and squares.) If using sashing, the length of short sashing is equal to side of each block plus seam allowances. (See diagrams at right.) Join to form rows. Join rows in pairs if it is a block-to-block setting or to continuous sashing. Add corner triangles to complete top. Press seams to one side.

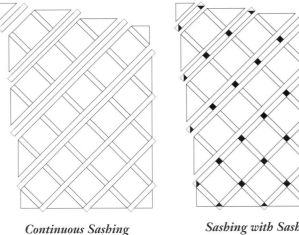

Continuous Sashing Diagonal Set

Sashing with Sashing Squares Diagonal Set

Making Setting Squares and Triangles for Diagonal Sets

Use either the quick-cutting or template method. The quick-cutting method is faster and well suited for machine piecing where the presser foot measures the ¼" seam. The template method is ideal when hand piecing because the setting pieces will have seam lines.

Template Method

1. For setting squares, make a square template equal to finished size of your block. Add seam allowances around pieces before cutting them from fabric.

—Setting Triangle

Place hypotenuse on straight grain.

2. For setting triangle, draw a square equal to finished size of your block and divide it in half diagonally to form two triangles, as shown. Use one triangle to make template for setting triangle and set aside second triangle for making corner triangle (step 3). Make template from triangle, adding seam allowances if machine-piecing. Place long side (hypotenuse) of triangle on lengthwise or crosswise fabric grain so outer edges of quilt will not be on bias.

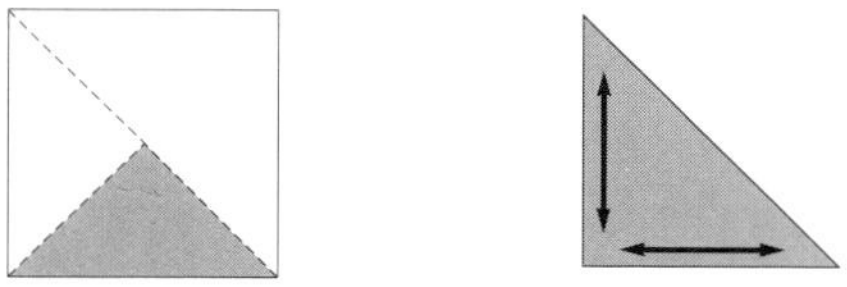

Place legs on straight grain.

3. For corner triangle, divide second triangle from step 2 in half as shown. (You will have two templates; discard one.) Make template from remaining triangle, adding seam allowances if machine-piecing. Use template to mark four corner triangles. Place template so that short sides (legs) of triangle are on straight of grain, and long side (hypotenuse) is on bias.

Quick-Cutting Method

Use large ruled square, plastic ruler, and rotary cutter to measure and cut pieces. The Quick-Cutting Chart for Setting and Corner Pieces at right gives frequently used measurements. Use blank lines in chart for your specific block measurements.

1. For setting squares, add ½" to finished size of block and cut needed number of squares. For example, cut 12½" setting squares for 12" finished-size blocks.

2. For setting triangles, a large square is divided into 4 triangles. To determine size of large square, first obtain diagonal measurement of finished size of block. This is easily done by multiplying finished length of one block side by 1.41 and rounding off to nearest ⅛" (.125"). (See Ruler to Decimal Conversion Chart, below right.) Add 1.25" (1¼") to diagonal measurement and cut a square with sides that size. Divide square in half diagonally both ways, as shown on chart, to make four setting triangles. Long side (hypotenuse) of each of these triangles is on straight of grain.

To figure how many large squares to cut, count number of setting triangles you need and divide by 4. Round off odd numbers to next highest number if necessary, and save extra triangles in your scrap bag.

3. For corner triangles, always cut two squares and then divide each in half diagonally to make two triangles each (four total). To determine size of square, divide diagonal measurement of finished block by 2, and add ⅞" (.875") to it.

Quick-Cutting Chart for Setting and Corner Pieces*

Finished Block Size	Finished Diagonal	Size To Cut Square for:		Size To Cut Setting Squares
		Setting ⊠ Triangles**	Corner ◲ Triangles***	
3"	4.25"	5.5"	3"	3½"
4"	5.625"	6.875"	3.75"	4½"
5"	7.125"	8.375"	4.5"	5½"
6"	8.5"	9.75"	5.125"	6½"
7"	9.875"	11.125"	5.875"	7½"
8"	11.375"	12.625"	6.625"	8½"
9"	12.75"	14.0"	7.25"	9½"
10"	14.125"	15.375"	8"	10½"
11"	15.5"	16.75"	8.625"	11½"
12"	17.0"	18.25"	9.375"	12½"
13"	18.375"	19.625"	10.125"	13½"
14"	19.75"	21.0"	10.75"	14½"
15"	21.25"	22.5"	11.5"	15½"

* Rounded off to the nearest ⅛" (.125).
Use blank lines to note your own block sizes.

** Finished Block Size x 1.41 = Finished Diagonal.
Finished Diagonal + 1.25 = Size of Square.

*** $\dfrac{\text{Finished Diagonal}}{2} + .875"$

Ruler to Decimal Conversion Chart

⅛	¼	⅜	½	⅝	¾	⅞
.125	.25	.375	.5	.625	.75	.875

Planning Simple Quilts

One of the reasons quiltmaking is enjoyable is that you can generate your own projects, not just make quilts that are already planned out for you. Planning your own quilt gives you control of not only the color and design, but also of the size. The quilt elements you can alter to change the size of a quilt are: block size, number of blocks, setting, sashing, and borders.

When planning a quilt, its use or purpose is an important starting point. Use graph paper, ruler, and pencil to sketch a plan for your quilt, changing the design elements as needed to come as close to your ideal size as possible. The charts below may help you determine the best quilt size for you.

Some Standard Quilt Sizes					
	Crib	Twin	Double (Full)	Queen	King
Mattress	27"x 52"	39" x 75"	54" x 75"	60" x 80"	76" x 80"
Quilt To Use with Dust Ruffle	30" x 54" / 30" x 45"	65" x 95"	80" x 95"	86" x 100"	106" x 106"
Batting Sizes	45" x 60"	72" x 90" / 81" x 96"	81" x 96" / 90" x 108"	90" x 108"	120" x 120"

Standard Mattress Sizes			
Bassinett	13" x 28"	Double	54" x 75"
Three-Year Crib	23" x 46"	Queen	60" x 80"
Six-Year Crib	27" x 52"	King	76" x 80"
Twin	39" x 75"		

Adjusting Quilt Size
Change Block Size

When considering changing block size, keep in mind the number of pieces within the block and their size. A nine-patch, for example, has only nine squares in it. In a 6" or 9" block size, it makes an attractive pattern. As a 12" or larger block, it would lose some of its charm. A complex pattern, such as Tree of Life, can be made quite large and still be attractive.

Also consider how changing block size changes the size of your quilt. If each block in a three-by-four block setting is 10", the finished size of the inner quilt would measure 30" x 40". Increasing the block size to 12" would increase quilt dimensions to 36" (3 blocks x 12") x 48" (4 blocks x 12").

Change Number of Blocks

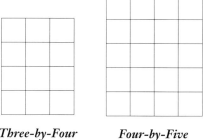

Three-by-Four
Block Layout   *Four-by-Five*
                        Block Layout

If the number of 10" blocks in a three-by-four- block setting (diagram on left) were increased to make a four-by-five-block setting (diagram on right) with eight more blocks, the quilt measurement would increase from 30" x 40" to 40" x 50".

Add Borders

Often quilts are planned so that the inner quilt is the part that covers the top of the bed, with the borders dropping over the side. The quilts shown in Quilt Diagrams A and B on page 52 show ways that borders can add to the size as well as enhance the design of a quilt.

Change the Setting or Layout

1	2	3	4
2			
3			
4			
5			

*Four-by-Five Block
Layout with Sashing*

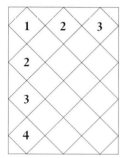

*Three-by-Four Block
Diagonal Layout*

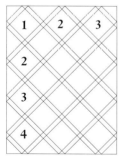

*Three-by-Four Block
Diagonal Layout
with Sashing*

Add sashing, straight set. If each piece of sashing is 3" wide, quilt would be 9" wider (3 sashing x 3") and 12" longer (4 sashing x 3") than without sashing.

Diagonal Set. The width measurement for blocks set on point is roughly 1½ times wider than when arranged in a straight set. When figuring diagonal measurement of a block, refer to Quick-Cutting Chart on page 55 for diagonal measurements of common-size blocks, or multiply finished size of block (square) by 1.41.

For example, a 10" block would be 14.1" on diagonal, or 14" rounded off. For a three-by-four diagonal block setting with 10"-square blocks, the inner quilt would measure approximately 42" x 56", as opposed to 30" x 40" if set straight. The diagonally set quilt would have six setting squares as well as setting and corner triangles to fill in around blocks. Another option would be to make six more pieced or appliquéd blocks to substitute for setting squares.

Add sashing, diagonal set. Sashing that separates diagonally set blocks adds more width and length, too. This diagram shows a diagonally set quilt with 18 blocks, set with sashing and squares. If block size is 10" and sashing 3" wide, the quilt would measure 54¾" x 73", as opposed to 42" x 56" without sashing.

To Find Finished Quilt Width, Diagonal Set with Sashing

1. **Find diagonal measurement of block:**
   10" (block finished size) x 1.41 = 14.1" (Round off to 14".)

2. **Find diagonal measurement of sashing:**
   3" (sashing finished width) x 1.41 = 4.23" (Round off to 4.25".)

3. **Find finished width of quilt:**
   a. Find total finished width of blocks:
      3 blocks x 14" (diagonal measurement) = 42".
   b. Find total finished width of sashing:
      2 sashing squares + 2 half sashing squares = 3 squares x 4¼" = 12¾".
   c. Add the two widths:
      42" + 12¾" = 54¾" (finished quilt width).

To Find Finished Quilt Length, Diagonal Set with Sashing

1. See step 1, above.

2. See step 2, above.

3. Find finished length of quilt:
   a. Find total finished length of blocks:
      4 blocks x 14" = 56".
   b. Find total finished width of sashing:
      3 sashing squares + 2 half-sashing squares = 4 x 4¼" = 17".
   c. Add the two lengths:
      56" + 17" = 73" (finished quilt length).

Determining Fabric Yardage

The best tool for estimating yardage for a quilt is a drawing or sketch of the project. A rough scale drawing on graph paper with the dimensions of the blocks and borders noted will take the guessing out of estimating the amounts of each fabric used in the quilt. Once you have a diagram, you can work with each fabric separately and come up with a list of yardage requirements to take to the fabric shop.

When estimating yardage, always work with a fabric width of 40", rather than the 44/45" width indicated on bolts of cotton. Most yardage is narrower than 45" and may shrink when washed. Also, you will not be using the selvage area, which subtracts width. This same rule applies when using 60"-wide fabric. Use 55" to figure yardage.

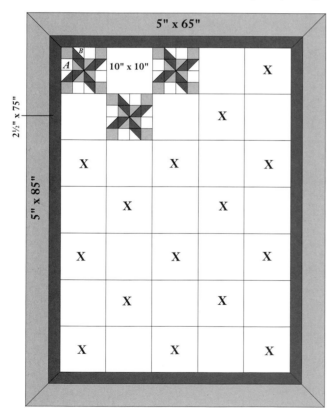

Quilt Diagram with Dimensions for Yardage Estimation

Estimating Yardage

1. Draw quilt to scale on graph paper. It is not necessary to draw in the piecing arrangement of individual blocks; instead, patchwork or appliqué blocks can be denoted by an X or by shading. (See Quilt Diagram at left.) However, drawing in all blocks will give you a good sense of how the finished quilt will look. Write in finished dimensions of blocks, borders, and setting pieces. Color or shade drawing to denote each fabric you will be using.

2. Determine cut size for pieces. **For borders and sashing**, add ½" to width for seam allowances and approximately 4" to length for insurance. **For setting pieces (if diagonal set)**, refer to Quick-Cutting Chart for Setting and Corner Pieces on page 55 for dimensions to cut squares, triangles, and short sashing pieces. **To cut individual pieces for blocks**, measure patterns with seam allowances to determine cut size of each piece. For triangles, nest two together to make a square for easy figuring. For appliqué pieces or odd-shaped pieces, such as hexagons, determine size square or rectangle needed to cut shape to make figuring easier.

3. Make a cutting chart for each fabric, listing cut size of pieces and number of pieces to cut. For pieces, determine number in one block and multiply by number of blocks to find number needed. Remember that for some blocks, the same pattern piece may be cut from more than one fabric.

Cutting Chart for Fabric		
	Finished Size	Cut Size
2 Side Borders	*5" x 85"*	*5½" x 89"*
2 Top & Bottom Borders	*5" x 65"*	*5½" x 69"*
72 A Squares (4 per block x 18 blks)	*2½"*	*3"*
72 B Triangles (4 per block x 18 blks)	*2½"*	*Cut 2 from 3⅜" square. (Use 3½" for estimate.)*

4. Draw a cutting diagram for each fabric, sketching in pieces to be cut. (See diagram on next page.) Draw borders and large pieces first; then estimate space allotment for smaller pieces from remaining cloth.

5. Double-check all figuring.

6. Allow an extra ¼ to ½ yard of each major fabric in quilt for accident insurance.

7. To estimate fabric for binding, see "Finishing Your Quilts," page 94. To estimate quilt backing fabric, see "Get Ready to Quilt," page 70.

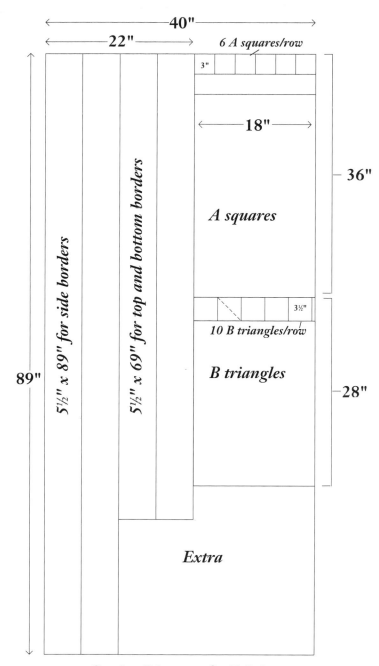

40"

22"

6 A squares/row

3"

18"

36"

5½" x 89" for side borders

5½" x 69" for top and bottom borders

A squares

89"

3½"

10 B triangles/row

B triangles

28"

Extra

Cutting Diagram for Fabric

More Yardage Rules of Thumb

Keep in mind that for patchwork quilts, the greater the number of pieces in the quilt top, the more fabric you will need to make it. That is because every patch has a ¼" seam allowance on all sides. The more pieces, the more seam allowances, and thus, the more fabric. Log Cabin quilts, for example, with their many seams, can require as much as 15 yards of fabric for a full-size quilt.

Appliqués for appliqué quilts have seam allowances, too, and the irregular shapes of many appliqués often prevent economical cutting. Therefore, appliqué quilts with lots of pieces sometimes require more yardage than you would expect.

Taking a look at the number of pieces in a quilt is a good way, also, to assess the difficulty of the pattern. The more pieces in a quilt, the harder it is to make.

A good principle to follow when estimating and buying fabric for a specific quilt is always to buy extra, and most quilters don't mind doing so. Always add an extra half yard when you are buying a yard or more of fabric.

Another rule of thumb is that it takes roughly 1½ to 2 times more fabric for a quilt top than it does for backing. A full-size quilt that requires 6 yards of fabric for the backing will probably need 9 to 12 total yards for the top. This rough idea provides a way to check your estimate.

Get Ready To Quilt

For many quilters, the thrill of completing a quilt top is equalled only by the joy of quilting it. But before you can take that first quilting stitch, some decisions need to be made—whether to hand-quilt or machine-quilt, what quilting designs you will use, and where they will go. You must mark the designs on the quilt top, prepare a quilt backing, choose the batting, and, finally, baste the three layers together.

Get Ready To Quilt

*In this chapter, we'll discuss quilting designs, strategies,
marking methods for both hand- and machine-quilting, backing and batting
choices, and how to layer and baste with thread or safety pins, so that
you are ready to hand- or machine-quilt in the best possible way.*

Choosing Between Hand and Machine Quilting

Hand-quilting and machine-quilting methods both have advantages and disadvantages. The unique stitch-space-stitch configuration of hand quilting has not yet been duplicated by machine, and the special status of fine hand quilting will probably never be diminished. Machine quilting is growing in popularity and acceptance. Machine-quilting advocates like the fact that they can quilt a full-size quilt in days.

Guidelines for Choosing a Quilting Method

Hand-Quilt If:

🏠 you have hand-sewn the top.

🏠 the pattern is a complex or difficult one that has taken a lot of time and skill to sew.

🏠 your quilt calls for curving quilting motifs. Unless you are a skilled machine quilter, hand quilting will be easier.

🏠 your quilt has open areas of solid, not print, fabric. Since quilting shows best on light, solid-colored fabrics, these are the preferred areas for hand quilting.

🏠 you have the time.

🏠 you like/love to hand-quilt. If so, the amount of time it will take is not a factor.

🏠 you want to create an heirloom-type quilt made in the tradition of American quiltmaking.

Machine-Quilt If:

🏠 your quilt is intended for steady use. Machine quilting is appropriate if it is a gift for a baby or a college student. The fact that you quilted it quickly will encourage the recipient to use, rather than save, the quilt.

🏠 the quilting won't show anyway. Patchwork quilts made primarily of prints are good candidates for machine quilting.

🏠 your quilt was quick-pieced. If you used quick-piecing techniques, why not speed-quilt as well?

🏠 your quilt is a small- to medium-size project. Machine quilting full-size quilts takes extra skill.

🏠 you are pressed for time.

🏠 you enjoy machine quilting and like the way it looks.

Combine Hand Quilting and Machine Quilting If:

🏠 your quilt has areas where quilting will show well and areas where it will not. Use hand quilting on the open, light-colored fabrics and machine quilting on the medium-value prints in patchwork areas.

🏠 your project is a baby quilt. Parents are sometimes reluctant to use a quilt that has a lot of hand quilting. Combination hand and machine quilting can produce a crib quilt that is utilitarian and special at the same time.

Types of Quilting Designs and Placement

Outline quilting follows the outline of the patchwork or appliqué pattern. There are several kinds of outline quilting: in-the-ditch, quarter-inch, and echo.

In-the-ditch quilting is quilting alongside a seam or an appliqué edge. No marking is needed for this type of quilting. In-the-ditch quilting is understated and is often the best choice for machine quilting.

Quarter-inch outline quilting is frequently used for patchwork patterns. Stitch ¼" from patchwork seams to avoid stitching through seam allowances. Mark quilting lines on the quilt top with a ruler or use a ¼"-wide masking tape as a guide. This approach to quilting works well if the pieces are 2" or more in size. If ¼" quilting is used for smaller patchwork, the quilting stitches end up crowded and may appear out of scale.

Echo quilting is a type of outline quilting for appliqué quilts. Hawaiian quilts are usually quilted this way. The appliqué motif is first quilted in-the-ditch around the shape. The next line of quilting is parallel to the first, approximately ¼" away, the third line the same distance away, and so on. *Kathy's Hawaiian Breadfruit* quilt on page 183 is echo-quilted. Some quilters do this type of quilting by eye, while others mark the lines.

Types of Outline Quilting

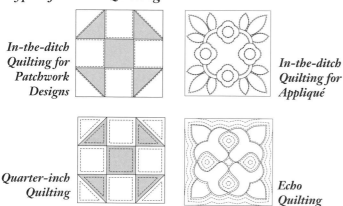

In-the-ditch Quilting for Patchwork Designs

In-the-ditch Quilting for Appliqué

Quarter-inch Quilting

Echo Quilting

Background quilting is stitching that appears to run behind or underneath a main motif, whether the motif is a larger quilting design or an appliquéd piece. Background quilting is often done in straight lines, such as a cross-hatch grid of squares or diamonds, or evenly spaced parallel lines.

Parallel Line Background Quilting

Unrelated, allover quilting ignores the pieced or appliquéd pattern. A grid of squares or diamonds, or units of concentric arcs, may be quilted over the entire quilt.

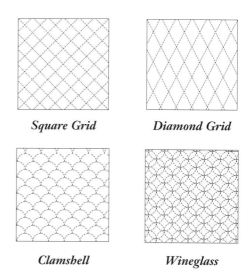

Square Grid *Diamond Grid*

Clamshell *Wineglass*

Fancies is the general quilting name for the elaborate designs used particularly in setting pieces, wide sashing, borders, and in the areas where blocks come together.

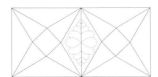

Plain Area Formed When
Blocks Are Combined

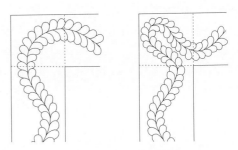

Undulating Feather Plume
Corner Options

Feather designs are among the oldest and best-loved fancy motifs. The classic curving lines of feather motifs can complement and relieve the hard edges of patchwork or mirror the curves of appliqué. Fancy designs are abundant in books of quilting patterns and collections of stencils.

Quilting designs for borders include clamshells, flower vines, grape-vines, grids, interwoven cables, and classic undulating feather plumes. Many antique Amish quilts display classic winding feathers. Creating cables and feathers involves forming repeats. (See the tip box on page 199 to learn how to determine repeats for your quilt.)

1. Create a center vein that trails along border.

2. Draw feather scallops on each side of vein, with right-hand sides of hearts on one side and left-hand sides of hearts on the other. Draw feathers on tracing paper patterns first and then either trace design on your fabric or make templates. (Two corner options are shown.)

Tips for Selecting Quilting Designs for Machine Quilting

🏠 Select straight-line quilting designs that can be quilted with a walking foot rather than curved motifs that require free-motion work for your first machine-quilting projects. Patchwork quilts can easily be quilted in-the-ditch along patchwork seams.

🏠 Outline-quilt close to appliqué shapes; then, just as with hand quilting, fill open areas with background quilting.

🏠 Select geometric grids, such as squares or diamonds, for large open areas on quilts.

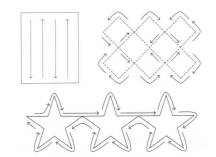

Examples of Machine-Quilting Strategies

🏠 Look for continuous designs that require little stopping and restarting or restitching.

🏠 Sketch a machine-quilting strategy or directional guide to save time and to organize your quilting. (See diagrams at left.) After you have inserted the quilt in the machine is not the time to decide which way you want to go.

Marking Quilting Designs

Marking quilting designs has always presented a dilemma—quilters want to be able to see the marks while quilting but have them disappear when they are done! Here is a list of options, both for marking tools and methods. Each quilt you make will probably require a different approach.

Mark Before or After Basting?

Generally speaking, you should mark your quilt top before you layer and baste it. Fabric is easier to mark when a hard surface, rather than a soft layer of batting, is beneath it. A sharp pencil point is more likely to poke a hole in a quilt top with batting behind it. Also, if the design is to be traced through the quilt top using a light box, it has to be done before basting. Sometimes, however, a quilt can be marked successfully as you quilt, by using adhesive templates or strips of masking tape as quilting guides.

Choosing a Marking Tool

Your choice of marking strategy and marking tools will often be determined by the color value of the fabric to be marked. Light-value fabrics are easier to mark. Most markers for dark fabrics are chalky or powdery, and the lines tend to rub off more easily than dark markings. The hardest fabrics to mark are medium-value prints. Neither a light nor a dark marker contrasts well. Experiment with the marking tool options we describe below to find the right marker for your quilt. The list includes marking tools that are used singularly or in combination by the majority of contemporary quilters.

Standard lead pencil. Keep the point sharp to draw thin lines on light-value fabric. The marks are somewhat removable with careful applications of soap and water. The harder the lead, the less likely the line is to rub off or smear.

Mechanical lead pencil. The best specifications are 0.5 mm (thin) leads, B (medium) or HB (medium-hard). Since the quilting thread covers the thin pencil line, washing is usually not necessary.

Artist's pencils. Use a silver-leaded pencil for successful marking of many light-, medium-, and dark-value fabrics. Also, experiment with other colored pencils. Silver washes out of most fabrics.

Tailor's chalk pencils. Use white to mark dark fabrics. Marks often rub off as you work.

Washable graphite pencil. This lead is soft and needs frequent sharpening, but the marks show well on light fabrics and can be removed completely by washing.

Soapstone pencil. This washable marker works well for dark fabrics, though the lead wears down quickly.

Chalk dispensers. These markers dispense tiny dots of white or colored chalk. White chalk usually rubs off easily (often too soon!), but some colored chalks are difficult to remove.

Soap slivers. Leftover bits of bar soap work well on dark fabrics and wash out easily.

The Importance of Testing Marking Tools

Before using any marker on a quilt top, test to make sure the marks will wash out of the fabric. Mark on a scrap of fabric from the quilt and wash it in the sink or along with other laundry.

Marking Methods

Choose your marking method in the same way that you select the marking tool—keeping the color values of your fabrics, the kind of designs you are using, and the intended use of your quilt in mind. Whatever instrument you choose, mark with a thin, light line.

Tracing. First, darken the outline of the quilting design on paper with a black permanent felt-tipped pen to make it easier to see through your fabric. For light-value fabrics, tape the pattern to a table top and then position and reposition the quilt top over the pattern as needed to complete marking. For dark fabrics, work at a sunlit window or use a light box. Tape the quilting pattern to the window pane. Then position the fabric over the pattern and tape it to the window pane, too.

For large projects use a light box. Art and photo-supply stores sell them, or you can improvise a light box by working on a glass-topped table with a lamp placed under it. A make-shift light box can be made with an open cardboard box, small unshaded lamp, and a square of clear plexiglass positioned on top of the box.

Stencils. On medium- and dark-value fabrics, marking a quilt top with stencils often works best. To transfer the design to the quilt top, place a plastic or cardboard stencil on the quilt top and mark through the slits in stencil. Connect lines after removing the stencil.

Quilting Templates

To make a template from a printed quilting design, transfer the pattern to tracing paper and then glue the paper to cardboard or trace the design on template vinyl. Cut out the motif. (Sometimes cutting the template into components will make marking easier.) Place the template on the quilt top and mark.

Tear-Away Paper Patterns for Machine Quilting

An alternative marking method for machine quilting is to mark your quilting designs onto pieces of tissue paper, tracing paper, or tear-away stabilizer. You will need to make a separate paper pattern for each time you intend to stitch the design. Pin the paper on top of the basted quilt. Stitch the designs through the paper and then tear away the paper. Use this method if your fabric is difficult to mark, if you don't want to make final decisions on quilting designs until after the quilt is basted, or you are concerned that marks may not wash out.

Marking Background Grids and Lines

When marking background quilting grids and lines, keep the illusion of continuity in mind. The background quilting should appear to run behind the patchwork, the appliqué, or the fancy quilting motifs. Here are some marking methods:

Gridded Sewing Board. Fabric stores sell inexpensive 36" x 60" fold-up cardboard cutting boards that can be used for marking a background grid.

Place the opened-out board on a large table and position the quilt top over it. Align the edge of a ruler with the printed grid lines and mark. Grids of squares are best positioned diagonally so that the squares are on point, and the quilting is on the bias of the fabric. Diagonal quilting remains solidly on the surface of the cloth. When planning and marking grids on your quilts, keep this advantage of diagonal lines in mind. Lines of quilting that run with the crosswise or lengthwise grains of fabric tend to embed themselves within the fabric threads.

Rulers. You can mark grids and parallel lines accurately with a ruler or straightedge if it reaches all the way across your quilt. For large projects, a household yardstick or a 6-foot length of wood lattice from the lumberyard works well. We often let the width of the straightedge determine the grid size or line spacing.

Alternative Quilting Guides

Quilting guides are used most often after the quilt has been layered and basted. The quilter simply follows along the edge of the guide with a quilting stitch, removes it after quilting, and repositions it on the quilt.

Adhesive Templates. Commercial adhesive-backed motifs are available, or you can make your own. Cut a shape from clear adhesive-backed paper, peel off the backing, and press the shape on the layered and basted quilt front. Don't leave the template on your quilt for more than a day, especially in warm temperatures. Sunlight or other heat can affect the adhesive and attach it permanently to your quilt or leave a sticky residue!

Masking or Drafting Tape. Use masking tape as a quilting guide when you want to quilt ¼" away from seams of straight patchwork pieces. With the quilt stretched in a frame or hoop, lay a strip of masking tape on the surface, aligning one edge with a patchwork seam, and quilt along the other edge of the masking tape. Peel and reposition pieces of masking tape until they lose their stickiness. Tape can be used as guides for quilting straight parallel lines or grids but may stretch too much to maintain accuracy for large areas.

The Quilt Back

The front of your quilt is the showpiece, but the back is important, too—it should complement the front.

The fabric for backing should be of the same quality, content, weight, and weave (thread count) as the fabrics used for the top. If your quilt top contains all printed fabrics, then a print is a good backing choice.

Quilt-backing fabric, 90" or wider for full-size quilts, is available in muslin and in solids and prints. Be cautious about using a bed sheet for a backing. Percale has a high thread count and is hard to needle.

Estimating Yardage for and Constructing a Quilt Backing

A quilt backing should be 2" or 3" larger than the quilt top on all four sides. This extra fabric is "accident insurance," in case quilt layers shift during quilting. Extra backing is also necessary for stabilizing and anchoring a quilt in a quilting frame. When quilting with a hoop, raw edges of the quilt are covered and protected with this extra fabric.

Small Quilts. For quilt tops 40" wide or less, use a single width of 44/45"-wide quilt-weight cotton broadcloth. Buy enough length to allow adequate margin at quilt edges, as noted above. For example, a quilt top measuring 40" x 45" would require around 1½ yards of 44/45"-wide fabric for backing.

Large Quilts. When your quilt is wider than 40", a sensible option is to use 60"-, 90"-, or 108"-wide fabric for the quilt backing. But since fabric selection is limited for wide fabrics, quilters generally piece the quilt backing from 44/45"-wide fabric. Plan on 40" to 42" of usable fabric width when estimating how much fabric to purchase. Make a sketch of how you plan to piece the backing. Plan your piecing strategy to avoid having a seam along the vertical or horizontal center of the quilt.

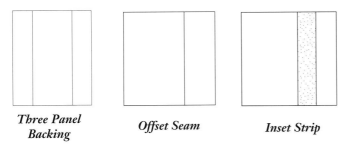

Three Panel Backing   *Offset Seam*   *Inset Strip*

For a bed quilt 81" to 120" wide, you will need three lengths of fabric, plus extra margin. For example, for a quilt 110" x 110", purchase at least 348", or 9⅔ yards, of 44-45"-wide fabric (116" + 116" + 116" = 348").

For a bed quilt 61" to 80" wide, most quilters piece a three-panel backing with vertical seams from two lengths of fabric. Cut one of the fabric lengths in half lengthwise, and sew the halves to opposite sides of the wide panel. Press the seams away from the center panel.

Horizontal Seam Back

For a bed quilt 41" to 60" wide, a backing with horizontal seams is usually the most economical use of fabric. For example, for a quilt 50" x 72", vertical seams would require 156", or 4⅓ yards, of 44/45"-wide fabric (78" + 78" = 156"). Horizontal seams would require 112", or 3¼ yards (56" + 56" = 112").

For a three-panel backing, pin the selvage edge of the center panel to the selvage edge of the side panel with edges aligned and right sides facing. Machine-stitch with a ½" seam. Trim seam allowances to ¼", trimming off the selvages from both panels at once. Press the seam to one side, rather than open, generally pressing away from the center of the quilt. Repeat on the other side of the center panel.

For a two-panel backing, join panels in the same manner as above and press the seam to one side.

Quilt Battings

Every quiltmaker seems to be on a quest to find the perfect batt. The information below is designed to inform you about the quilt battings currently on the market. We encourage you to read the product information included on batting packages.

Loft: the thickness of a batt. The more loft, the warmer the bed covering. Use low loft for hand and machine quilting and for quilted garments. Use high or ultra loft for tied comforters.

Needling: putting the needle through the fabric as you quilt. Synthetic batts needle more easily than cotton. Advocates of wool batting say the natural lanolin of wool fibers lubricates the needle as you quilt.

Glazing and Bonding: processes that stabilize loose fibers and retard or prevent fiber migration. A glazed batt is coated on both sides with resin that holds the batt together and discourages fiber migration. A bonded batt is sprayed with resin. Both of these processes are used on cotton, polyester, and cotton/poly blend batts.

Needlepunching: another method for stabilizing loose fibers. A machine with barbed needles pounds the batt, twisting and tangling the fibers together.

Fiber Migration and Bearding. Loose fibers of batting tend to work their way out (or migrate) through the spaces between threads of woven cloth. When the strong synthetic fibers migrate through a quilt top, they don't break off as natural fibers do. Instead, they beard or rest on the quilt top.

Shrinkage. Synthetic battings do not shrink significantly when laundered, but cotton battings do if exposed to hot water and dryers. Quilts with wool batting should always be dry-cleaned.

Batting Sizes

Standard batting sizes are:

Craft: 36" x 45"	Full: 81" x 96"
Crib: 45" x 60"	Queen: 90" x 108"
Twin: 72" x 90"	King: 120" x 120"

Rolled batting by the yard: 45", 48", and 90" widths

Types Of Batting Fibers

The majority of quilters today use either polyester, cotton/polyester blend, or cotton batts. Wool and silk batting are also available but aren't as popular. Here are some facts about each option.

Polyester

Synthetic battings are available in many loft levels. Fiber migration and bearding are more prevalent with polyester, but bonding, glazing, and needlepunching processes are used to reduce these problems. Polyester battings are warmer than cotton and needle very easily. The amount of quilting recommended varies among manufacturers, ranging from 3" to 6" intervals, depending on the brand. These batts shrink very little, if at all, when laundered.

Cotton/polyester

Blended batts (80% cotton/20% polyester) are low loft, combining the flat, old-fashioned look of cotton fillers with the stability of synthetic fibers. Read the

Types of Batting: (Top row, left to right) 100% glazed cotton; 100% cotton; 100% cotton; and 100% wool. (Bottom row, left to right) 80% cotton, 20% polyester; 100% needlepunched polyester; 100% polyester; 100% low-loft polyester.

manufacturer's instructions and soak batt before layering to shrink the batting and to improve ease of needling. Quilting can be at 2" intervals or to manufacturer's recommendations.

Cotton

Cotton batts are low loft and result in a flatter, more old-fashioned look than a polyester batt. Cotton batting provides less warmth than polyester and is harder to needle. Quilt unglazed cotton batting at ½" to 1" intervals and glazed cotton at up to 2" intervals, or according to manufacturer's specifications. Wash quilts in cold water to prevent batting shrinkage.

A single layer of prewashed, cotton flannel can be used in place of batting. Virtually without loft, it works well for miniature quilts, wall hangings, and clothing.

Wool and Silk

Wool batts make warm quilts since they are medium to high loft. Needlepunching prevents fiber migration. Although often used for tied quilts, they needle easily for hand quilting too.

Silk filler is manufactured in small leaves, which are unfolded and layered by hand to form a batt. Silk needles with great ease because it is low loft and lightweight. It gives luxurious sculpted results, and shrinkage is minimal.

Layering

Layering a quilt is the process of spreading out and aligning the three layers that make up a quilt—the backing, batting, and top—so that they can be basted together in preparation for quilting.

The day before you layer your quilt, open the batting to relax any deep creases or folds. Relax polyester batting by tumbling it in a clothes dryer on the air-dry setting. Clip threads on the quilt top and give it a final pressing. Fold the backing in half lengthwise and lightly press a center guideline for aligning the layers.

Layering a Quilt for Insertion in a Hoop or a Two-Rail Floor Frame

1. Press center lengthwise guideline on backing. Open it wrong side up and align center guideline with lengthwise center of table, or with junction of two tables.

2. To ensure a smooth backing, clip it to table edge with large binder clips. (These can be purchased from an office supply store.) If you are working on floor or another surface, tape backing to surface to keep it from slipping.

3. Fold batting in half lengthwise. Align fold with center guideline of quilt backing. Open batting. Smooth out any lumps or baggy areas on batting with your hands, working any fullness toward outside edges. Remove loose threads or foreign matter that may be on batting. Trim excess batting even with or slightly smaller than quilt backing but larger than quilt top.

4. Fold quilt top in half lengthwise with right sides together. Align fold with lengthwise center of batting and quilt backing. Open quilt top. Smooth layers gently with hands, starting at center and working excess fullness toward outer edges. Check to be sure batting and backing are 2" to 3" larger than quilt top all the way around and that layers are straight.

Basting

If you plan to quilt in a hoop or on a two-rail frame on which the quilt is rolled, thread-baste the layers together. (Some types of quilting frames are designed to eliminate layering and basting; follow the instructions accompanying your frame if you have one of this type.) If you plan to machine-quilt, pin-baste with safety pins to hold layers together securely.

Thread Basting

Use white thread for basting since colored thread can leave colored fuzz. Choose a long, thin needle, such as a size 7 sharp or long darner. Before basting, make sure all layers are smooth.

Begin basting at the center of the quilt and work toward the outside edges, smoothing layers and working any excess fullness to the outside as you go. A radiating pattern,

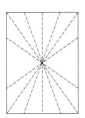

Radiating Pattern

shown at left, is a good basting layout for many quilts. Basting stitches should be every 4" to 6". If your quilt has blocks, sashing, or other regularly spaced elements, baste along seams first and then fill in with more basting, as shown in the grid pattern.

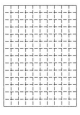

Grid Pattern

If you plan to quilt in a hoop, baste at 4" intervals and roll outside edges. (See page 74.) If you plan to put your quilt in a frame, add a line of basting around outside edges.

We recommend a tailor's padding stitch for basting. This stitch has some give, and it can be made easily from the top of the quilt without reaching under the quilt and possibly wrinkling or misaligning the layers. Put plenty of thread (several yards) in your needle. The stitches on the top will be long and diagonal; the stitches on the back will be short and horizontal.

Steps in Thread Basting

1. Insert needle at center of quilt. Make about a 1" horizontal stitch through all layers.

2. Bring needle toward yourself 3" to 4" and then take another stitch as above. Baste to edge of quilt. When finished, clip thread, leaving 3" to 4" unknotted tail.

3. When basting is complete, turn quilt over to make sure backing is as smooth as top. If necessary, re-baste any areas that may not be smooth. Trim excess batting 2" to 3" outside quilt top edges.

Safety Pin Basting for Machine Quilting

Safety pin basting, sturdier than thread basting, is necessary to keep quilt layers from shifting during machine quilting. The pins can be removed as you quilt. Use only the best quality size 1 (1"-long) brass or nickel-plated safety pins.

Layer batting and backing, taking extra care to get the quilt backing smooth and wrinkle free. (When hand-quilting, it is easy to check on and smooth the quilt backing as you go, but when machine-quilting, no such opportunity exists.) Check the backing after pinning each section and reposition the pins as necessary.

Begin pinning at the center of the quilt and work to the outer edges. Place a safety pin approximately every 3" to 4". Check spacing by placing your fist randomly on the quilt top—the edges of your fist should always touch pins. Work entirely from the quilt top, pinning through all layers, without reaching under the quilt and possibly misaligning the layers.

Folding a Quilt for Machine Quilting

1. To control bulk of a large quilt after basting and to make manipulation easier, tightly roll outside edges inward, leaving approximately 12" of material exposed in section you are going to quilt. Use at least two bicycle clips on each rolled portion to keep fabric from unrolling.

2. After sides are rolled and clamped, fold over about 12" to 18" of the edge where you will end quilting. Continue to fold quilt over on itself until it is a manageable size. You are now ready to machine-quilt. As you quilt, repeat these steps to re-roll and re-fold quilt as needed.

Quilting Hoop

A hoop keeps the quilt layers close together and smooth, which facilitates quality stitching. Quilts in a hoop are portable. Wooden quilting hoops have wider bands than embroidery hoops. Use a 10" circular or an oval hoop for small projects and a 14" hoop for larger projects and for full-size quilts. A hoop with a lap attachment keeps the quilt's weight off your lap. Half-circle hoops are best for borders. Plastic frames are lightweight and easy to adjust.

Types of Quilting Hoops: *1) Wooden Circular Hoop, 2) Half-circle Hoop, 3) Plastic Frame, 4) Wooden Oval Hoop.*

Rolling the Edges

If you quilt with a hoop, roll the edges to protect them from fraying and stretching while quilting. To roll edges,  fold backing over batting until the edge of the backing meets the edge of the quilt top. Bring the folded edge over the batting and onto the quilt top. Baste the rolled edge to the quilt to secure.

Floor Frames

Many modern quilters like a full-size frame, partly because several quilters can work at once and partly for the aesthetic beauty of a quilt in a frame. Some floor-frame advocates feel that a super-smooth backing can be achieved only by using a frame. When choosing a frame, send for the offered literature and get advice from experienced quilters about their preferred frames.

Four-Rail Frames. Probably the earliest type of floor frame is one that consists of four long boards (rails), four common C-clamps, and four chairs or sawhorses. The backing is stretched taut on the boards; then, the batting and quilt top are added and pinned to the stretched backing. (No basting is required.) Quilting is done from the outer edge of the quilt to the inside. Quilted portions are rolled on rails so that the quilter can reach the center for quilting.

Two-Rail Frames. Because of space limitations, most modern quilt frames, such as the one we show here, consist of two long boards or rails supported by stands at the ends. The frame rails should be as long as the quilt is wide, plus extra length for setting into the stands. Opposite ends of the quilt are tacked to the two rails. An equal amount of the quilt is rolled on each rail; quilting is done from the center out to one end. The quilted end is then rolled back to the center, and the quilt is quilted to the opposite end. For most two-rail frames, layer and thread-baste quilt before installing it in the frame.

1. Attach quilt to tacking strip. Place rails in frame or parallel to each other on floor. Match center of quilt width to center point on one tacking strip, the piece of fabric that is permanently attached to rail. Working from quilt's center toward ends, pin or baste quilt to tacking strip. Repeat for other rail. If rails are not inserted in frame, basted quilt will be on floor between rails.

If rails for your frame do not have fabric tacking strips attached, you will need to add them. From muslin or other sturdy fabric, cut 8"-wide strips; piece them together so that they are almost as long as rails. You will need to leave ends of rails uncovered where they attach to main part of frame. Press fabric strips in half lengthwise so that they are 4" wide. Use hammer and tacks or staple gun to fasten strips along rails. Mark tacking strip at center of rail length to use as guide for positioning quilt evenly on both rails.

2. Roll quilt. Starting with one rail, roll the quilt evenly and smoothly around rail to center of quilt, rolling quilt so that quilt top is facing out. Roll second rail in opposite direction so that quilt back is facing out. Rolling rails in opposite directions will keep an even tension on quilt top and back. Now secure rails in frame. Many frames have pegs or ratchets to keep rails from rolling. The center section of quilt should be firm and fit evenly between rails.

3. Attach sides of quilt to frame. Cut several 2"-wide strips of muslin or some other sturdy fabric. Beginning near one rail, pin fabric strip to edge of quilt through all layers. Wrap fabric strip around side of frame or pull to reach tacking strip on side of frame. Pull strip snug. Pin strip to quilt again a short distance from first pin. Continue to wrap and pin until entire side is attached. Repeat for other side.

Ins and Outs of Quilting

Quilting refers to the small running stitches that hold the three layers of a quilt—top, batting, and backing—together. This stitching, which can be done by hand or by machine, adds the extra dimension that makes a quilt a quilt. The best way to learn to quilt is to practice, practice, practice. Your quilting will improve in proportion to the time you spend on it.

The Ins and Outs of Quilting

In this chapter, you'll learn the techniques for hand quilting, machine quilting, and tying a comforter. We will also introduce you to three distinctive quilting techniques—stippling, trapunto, and corded quilting.

Learn These Hand-Quilting Skills While Quilting a Feathered Star

- 🏠 *preparing to quilt*
- 🏠 *securing knot in quilt*
- 🏠 *using a quilting hoop*
- 🏠 *making quilting stitches*
- 🏠 *beginning and ending quilting*
- 🏠 *traveling*

Materials:

½ yard 100%- cotton muslin
Batting, low-loft, 18" square
Quilting hoop
Needles (betweens)
Tracing paper
Black permanent marking pen
Pencil
Thimble
Quilting thread, off-white*

Finished Size: 14" square

*Red quilting thread is used in the photos so that quilting stitches can be seen easily.

1. Use tracing paper and permanent pen to make master pattern of feathered star on page 83. From muslin, cut or tear two 18" squares; set one aside for backing. Fold the other in half both ways and

lightly press folds to form positioning lines. Trace quilting design onto square and then layer and baste. (Not basted in photos 2 and 3.)

2. Spread layered square out smoothly. Position inner hoop under area to be quilted. (Always begin quilting at center of project and work to edges, smoothing out any fullness as you go.) Then, slip outer hoop in place. Tighten hoop nut so bands hold quilt loosely.

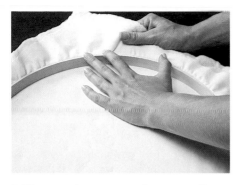

3. Turn work over to make sure quilt backing is smooth and wrinkle free. Adjust backing as needed. Now, tighten hoop again so that it holds work securely. The degree of tautness is a matter of personal choice. Some quilters like their work stretched tight; others like some give. Experiment to find right tension.

4. To begin, thread the quilting needle with about a 27" length of thread. Tie a quilter's knot at end of thread. Insert point of needle in quilt top ½" to ¾" from where you want to begin quilting. Run needle through batting only and bring point of needle out through top where quilting is to begin.

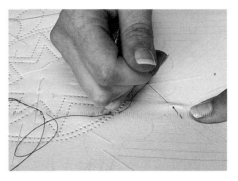

5. Pull needle and thread until knot rests on surface of quilt top. Tug on thread to pop knot through fabric and into batting layer. If knot is stubborn, hold thumbnail of free hand against knot while tugging on thread.

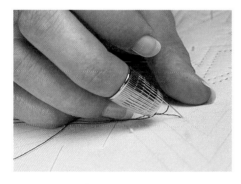

6. Grasp needle between thumb and index finger and insert needle into quilt. Position index or middle finger (whichever is more comfortable) of other hand under quilt where needle will come through. Push needle straight down through all layers until you feel needle point brush against your underneath finger. Balance needle point on underneath finger and stabilize needle by placing thimble on eye end.

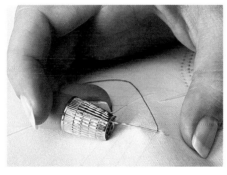

7. Rock needle down and away from you into a horizontal position. At same time, push needle point up while pressing down on quilt top with thumb of your top hand, just ahead of place where you expect needle to appear; small swell will form. Drive needle forward slightly through swell, keeping needle parallel to work surface, until needle point is barely visible. The amount of needle showing determines length of next stitch.

8. To make next stitch, rock needle up so that it is nearly vertical. Push needle straight down into quilt until you feel needle point with bottom hand.

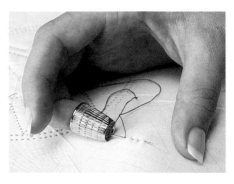

9. Rock needle down and at same time push needle point up from underneath and press on quilt ahead of needle with thumb. Continue in this way, rocking needle up and rocking it back down, until it is loaded with three to five stitches. Drive needle forward with thimble and pull needle and thread through fabric to complete series of stitches. (When quilting curved lines, you will not be able to load as many stitches on needle as when you are quilting straight lines.) Repeat procedure for loading needle and follow quilting design.

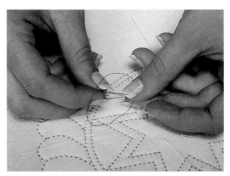

10. Form a loop with thread and take needle through center of loop. Slide loop down to ¼" or less from quilt top. (Needle remains threaded.) Then, tighten knot.

11. To hide knot, insert needle in quilt top one stitch length from where thread comes out. Push needle into batting layer only and bring needle out about ½" away.

12. Pull knot through quilt top and into batting. Gently pull up on thread and clip it close to quilt top. Clipped end will slip into batting.

Traveling

Traveling is a way to move from one area of the quilt to another without knotting your thread and starting over. Use this technique when you have finished a line of quilting, still have plenty of thread in your needle, and want to begin quilting again within 2".

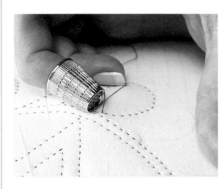

1. To travel, run needle into batting in direction of next quilting line and bring needle point out one needle length away. If you have reached new place to quilt, pull needle through and begin quilting.

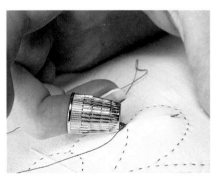

2. If you have not reached new beginning point, bring only point of needle out and grasp it. Without pulling eye out of quilt, pivot needle eye around inside batting and point eye toward new quilting line.

Place thimble on needle point and push needle, eye first, toward new starting point. If you have reached new starting point, push entire needle through. If not, bring only eye of needle out, leaving needle point in fabric, pivot, and travel forward again. If thread is darker than quilt top fabric, be sure thread goes deep into batting.

Directional Map for Feathers

Traveling is frequently employed when quilting feather patterns. A continuous quilting strategy (directional map) expedites all methods of quilting.

Tips on Hand Quilting

Preparation

Position a lamp on your left side if you are righthanded and vice versa if you are lefthanded so that your hand does not cast a shadow on your stitching.

Some quilters wrap hoop rims with muslin strips to form a barrier between the quilt and the wood. Remove work from hoop after quilting. Leaving it in the hoop might stretch the fabric, and the acid pH of wood can discolor the fabric.

When using a round hoop, pin a terry cloth towel to the quilt edge and insert the quilt in the hoop so that the whole hoop is filled. This keeps the work stretched evenly, prevents the edges from stretching, and allows you to quilt easily on the edges of your quilt.

Warm up on a practice piece before starting.

Thread

Match quilting thread to color of quilt backing so that uneven stitches are less noticeable. Print backings also camouflage uneven stitching.

If you wish to substitute regular sewing thread for quilting thread, coat lengths of thread with beeswax to stiffen and strengthen them.

Quilting

After loading needle with stitches, look at them with a critical eye to see if they are straight and evenly spaced. If they don't look satisfactory, back the needle out and start again. Unloading a needle is much easier than removing stitches.

Quilting stitches made on the diagonal (bias) fabric weave will always look better than those stitched with the grain. On-the-grain stitches fall into and blend with the threads of the fabric.

Keep several needles threaded and ready to use to keep your quilting process running smoothly.

Discard the needle if any rough spots develop or if the needle becomes bent.

Plan your quilting route before starting to quilt.

When quilting complex designs, insert several threads at various places in the design. As you move the hoop to a new section, re-thread your needle with each of the threads in turn to continue the quilting lines. Also start multiple threads when quilting grids.

Experiment with shorter quilting needles. Master quilters believe a shorter needle produces smaller stitches.

Use a similar amount of quilting on all areas of a quilt so that one area is not flatter or puffier than another.

Knots

If fabric is tightly woven, making it hard for the starting knot to pop through, make a quilter's knot with just two wraps of thread instead of three so that knot will be smaller.

When quilting patchwork projects, secure thread with backstitches hidden in a seam, instead of making a knot.

Start quilting at the center of the thread, without making a beginning knot, and quilt off both long ends of thread.

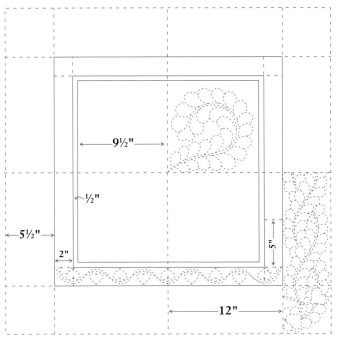

Practice Straight and Curved Hand-Quilting Stitches While Making a *Little Princess* Whole-Cloth Baby Quilt

American folklore includes a tradition of presenting a newborn child with a yard of cloth.

Materials:

2⅜ yards light solid (not print) fabric
½ yard fabric for single bias binding
Batting, low-loft, 40" square
Tracing paper
Black permanent marking pen
Silver pencil
Rulers, large ruled square and 6" x 24" straight edge

Finished Quilt Size: *36" square.*

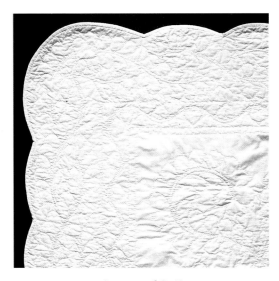

Quarter of Quilt

1. Use photocopy machine to enlarge patterns. Darken lines with pen to make them easier to trace.

2. Cut two 40" squares from solid fabric; set one aside for backing. Fold square for quilt top in half both ways and lightly press to form positioning lines.

3. On fabric, mark three squares, indicated by straight solid lines on Quilt Diagram, as follows. Do not mark any straight dashed lines; they indicate pattern sections.

Begin by marking a 19" center square (9½" quadrants). Next, mark a 20" square ½" outside first square. Mark another square 2" from 20" square. Referring to Quilt Diagram, position patterns under quilt top and trace designs onto fabric, repeating patterns as indicated.

4. Layer and baste to prepare for quilting. (See sections on layering and basting in "Get Ready to Quilt.")

5. Position work in hoop or frame. Working from center out, quilt marked designs.

6. The Little Princess quilt has scalloped edges. Use a 15" square of fabric to make 1"-wide single bias binding. (See pages 95 through 100 in "Finishing Your Quilts."

Quilt Diagram

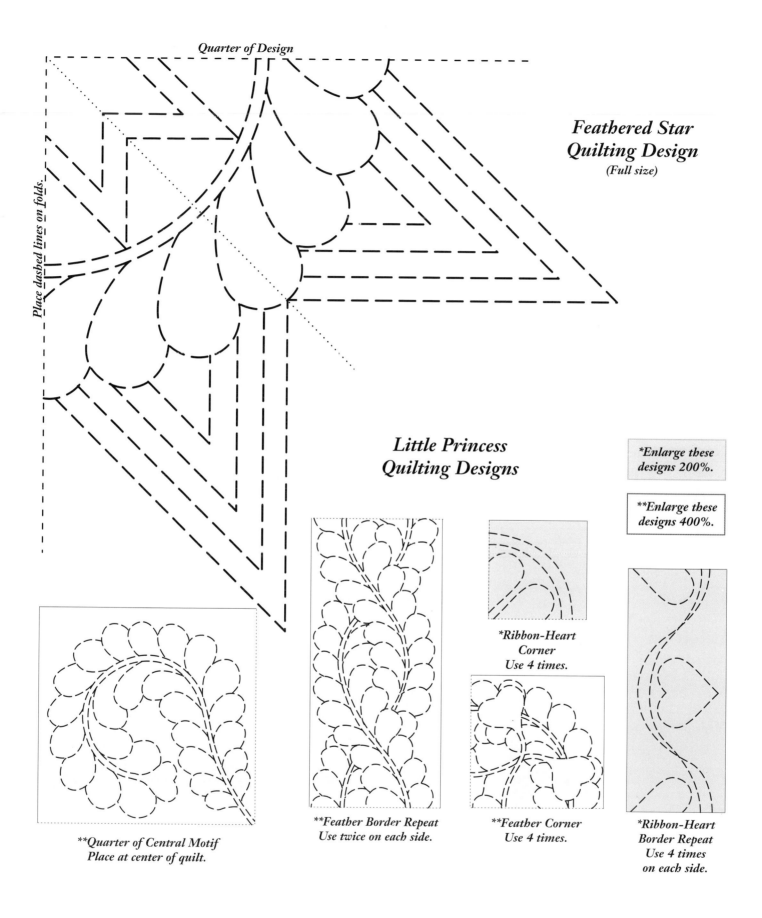

Quarter of Design

Place dashed lines on folds.

**Feathered Star
Quilting Design**
(Full size)

**Little Princess
Quilting Designs**

**Enlarge these
designs 200%.*

***Enlarge these
designs 400%.*

**Ribbon-Heart
Corner
Use 4 times.*

**Quarter of Central Motif
Place at center of quilt.

**Feather Border Repeat
Use twice on each side.

**Feather Corner
Use 4 times.

***Ribbon-Heart
Border Repeat**
Use 4 times
on each side.

Additional Hand-and Machine-Quilting Techniques

Stippling, trapunto, and corded quilting are traditional needlework techniques that have been used for centuries to enhance the basic quilting stitch on quilts and clothing.

Stippling

Stippling is very close background quilting that can be done by hand or machine to create surface texture. This dense quilting flattens the background, which results in raising the motif it surrounds. Stippling creates ridges in the fabric that give rich visual texture similar to that created when paper is embossed.

Traditionally, stippling is done with thread that matches the background fabric, which is usually white or a light shade. Choose a lightweight batting. When using stippling, distribute the amount of stippling evenly over the quilt. If stippling is used on only one block, it is likely to draw up and be out of balance with other areas. Keep in mind that heavy stippling will decrease the overall size of a quilt.

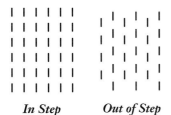

In Step   **Out of Step**

The distance between rows of stippling dictates the configuration of the ridges. Stitches can be "in step" or "out of step," as shown in the diagrams at left. Stippling rows can be in an echo pattern that eventually reaches the edge of the piece or in a meandering pattern that winds around randomly, with lines of quilting that neither touch nor cross each other. Other stippling patterns are tiny fan shapes, herringbones, and hanging diamonds.

When **stippling by hand**, use a frame or hoop to hold work taut and prevent it from being pulled out of shape by dense quilting. Pull stitches snug to create tiny dimples, ridges, or indentations. As closely spaced stippling flattens the batting loft, stitches tend to loosen; therefore, make stitches slightly tighter than ordinary hand-quilting stitches. The lower the batting loft, the flatter the finished result.

Machine stippling duplicates the look of hand stippling in a fraction of the time. It is like doodling on fabric with your sewing machine; there are no marked quilting lines to follow. A pattern is created by eye and is either echo-quilted in closely spaced rows around the existing design or meander-quilted to fill in open areas. Curving lines of meander quilting should not touch or cross each other.

To do either type of stippling (echo or meander) on a sewing machine, use a darning presser foot and follow suggestions included in section on free-motion machine quilting later in this chapter to give you maximum freedom of movement while stitching.

Trapunto

Trapunto is a stuffed quilting technique that raises the quilting design in relief. The trapunto is often further accentuated by stipple quilting (see above) that flattens areas surrounding it.

Quilters today are experimenting with quicker, easier methods for doing trapunto. Some use a compressed-air apparatus to blow fiber into the areas to be stuffed. Others machine-quilt designs to speed-up the process. However, the two most commonly used methods today are the **stuffing method** and the **yarn-and-needle method.**

With the stuffing method, the trapunto work is done before layering and basting the quilt. A special lining piece is added beneath the quilt top, and loose filler is inserted through slits in the lining.

The yarn-and-needle method involves using a long, blunt needle to fill areas with yarn after the quilt has been quilted.

The stuffing method is preferred by those who want their quilt backing to remain free from the small misalignments of backing threads caused by the insertion of a trapunto needle. Laundering will realign most threads, but many quilters do not want to launder their project immediately after completing it.

Stuffing Method for Trapunto

Materials:
Embroidery floss
Embroidery hoop
Knitting needle or orange stick
Lining (batiste or lightweight fabric)
Polyester stuffing

1. For lining, cut a piece of batiste equal to size of area to be stuffed. For example, if entire quilt top has areas for trapunto, cut a piece of batiste equal to size of quilt top. Baste lining to quilt top, making sure to place basting stitches only in areas for quilting and not for trapunto. (Not basted in photos.)

2. Quilt design or backstitch along marked lines with one strand of floss. Backstitches should be even and approximately ⅛" long. Use small embroidery hoop to hold work. Complete all backstitching before stuffing since hoop cannot be placed over any area that has been stuffed.

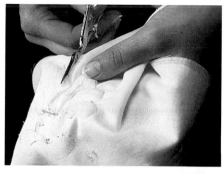

3. Turn work to back and snip small slit in lining only, behind area to be stuffed. Fill area with stuffing using blunt-ended instrument, such as orange stick. Stuffed area should be full but not firm.

4. Use sewing thread to make loose stitches across slit to secure stuffing. It is not necessary to tightly close opening.

5. If any puckering has occurred in trapunto, make tiny snips in lining to relieve it before layering. Once trapunto is complete, quilt top is ready to be layered and quilted.

Yarn-and-Needle Method for Trapunto

Materials:

Lightweight backing
Trapunto needles
Yarn, 100%-acrylic three-ply (white)

1. Mark trapunto and quilting designs on quilt top. Layer quilt top, batting, and backing; baste. Hand- or machine-quilt marked quilting designs.

2. When quilting is complete, you are ready to stuff areas for trapunto. Thread trapunto needle with a 12" to 15" length of single-ply yarn. See page 91 and make your own needle threader for yarn. Do not knot yarn.

3. Working from back, insert needle between threads of backing fabric. Gently rubbing backing fabric with needle point will help to separate threads. Run threaded needle between batting and backing, into quilted area. Twisting or rolling needle will help ease eye of needle through batting. Carefully exit needle through backing.

4. Pull single length of yarn into narrow channels. For wider channels or larger areas, double the yarn strand. Keep pulling needle gently until yarn tail or tails disappear into hole.

5. Clip yarn close to needle exit point. Use tip of needle to poke yarn end into hole. Repeat until area is uniformly filled. Realign threads of backing with fingernail. Laundering will align most threads and close needle holes.

Tips on Yarn-and-Needle Method for Trapunto

⌂ When stuffing channels longer than 4" or 5", such as stems or feather veins, overlap yarn ends by about ½" to avoid hollow spaces between lengths, caused by yarn shrinkage after washing and drying.

⌂ For curved channels, run needle as far as you can through curve without damaging backing fabric. Bring needle out and clip yarn. Re-insert needle, beginning ¼" to ½" behind exit point so that yarn ends will overlap.

⌂ To fill large areas, run the needle through each area repeatedly, pulling two plies of yarn into area each time.

⌂ After inserting several lengths of yarn in an area, use blunt point of needle to distribute the yarn evenly.

⌂ Check front of work and add lengths of yarn until design is raised to desired height. Designs should be firm and full, but not hard.

Corded Quilting

Another type of relief quilting is corded quilting. This involves inserting a length of yarn or cording into a quilted channel. The channel is usually no more than ¼" wide, and is most frequently a stem or a vine in a floral motif. The width of the channel must be uniform, and it must be equal to the size of cording/yarn being used. If the channel is too wide, the filled channel will not appear to be raised. If the channel is too narrow, the work will pucker. The yarn/cord is drawn through the channel with a tapestry or a trapunto needle. Ends of the yarn/cord are clipped, and the backing is closed as with yarn-and-needle trapunto.

Corded Quilting Supplies

Needles. Use a 6" weaving or trapunto needle with a blunt point and large eye for long channels. A tapestry needle works best for short or curved channels.

Cording or yarn. White polyester or preshrunk cotton cording in a variety of diameters can be purchased in the drapery department of most fabric stores. The cording is easy to use and will not beard as yarn may. For a softer feel or finish, use yarn instead of cording in the channels. (See Yarn-and-Needle Method on page 86.)

Machine Quilting

When the current American quiltmaking revival began in the mid-1970s, the only machine quilting we were familiar with was the kind done on a large commercial machine. The general attitude at that time among hand quilters, ourselves included, was that machine quilting was grossly inferior to hand quilting and always would be.

In the mid-1980s, however, quilters began to experiment more with machine quilting on their home machines and began to achieve remarkable results.

We have machine-quilted quite a few of the projects in this book, and we encourage you to try it, too. Machine-quilting a few quilts doesn't mean you won't hand-quilt others. Straight-line machine quilting is an easy skill to master, especially for relatively small projects. Free-motion machine quilting of curved designs requires more practice and skill. An alternative is to combine straight-line machine quilting with hand quilting for curves.

Keep in mind that, even though machine quilting is faster than hand quilting, it can still take anywhere from hours to several days of concentrated effort to machine-quilt a large quilt.

Machine-Quilting Supplies

Sewing machine. A special sewing machine for machine quilting is not necessary, but you will need a machine that makes an even straight stitch. For free-motion quilting, you must be able to lower the feed dogs on the machine or to cover them with a special throat plate. (Refer to your sewing machine manual.)

Straight-stitch throat plate. A straight-stitch throat plate will provide a more even stitch. The tiny hole in this plate, instead of a slit opening, keeps the quilt from being pulled into the throat plate while stitching.

Even-feed or walking foot. A walking foot has a feeding mechanism that moves the top fabric through the machine at the same rate that the feed dogs feed the bottom fabric. Use a walking foot for straight-line stitching to prevent wrinkles and puckers from forming.

Darning foot. A darning foot is designed for use when the feed dogs are either lowered or covered. The foot has a light touch, allowing you to guide and move the fabric freely as you stitch curved designs. Although you can free-motion-stitch without a presser foot, a darning foot protects your fingers and prevents skipped stitches.

Bicycle clips. These clips are used to keep a large quilt tightly rolled.

Thread. For the top thread, use either regular sewing thread, machine embroidery thread, or monofilament clear nylon machine-quilting thread. Nylon thread blends with the fabrics on the quilt top so that any stitch irregularities will be less noticeable than with regular thread. If your quilt top and backing are both made from dark fabrics, smoke-colored thread may show less.

For the bobbin, use either nylon thread or regular sewing thread in a color that blends with the quilt backing. If you use regular thread in the bobbin and nylon top thread, you may need to loosen the top thread tension to prevent loops of bobbin thread from showing on the quilt top.

Quilting guide. A quilting guide is a bar that helps to space rows of straight stitching more evenly. This guide fits into a hole on the needle bar of some machines.

Cotton batting. The quilt layers tend to adhere to cotton batting and shift less during machine quilting than with polyester batts.

Preparation for Machine-Quilting

1. Mark quilting designs.

2. Layer and pin-baste quilt with safety pins. (See page 73 in "Get Ready to Quilt.")

3. Roll and fold quilt if machine quilting a large quilt. Some machine quilters skip the folding process, preferring to sling the rolled quilt over their left shoulders!

4. Make a continuous-line quilting-strategy diagram (or directional map). (See pages 80 and 89 for examples.)

5. Test-stitch on a sample of layered fabrics and adjust thread tension as needed.

6. If machine-quilting a large quilt, set up a table behind your sewing machine cabinet or table to support the weight of the quilt as you feed it through the machine.

Straight-Line Machine Quilting

We often begin machine-quilting along border seams, and then add stitching along the seams joining the rows of blocks. Stitch along the center row of blocks; then machine-quilt rows to the right of that row, unrolling the quilt as you work. Turn the quilt completely around and work the remaining rows from the center to the right. This stabilizes the quilt. Now you can quilt individual blocks, borders, or other sections of the quilt.

1. Attach a walking foot to machine and adjust stitch length to approximately six to ten stitches per inch, or between three and four on European-made machines.

2. Bring bobbin thread to top by turning handwheel to take a stitch. With needle at its highest position, pull on tail of top

thread. This will pull bobbin thread to top. Hold both thread tails as you begin stitching to prevent threads from tangling.

3. Set needle to stop in down position to avoid having fabric shift while repositioning your hands or fabric. If your machine does not have this option, try to stop stitching with needle in fabric.

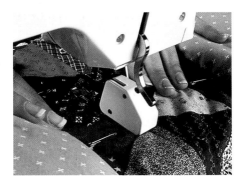

4. To lock stitching at beginning and end of each line of quilting, reduce stitch length to a very short stitch for approximately ¼". Use this method to secure all lines of machine quilting.

5. As you quilt, use your hands to assist walking foot. Spread fabric slightly with hands and gently push fabric toward walking foot to reduce puckering.

Free-Motion Machine Quilting

Free-motion machine quilting is a skill most of us must practice in order to master. Keep your first projects small so that they are easier to manipulate. Do not be discouraged if your first attempts are less than perfect. Jerky, uneven movements and inconsistent machine speed both cause uneven stitches. At first, concentrate on following the design; even stitches will come with practice.

1. Attach a darning foot and lower or cover feed dogs. No stitch length adjustment is necessary; you will control stitch length by manually moving fabric. Position project under darning foot and bring bobbin thread to top (see Straight-Line Machine Quilting at left).

2. Rest fingertips lightly on fabric, with a hand on each side of presser foot. Spread fabric slightly with hands and move fabric freely and evenly. To make even stitches, run machine at a steady, medium speed and move fabric smoothly and evenly so that needle follows design. Do not rotate quilt; simply move fabric forward and backward and side to side.

3. To keep quilt from shifting when repositioning hands or fabric, stop with needle in fabric or at least with needle in downward position. To lock stitches at beginning and end of machine-quilting, move fabric very slowly to make tiny, closely spaced stitches for approximately ¼" and then clip thread.

Learn To Free-Motion Machine-Quilt While Making a Four Hearts Block

Materials:

2 (6" or larger) fabric squares for top and backing

Darning foot

Black permanent marking pen

Safety pins, size 1, brass

Thread, clear nylon for machine-quilting or colored thread that matches fabric

Batting, cotton, 6" square

Finished block size: *6" square*

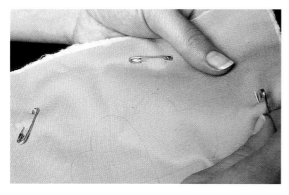

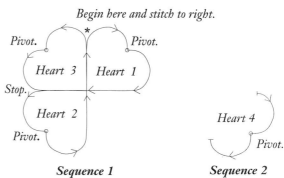

Begin here and stitch to right.

Pivot.   *   *Pivot.*

Heart 3   *Heart 1*

Stop.

Heart 2   *Heart 4*

Pivot.   *Pivot.*

Sequence 1   *Sequence 2*

Quilting Strategy Diagrams

1. Center and trace Four Hearts quilting pattern (page 132) on fabric square for top. Layer top, batting, and backing square and pin-baste with safety pins, spacing them approximately 3" apart. Try to position pins so that they will not interfere with quilting.

2. Four Hearts quilting design is a continuous-line design that is machine-quilted in two steps. Using a darning foot and free-motion techniques, begin quilting design at position marked with * in Sequence 1 diagram and follow arrows to complete three hearts in numerical order, as shown. For Heart 4, refer to Sequence 2 diagram.

Tying a Comforter

Tied quilts are usually called comforters. Yarn or thread ties, instead of quilting stitches, secure layers. Choose a stable batt, such as bonded or needlepunched polyester, so that batting will not separate when comforter is used or laundered. High-loft batts are intended for tied comforters.

For ties, choose strong cotton or synthetic sport, baby, or worsted weight yarn, pearl cotton, or embroidery floss in a color that complements your fabrics. The yarn should be thin enough to pull through the fabric without damaging it. Synthetic yarns tend to stay tied better than natural fibers. The only other supplies that you will need are scissors and a darning or tapestry needle with an eye large enough for your yarn.

Determine the positions for ties. Space ties evenly, no more than 4" apart. Tie pieced comforters at the corners of specific shapes, such as corners of blocks and at the corners of pieces within blocks. Prepare comforter by layering and basting with thread or safety pins to keep layers stabilized while working.

How To Tie Knots on Quilt Front

1. Thread needle with long length of yarn; do not knot end. Take small stitch through all layers at position for tie. Pull up yarn, leaving 3" to 4" tail. Do not cut yarn.

2. Move to next tie position and take another small stitch through all layers, leaving long, loose length of yarn between tie positions on quilt top. Length of yarn between stitches will ultimately be cut and become tails of yarn used to tie knot; therefore, be generous with amount of yarn left between stitches. Continue to make small stitches at tie positions, rethreading needle as necessary.

3. Cut each length of yarn between stitches in half. If you wish to add extra yarn to make a fuller tuft or tie, cut one or more 6" lengths of yarn and lay them on top of small stitch and perpendicular to stitch tails. Wrap right yarn tail of stitch around left tail of stitch, forming half square knot over perpendicular lengths. Tighten half-knot.

4. Treating yarn tails of stitch and added yarn lengths as one, tie second half of square knot by wrapping left tails around right tails. Using added yarn lengths to form knot keeps yarn lengths from pulling out. Tighten knot. Clip tails to desired length.

How To Tie Knots on Quilt Back

1. Follow step 1 for knots on quilt front (left). Then make an additional small stitch in same position as first stitch. One small stitch will show on front and two small stitches on back. Continue to make double stitches in this manner until all ties are in place. Clip yarn between stitches.

2. Turn comforter over. Bring yarn tails to back by pulling on small stitches with an unthreaded needle.

3. Tie square knots. Clip yarn ends, adding extra yarn if desired.

Make Your Own Needle Threader

To make threading a needle with yarn easy, make your own needle threader with a length of quilting or buttonhole thread. Fold thread in half and insert folded portion through needle eye. Slip yarn end into thread loop and pull thread back through needle eye, drawing yarn through needle eye.

Finishing Your Quilts

The final steps in making a quilt are finishing the edges and signing your work. If you plan to hang the quilted piece, you'll also need to add a hanging sleeve. Take as much care in finishing your quilt as you did in making it. Often, otherwise fine quilts are spoiled by poorly finished edges.

Finishing Your Quilts

In this chapter, we'll cover techniques for making both straight-grain and bias bindings, sewing binding to your quilt, mitering corners on the binding, and hand-finishing the binding. Other edge finishes, such as single-fold binding, overlapped corners on binding, self-finished edges, and prairie points, as well as binding quilts with scalloped edges, are discussed later in the chapter.

Binding Your Quilt

Strips for quilt binding may be cut either on the straight of grain or on the bias. Straight-grain binding can be used on all quilts, unless there are rounded corners or scalloped edges. Curved edges require the stretch of a bias binding. Straight-grain binding is quicker and easier to make than bias binding. Bias binding strips, however, are not difficult to make, and a bias binding is more durable than a straight-grain binding. Both straight-grain and bias strips can be used to make single or French (double) bindings.

Estimating the Amount of Binding Needed

To determine the amount of continuous binding needed for your quilt, measure the perimeter of the quilt and add approximately 15" for mitered corners and finished ends. As a rule for a large quilt, allow approximately ¾ to 1 yard of fabric to make all types of binding, unless the quilt has scalloped edges.

Making Straight-Grain Strips for Binding

To make strips for straight-grain binding, select the width of finished binding and the type of binding (single or French). Cut strips on either the crosswise or lengthwise grain of the fabric. (Strips cut on the crosswise grain have more give and are easier to work with than those cut on the lengthwise grain.)

To join strips, layer strips perpendicular to each other with right sides facing. Stitch across strips to make a diagonal seam. Trim to ¼" seam allowance and press open.

Estimating the Amount of Bias You Can Cut from a Square

Bias Strip Formulas

To estimate length of bias strip that can be cut from a square:

1. $\dfrac{\text{Width of}}{\text{Square}} \times \dfrac{\text{Length of}}{\text{Square}} = \text{Area of Square}$

2. $\dfrac{\text{Area of Square}}{\text{Width of Binding Strip}} = \dfrac{\text{Length of}}{\text{Bias Strip}}$

To estimate size of square given length of bias strip:

1. $\dfrac{\text{Length of}}{\text{Bias Strip}} \times \dfrac{\text{Width of}}{\text{Bias Strip}} = \text{Area of Strip}$

2. $\sqrt{\dfrac{\text{Area of}}{\text{Strip}}} = \dfrac{\text{Size of}}{\text{Square}}$

Making Continuous Bias Strips for Binding

Cut a large square from binding fabric. (The formula for estimating amount of bias that can be cut from a square is in tip box on page 94.). To make approximately 13 yards of 2¼"-wide binding, cut a 36" square. (See Choosing Between Single and French Binding on page 96 to determine width of your strip.)

1. Place pins at opposite sides of square. Point pin heads toward center on top and bottom of square. Point pin heads toward outside on remaining sides.

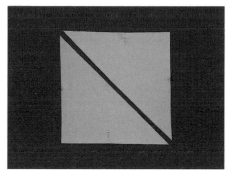

2. Cut square in half diagonally into two triangles.

3. With right sides facing and raw edges aligned, pin together edges with pin heads pointed to outside. Join with ¼" seam and press seam open.

4. Mark cutting lines parallel to long bias edges (edges without pins), spacing lines equal to width of binding strip. For example, if you need a 2¼"-wide binding strip, space lines 2¼" apart.

5. With right sides facing and raw edges aligned, pin together edges with pin heads pointed to the inside, offsetting one width of binding strip. This forms a fabric tube. Join edges with ¼" seam and press seam open.

6. Begin cutting at an extended edge and follow cutting lines, rolling tube around as you cut, until all fabric is cut in one continuous strip. Trim ends of strip square.

Choosing Between Single and French Binding

Single binding or single-thickness binding is a binding strip that requires little or no preparation before joining it to a quilt. Many quilters turn and press one long edge in ¼" before joining. This edge will be blindstitched to the backing. Since there is essentially only one layer of fabric protecting the quilt edge, a single binding is recommended for wall hangings or quilts that will not be used frequently. It should also be used for scalloped-edge quilts, because it is less bulky.

A single binding is cut narrower than French binding and, therefore, requires less fabric. Cut single binding approximately twice the width of the desired finished binding plus ½" for seam allowances. For example, for ⅜"-wide finished binding, cut binding strips 1¼" wide. Test the width on layered scraps of fabrics and batting of the weight used in your quilt before cutting the binding for your quilt.

French binding or double binding is the most common and most durable edge finish for bed quilts because

of its extra thickness. To prepare French binding, press binding strip in half lengthwise with wrong sides facing. If binding strip is 2¼" wide, French binding will be 1⅛" wide after folding. French binding can be made from either straight-grain or bias strips. Its pressed fold (see photo) also provides a smooth, straight edge that is easily blindstitched to backing.

Binding strips for French binding can be cut 2", 2¼", or 2½" wide, depending on the thickness of the batting and how wide you want your finished binding. We recommend 2"-wide binding strips for quilts with cotton batting and 2¼"-wide binding strips for most quilts with polyester batting. Before making all binding, test the width on layered scraps of fabrics and batting.

Attaching the Binding

If you own an even-feed or walking presser foot, install it before sewing binding to quilt. This presser foot prevents puckering when sewing through quilt layers.

1. Use large ruled square to check that all corners are square. If they need correcting, draw along ruled square to mark binding placement line. Wait to trim any excess batting and backing until binding has been attached. If corners are to be rounded, use curved object such as dinner plate, cup, or saucer to mark curved corner placement lines.

2. If using regular machine presser foot, either hand-baste close to edge, within seam allowance, or place pins at 2"intervals around quilt to keep layers from shifting and to prevent puckers from forming. If closely spaced quilting reaches edges of quilt, this step can be omitted.

3. Choose beginning point along one side of quilt. Do not begin at corner. With right sides facing, align raw edge of binding with raw edge of quilt top or marked line from step 1. If using single binding, folded and pressed edge will be free and to left of seam line. If using French binding, the two raw edges of binding strip will be matched to raw edge of quilt top. The folded edge will be free and to left of seam line. (See photo for step 4.) Leave 4" or more tail of binding strip dangling free from beginning point. Start stitching approximately 4" from beginning edge of binding strip, taking ¼" seam through all layers.

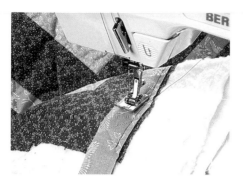

4. For **mitered corners**, stop stitching ¼" from corner or marked corner line, backstitch, and remove quilt from sewing machine. (Placing pin at ¼" point will show you where to stop stitching.)

5. Rotate quilt quarter turn and fold binding straight up, away from corner, forming 45°-angle fold.

6. Bring binding straight down in line with next edge to be sewn, leaving top fold even with raw edge of previously sewn side. Begin stitching at top edge, sewing through all layers.

Finishing

As you approach beginning point, join ends of binding either with a folded edge or with a seam. (We use both methods to finish binding on our projects. The folded finish is the fastest but creates a slight bump because of the extra thickness. The stitched finish is a bit more difficult but is smoother and less noticeable.)

Finishing with a Fold

To finish or end binding with a folded edge, fold beginning end of binding as shown. Lay binding end over the fold and continue stitching through all layers ½" to 1" beyond beginning fold. Trim extra binding. When binding is turned to quilt back, the beginning fold will conceal ending raw edge.

Finishing with a Seam

1. To finish binding with a seam, leave approximately 8" total of binding unsewn between beginning and ending stitching. Open out binding and form 45°-angle folds; crease folds.

2. Open folds. With right sides facing, match fold lines. Stitch on fold lines, creating a diagonal seam. Check to see that length of newly seamed binding is equal to length of quilt edge. Adjust seam allowance, if needed.

3. Trim excess binding, leaving ¼" seam allowance; press seam open. Stitch binding to quilt.

Hand-Finishing Binding to Quilt Back

1. Trim any excess batting and quilt backing, leaving enough to fill binding uniformly when it is turned to quilt back. Trim excess with scissors or with a rotary cutter and ruler.

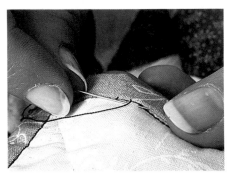

2. Bring folded edge of binding to quilt back so that it covers machine stitching. Blind-stitch folded edge to quilt backing, using a few pins just ahead of stitching to hold binding in place.

3. Blindstitch to corner. Fold un-stitched binding from next side under, forming a 45° angle and a mitered corner. Stitch on mitered folds on quilt front and back.

Spiral Binding

1. To make pieced spiral binding, begin by cutting 2"-wide strips across fabric width from several different fabrics. Sew strips together lengthwise into a strip set. Press seams to one side. Using rotary cutter and ruler, trim one end of strip set at 45° angle. Make 45°-angle cuts that are parallel to first cut, cutting segments the width of binding. (See *Tessellated Star* wall quilt on page 147.)

2. Join segments with ¼" seams (A) to form a long binding piece (B).

Attaching Binding with Overlapped Corners

1. Sew binding to two opposite sides of quilt. Trim excess binding, batting, and backing and hand-finish. Allowing approximately 2" excess binding at each end, machine-stitch binding to remaining two sides.

2. Trim end of unfinished binding ½" longer than adjacent bound edge. Working with back of quilt toward you, fold end of binding over, even with bound edge.

3. Fold binding over to cover machine stitching and raw edge of binding corner. Blindstitch binding to quilt backing, adding extra stitches to secure corners.

Binding with Accent Piping

Narrow piping or flange inserts, made from fabric that contrasts with binding and quilt border, can add interest to the edge of your quilt. This tailored finish was used on *Floral Wreath* wall quilt, shown on page 136.

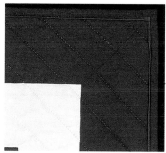

To make accent piping, cut ¾"-wide strips across fabric width. Piece strips together with diagonal seams and make four strips, each approximately 3" longer than side of quilt. (See Making Straight-Grain Strips for Binding on page 94.) Press strips in half lengthwise with wrong sides facing.

Pin pressed piping strips to quilt top sides, placing raw edges even with quilt edges and overlapping strip ends at corners. (See photo above left.) With right sides facing and raw edges aligned, place binding on piping and quilt top. Stitch through all layers, taking extra care to keep stitching straight since it will determine the width of the piping. (See photo at left.)

Attaching Machine-Finished Binding

1. To finish utilitarian projects quickly, binding can be attached entirely with sewing machine. Begin by trimming excess batting and backing even with raw edges of quilt top. With right sides facing and raw edges aligned, pin binding to quilt **back**, instead of quilt top, and machine-stitch through all layers. Miter at corners, as described in step 4 on page 97.

2. To finish binding, bring folded edge of binding over to quilt top to cover machine stitching. Using thread to match binding or clear nylon thread, machine-topstitch binding through all layers. Add hand stitching to secure binding corners.

Attaching Binding to Quilts with Scalloped Edges

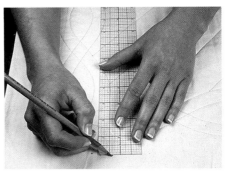

1. If scallops are to reflect curved appliqué or quilting motifs in borders, simply measure and mark a uniform distance from curves of appliqué pieces or quilting and mark placement guides for binding. Measure along placement line to estimate amount of 1¼"-wide single-thickness bias binding you will need.

2. With right sides facing, pin raw edge of binding to placement line just ahead of where you will stitch. As you stitch, ease binding on outer curves. If binding is stretched around outer curves, edges will cup when binding is finished. At cleft or inside junction between scallops, raise presser foot and stitch, taking care not to allow pleats or puckers to form in the binding.

3. After binding is attached, trim batting and backing even with raw edges of quilt top. Clip seam allowance to stitching at cleft of each scallop. Turn binding to quilt back and blindstitch to backing.

Self-Finished Edges

Although binding is the most durable edge finish for quilts, quilt edges can be finished without a separate binding. Quilts can be finished by either bringing the quilt backing to the front to cover the raw edge and batting, folding it under, and stitching it in place, or turning the quilt top to the back and folding the raw edge under.

Bringing Backing to Quilt Front

1. This edge finish creates a false binding. If quilting does not extend to edge of quilt top, baste through all layers close to raw edge of quilt top. Trim batting even with quilt top edges; trim backing so that it is 1" larger than quilt top. Fold edge of backing under ½".

2. Bring folded edge over to cover batting and raw edge of quilt top. Blindstitch folded edge to quilt top or machine-topstitch folded edge through all layers.

Stitching Quilt Edges Together

Stop quilting at least ½" from quilt edge. Trim backing and batting even with raw edges of quilt top; then trim batting approximately ¼" more. Turn in raw edges of quilt top and backing and blindstitch together.

Prairie Point Edging

Folded fabric triangles, known as prairie points, are particularly attractive on quilts with patchwork triangles or simple quilts that need perking up. Add prairie points to the quilt top before it is quilted. You can also add them after quilting if the quilting does not extend to the edges of quilt top.

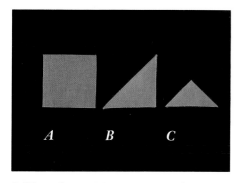

1. To make prairie points, cut 3½" squares of fabric (A). These can be cut from the same fabric or several different-colored fabrics.

To estimate how many squares to cut, assume that each prairie point will cover approximately 2½" to 3" of quilt edge. Fold each square in half diagonally with wrong sides facing; press (B). Fold in half again, as shown, forming a smaller triangle; press (C).

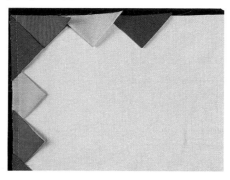

2. With right sides facing, align long raw edge of each prairie point with raw edge of unquilted quilt top. Begin at center of quilt side. Slip folded edge of triangle (prairie point) into open side of adjacent triangle so that they overlap slightly. Adjust overlap, as needed, to position triangles at corners and machine-stitch.

3. After quilting is complete, trim backing and batting even with raw edge of quilt top. Trim an additional ¼" of batting. Turn prairie points so that they face out from quilt top, bringing raw edge of quilt top to inside. Turn in ¼" of quilt backing. Blindstitch folded edge of backing to prairie point edges, concealing machine stitching (A). Photo (B) shows the finished quilt front edge.

Attaching a Hanging Sleeve*

1. Choose muslin or fabric that matches quilt backing for hanging sleeve. For a 4"-wide sleeve, cut and piece together 8½"-wide straight-grain strips to make a piece 2" shorter than quilt width. Turn ½" to wrong side on both narrow ends and machine-hem, making sleeve 3" shorter than quilt width.

2. Press sleeve in half lengthwise with wrong sides facing. On side that will face away from quilt, machine-baste a ¼"-deep pleat along length of sleeve. (See photo.) Basting can be removed to release pleat if quilt is hung on a thick pole. Pleat also gives extra fullness on back of sleeve to keep quilt front from bulging out.

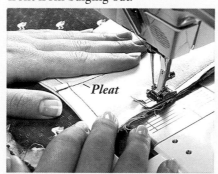

3. Machine-stitch binding to quilt; trim excess batting and backing. Center and pin sleeve to quilt backing, aligning raw edges of sleeve with top edge of quilt. Machine-stitch on top of binding stitching.

4. Blindstitch binding to quilt, covering raw edges of sleeve. Blindstitch bottom fold of sleeve to quilt backing, being careful not to stitch through to quilt top.

*Instructions are for an unfinished quilt. If your quilt is bound, follow steps 1 and 2. Sew sleeve into a tube. Position sleeve near top of quilt and center sleeve seam so that it faces quilt backing. Blindstitch folds of sleeve to quilt backing.

Signing Your Quilt

Signing and dating your work is an important step in finishing a quilt. In addition, you may add other information, such as the occasion for which the quilt was made, the length of time it took to make the quilt, the recipient of the quilt, your age, the number of quilts you have made, or a list of awards the quilt has won. Think of it as a diary of the history and ownership of the quilt. Here are some ways to document your quilt.

(Top) Quilted Name and Date. This is a discreet but permanent way to sign your work.

(Bottom) Machine-Stitched Signature Documentation. If your sewing machine can be programmed to stitch letters, machine-embroider a label with your name and date.

(Top) Embroidered Signature. A signature embroidered in outline or cross-stitch, either on the quilt top or back, is another popular way to sign.

(Bottom) Ink Signature Documentations. Here, we signed and dated the Memory block from our *Americana* sampler quilt. In addition, always attach a signature document on the back.

(Top) Typed Signature Documentation. A manual typewriter works best, but an electric one can be used. Press muslin with a hot iron and a pressing cloth after typing to set ink and prevent smearing.

(Bottom) Ink on Muslin. Stabilize muslin by pressing freezer paper to back of muslin before writing on it. Remove paper before stitching label to quilt back.

Learn These Skills While Making a
Ribbon Star Wall Quilt

- 🏠 *arranging multiple identical blocks*
- 🏠 *adding borders with corner squares*
- 🏠 *chain-piecing block units and rows*
- 🏠 *attaching straight-grain French binding*

Materials:

1¼ yards pink/blue print for blocks,
  backing, binding, and hanging sleeve
¼ yard pink print for stars
⅝ yard navy print for blocks and borders
Basic sewing supplies
Batting, low-loft, 28" square

Finished Block Size: *9" square*
Finished Quilt Size: *24" square*

1. *Note:* Measurements include seam allowances. From pink/blue print, cut three 2¼"-wide strips across fabric width for straight-grain French binding and one 28" square for backing. Cut 16 triangle As for blocks and four square Bs for border corners. (See page 41 for patterns.)

From pink, cut 16 triangle As and four square Bs. From blue, cut two 3½"-wide strips across fabric width for borders.

(Borders will be cut to length when added to quilt top.) Cut 32 triangle As for ribbons around stars.

2. Refer to Ribbon Star Block Piecing Diagram and arrange pieces for blocks, stacking them atop each other. Using assembly-line methods, piece four Ribbon Star blocks. (See page 39.)

3. Sew two blocks together to form a row. Make two rows.

4. Measure through center quilt top. (Quilt top should measure 18½" across.) Cut four borders 18½" long from border strips cut in step 1. If quilt top is slightly larger or smaller, cut borders equal to your measurement. Sew a border to two opposite sides of quilt top; press seams toward borders. Sew a border corner square to each end of remaining two borders; press seams toward borders. Sew borders to remaining two sides. Press completed quilt top.

5. Prepare quilt for quilting. Outline-quilt in-the-ditch around stars, ribbons, and inside edge of borders and corner squares.

6. Bind edges with French binding. Add hanging sleeve. Make signature label and attach to quilt back.

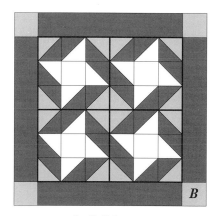

Quilt Diagram

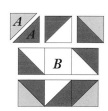

***Ribbon Star
Block
Piecing Diagram***

First Steps in Quick-Cutting and Quick-Piecing

The invention of the sewing machine in 1846 changed the way people sewed. Individuals who made quilts immediately recognized the speed and accuracy it made available to them. They began to use the machine to piece their quilts. Over time, the sewing machine has inspired many time-saving piecing methods that are uniquely suited to machine stitching. The introduction of the rotary fabric cutter with a cutting mat and special rulers was a direct response to the demand for faster and easier methods of machine piecing.

First Steps in Quick-Cutting and Quick-Piecing

*In this chapter, we discuss how to use a rotary cutter, how to cut fabric strips,
and how to quick-cut and quick-piece squares, rectangles,
and triangles. We also cover some forms of strip or string patchwork.*

The first step in many quick-cutting and quick-piecing methods is to cut fabrics into strips. Often, the next step is to sew combinations of strips together lengthwise into strip sets. Then the strip sets are cut into smaller segments, such as squares, rectangles, triangles, and other shapes. These smaller segments are joined to form block units or blocks. Pieces cut using quick-cutting methods include ¼" seam allowances.

Because strip sets will be made before being cut into other shapes, visualizing how a finished block or project will look is often difficult. Sketching your quilt with colored pencils is a worthwhile use of time. With practice, you will gain skill in forecasting your results. Sometimes, you may want to piece one block in the traditional way to see how the fabrics work together before you quick-piece an entire quilt.

Learn These Quick-Cutting Skills While
Piecing a St. Louis Block

🏠 *straightening or squaring-off end of fabric*
🏠 *cutting fabric strips with rotary cutter and ruler*

🏠 *sewing and pressing strip sets*
🏠 *cutting strip sets into smaller sections*

Materials:
¼ yard each of 3 fabrics
Basic sewing supplies
Rotary cutter, mat, and ruler
Ruled square, large

Finished Block Size: *9" square*

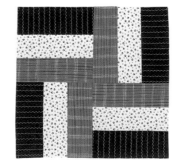

Squaring-off End of Fabric

Since most cotton fabrics are treated with a permanent press finish, it is pointless to try to straighten them in the traditional way by pulling on opposite corners. The built-in memory of the permanent press finish will return the fabric to its original shape after washing. Instead, before strips or other pieces are cut, straighten or square-off one end of fabric by trimming it so that the edge is perpendicular to the center fold.

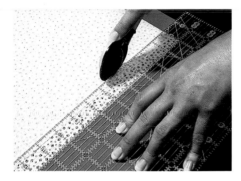

1. Begin by folding fabric in half lengthwise, matching selvage edges. You may need to misalign cut edges to get selvage edges to line up; pressing out creased center fold will make this easier.

Lay folded fabric on cutting mat with selvages nearest you; fold fabric in half lengthwise again, bringing selvages to center fold. By folding fabric in fourths, cuts will be approximately 11" long (44" width of fabric ÷ 4 = 11"). Short cuts like these are generally more accurate and easier to make than longer ones. Adjust fabric on cutting mat so that uneven edge is on left side if you are right-handed or on right side if you are left-handed.

2. To square off fabric edge, place large ruled square on fabric so that bottom edge of square is even with folded edge and side of square is approximately ½" from uneven fabric end. Butt long ruler against left edge of square. Remove square but keep ruler in place.

IMPORTANT:

Never let children or anyone unfamiliar with proper and safe use of a rotary cutter handle it. Cover blade with guard whenever it is not in use.

---

3. Holding ruler firmly in place with your left hand (if you are right-handed), cut along right edge of ruler, trimming uneven fabric edge from end.

To cut, roll cutter away from yourself, exerting firm and even pressure. As you cut, "walk" other hand along ruler to hold it firmly in place. Most people find that cutting is easiest when they cut away from themselves and when they stand to cut. If working on a gridded mat, use lines on mat to make a square cut. Align folded edge of fabric with horizontal grid line. Align ruler with vertical grid line; cut along ruler, straightening and squaring off fabric edge.

Cutting Fabric Strips

Perfectly straight and accurately cut strips are essential for many quick-piecing methods. Cut all fabric strips across fabric width, unless instructed otherwise.

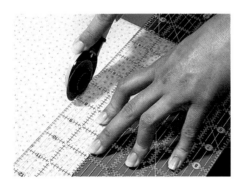

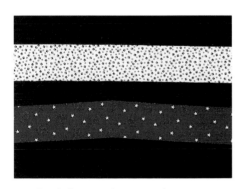

1. Cut one (2"-wide) strip from each of three fabrics. With fabric folded into fourths, place ruler atop folded fabric so that it measures desired strip width. Cut through all layers, guiding cutter along edge of ruler.

2. Check frequently to see that cuts remain perpendicular to fold. If strips are not cut exactly perpendicular to fold, they will bow where they were folded. The strip shown on top is a properly cut, straight strip; strip on bottom is a poorly cut, crooked one.

Sewing and Pressing Strip Sets

A **strip set** is a group of strips that have been sewn together lengthwise in a particular sequence. Often completed strip sets are later cut into smaller segments to use as blocks or as portions of blocks.

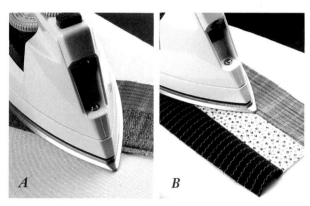

1. To make a strip set, pair two different strips with right sides facing and raw edges aligned. Machine-stitch with ¼" seam. Add third strip to complete strip set. (If making sets with more than three strips, join strips in pairs and then sew pairs to other pairs.)

Pinning strip edges in a few places before sewing or holding unsewn edges of strips together as you sew will prevent bottom strip in pair from drawing up. If your sewing machine tends to draw up bottom strip as you sew, try stitching alternate strips in opposite directions. Try not to pull or stretch strips.

2. Press seams of strip set. Begin by pressing strips flat, just as you have sewn them, to set stitching (A). Fold top fabric strip back, revealing right side of seam and strip set (B). Gently, with side of iron, press seam open on right side with seam allowances to one side. Pick up iron to press so that you do not risk stretching fabric.

Check to be sure that there are no folds or tucks and that seams are fully open. Turn strip set wrong side up; correct any spots where seam allowances are pressed to incorrect side. Strip set should be straight, without any distortion along outside edges.

Cutting Strip Sets into Smaller Sections

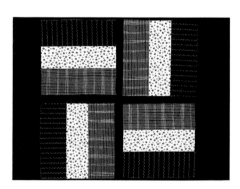

1. The St. Louis block is made of four three-bar units joined together. Align horizontal mark on ruler with long edge of strip set. Cut along ruler edge, trimming uneven end of strip set.

2. Turn strip set around so trimmed end of strip set is near left edge of mat. Keeping horizontal line on ruler aligned with long edge of strip set, measure 5". Cut along ruler edge, cutting a 5" square. Cut four (5") squares from strip set. ·

3. Lay out three-bar units to form block. You have two options for arranging the three-bar units. We placed strip sets so that blue edges meet. The alternative would have been to place them so that brown edges meet. Join strip sets.

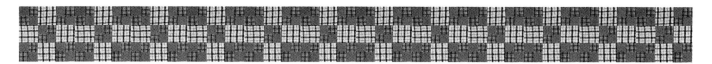

Learn These Quick-Cutting and Quick-Piecing Skills
While Making a Four-in-Nine-Patch Block

🏠 *quick-cutting squares*   🏠 *quick-piecing four-patch units*

Materials:
¼ yard each of 3 fabrics
Basic quick-cutting and sewing supplies

Finished Block Size: *9" square*

Quick-Cutting Squares

To quick-cut squares, first add ½" to finished size of square for ¼" seam allowances. Cut strip equal to this measurement across fabric width. Unfold strip so that it is doubled, rather than folded in fourths. Trim selvages, squaring off ends.

Measure across strip distance equal to strip width measurement to make square. For this block, cut four 3½" squares from a 3½"-wide strip.

Quick-Piecing Four-Patch Units

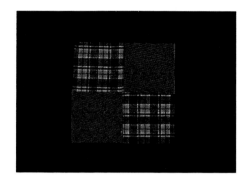

One common arrangement of squares is called checkerboard because it is made of same-size contrasting squares, arranged in regular sequence. This four-patch unit contains two fabrics, but up to four different fabrics may be combined in a unit. Four-patch and nine-patch units are examples of checkerboards. (Turn page for Block Assembly.)

Bonus Checkerboard Blocks

Often when quick-cutting, you will have segments left over. These segments can be joined to make more four-patch units or combined with squares as we did for the Four-in-Nine-Patch. The diagrams below illustrate a few block ideas.

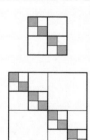
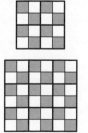
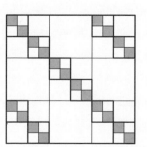
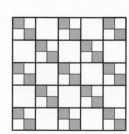
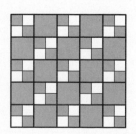

Block Assembly

1. Count number of squares of each fabric in the checkerboard. Cut one strip for each square, cutting each strip ½" wider than finished-size square. Cut a 2"-wide strip from each of two fabrics for block. Finished size of small square will be 1½".

2. Join strips lengthwise in pairs to form strip set and press seam allowances to one side. Cut across seam line of strip set at 2" intervals and cut 10 segments. When cutting large number of segments from several strip sets, stack pair with right sides together so that segments are paired and ready to sew as they are cut. After every few cuts, check to see that cuts are at right angles to strips. If necessary, square off end of strip sets again before cutting more segments.

3. Pair 10 segments, reversing positions of segments so that contrasting fabrics alternate in checkerboard. Chain-piece pairs. Your sewing machine will almost automatically match seams for you if you arrange pairs so that seam allowances on top piece are pointed away from you and seam allowances on bottom piece are toward you.

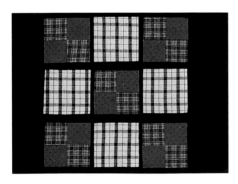

4. Lay out five four-patch units and four squares to form block. Sew units into three rows with three units in each row; join rows.

Cutting Borders

For quilts with finished size smaller than width of your fabric, cut borders across fabric width.

For larger quilts, cut strips across fabric width and piece to achieve needed length. For continuous borders, cut borders lengthwise first, before cutting smaller pieces or strips, so that you will not run short of fabric.

1. To cut lengthwise borders, open fabric to its full width. Fold fabric in half widthwise so that doubled fabric is a little longer than half as long as borders will be. (Selvages will be on both sides of fabric.) For very long borders, fold fabric in half widthwise again. For example, for borders 100" long, fold fabric so you will make four cuts approximately 25" long.

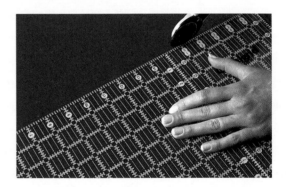

2. Trim away selvage edge on one side. Measure and cut borders parallel to trimmed edge. Since you will probably be working with a lot of fabric, reposition cutting mat and ruler as you cut. For wide borders, use large ruled square or ruler in combination with ruled square.

For lengthwise striped borders, do not fold fabric. Instead, use one stripe as cutting guide and cut through single thickness of fabric.

3. After cutting, unfold border and straighten one end. Measure border length and trim opposite end to several inches longer than desired length. Trim borders to exact length when you are ready to sew them to quilt. Before setting borders aside, pin label on them so that you will not cut them into smaller pieces by mistake. (See "Basic Settings and Borders for Quilts," page 50, to sew borders to quilt.)

Learn These Quick-Piecing Skills While
Making a Nine-Patch Block

🏠 *determining strip width*

Materials:
¼ yard each of 6 fabrics
Basic quick-cutting and sewing supplies

Finished Block Size: *4½" square*

Nine-Patch blocks are usually shaded in one of two ways. Many have five dark squares and four light squares, (left); others have five light squares and four dark squares (right).

🏠 *quick-piecing a Nine-Patch block*

1. Each small square for a 4½" Nine-Patch block is 1½" (4½" ÷ 3 squares/row = 1½"). Add ½" to 1½" for seam allowances and cut strips 2" wide.

2. Cut nine strips, one for each square in block. To make a Nine-Patch with five dark squares and four light squares, cut five strips from dark fabric and four from light fabric.

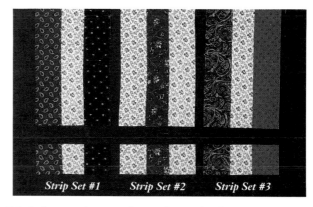

Strip Set #1   Strip Set #2   Strip Set #3

3. Stitch three strip sets, alternating strip placement to match a row in finished block. Press seams toward dark strips. Cut across seam lines of each strip set at 2" intervals to form segments. (Or, for another size block, use same width measurement that you used when cutting strips.) If you stack strip set for first row atop strip set for second row with right sides facing before cutting, first two rows of squares will be paired and ready to sew.

4. Arrange segments into rows. Stitch row 1 segment to row 2 segment; add row 3 segment to row 2.

Working with Triangles

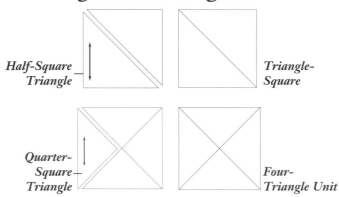

Half-Square Triangle

Triangle-Square

Quarter-Square Triangle

Four-Triangle Unit

After squares, 45° right triangles are probably the most frequently used shape in patchwork designs. These triangles can be cut in two different ways. The most common way to cut them is with the short sides (the legs) on the straight of grain. These triangles are often called **half-square triangles** because they are quick-cut by dividing a square in half diagonally into two triangles. Pairs of half-square triangles joined on the long sides (hypotenuse) into a square unit are called **triangle-squares**. In this section we'll illustrate the two basic quick-piecing methods for making triangle-square units.

The second cutting arrangement for triangles puts the long side of the triangle on the straight of grain. These triangles are often called **quarter-square triangles** because they are quick-cut by dividing a square diagonally in both directions into four triangles. Use quarter-square triangles whenever the long side of the triangle is on the outside edge of a block, on the outside edge of a block unit, or on the outside edge of the quilt. The straight of grain on the outside edge adds stability and prevents the outside edge from stretching or giving as it would if cut on bias. **Four-triangle units** are squares formed by joining four quarter-square triangles. Quick-piecing these units makes constructing blocks like Ohio Star a breeze.

Quick-Cutting Half-Square Triangles

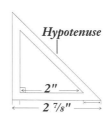

Hypotenuse

2"

2 ⅞"

When ¼" seam allowances are added to each side of a right triangle, the measurement of each leg (short side) is ⅞" longer than leg of finished-size triangle. (See diagram at left.) For example, a triangle with 2" finished legs will have a leg measurement of 2⅞" when seam allowances are added.

1. To quick-cut half-square triangles, measure finished size of one triangle leg. Add ⅞" and cut squares that size. For example, cut 4⅞" squares for triangles with 4" finished-size leg.

2. Cut each square in half diagonally from corner to corner into two triangles. To cut multiple triangles, stack several strips and cut them into squares and then triangles.

3. For large half-square triangles, use a large ruled square to measure and cut squares; then cut squares in half diagonally into two triangles.

Quick-Cutting Quarter-Square Triangles

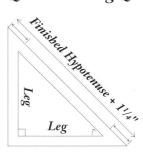

Finished Hypotenuse + 1¼"

Leg

Leg

When ¼" seam allowances are added to all three sides of a triangle, the long side is ⅝" longer on each end or a total of 1¼" longer than original triangle. (See diagram at left.)

1. To quick-cut quarter-square triangles, measure length of long side of triangle. Cut squares 1¼" larger than this measurement. For example, cut 4¼" squares for triangles with long side equaling 3" finished size.

2. Cut each square in half diagonally in both directions, cutting in an X, to make four triangles. To cut multiple triangles, stack several strips and cut multiple layers.

3. To cut large quarter-square triangles, such as triangles used as setting triangles for a diagonally set quilt, use a large ruled square to cut individual squares, rather than cutting squares from fabric strips.

Grid Method

With the grid method, two fabrics are placed with right sides facing, a grid of squares is marked, diagonal lines are marked through the squares, and diagonal seams are sewn. The grid method is much faster, easier, and more efficient than marking, cutting, and stitching individual triangles. Sewing before cutting also helps prevent stretching the long bias edges of the triangles. If you mark, stitch, and cut accurately, the resulting triangle-squares are as accurate as those pieced by traditional methods.

1. Cut rectangle no larger than 18" x 22" from each of two fabrics that are to be joined into triangle-squares. (Larger pieces are difficult to handle.) With right sides facing and raw edges aligned, press fabrics. These paired fabrics are referred to as a fabric combination.

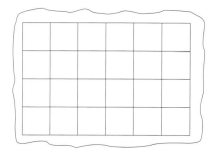

Diagram Showing Grid Drawn

2. Mark grid of squares on wrong side of lighter fabric in fabric combination. To make marking and sewing easier, draw grid so it is at least ½" from raw edges of fabric. Each square in grid should be ⅞" larger than finished size of triangle-square. For example, draw grid of 3⅞" squares to make triangle-squares with 3" finished-size leg.

To determine number of squares to draw, divide number of triangle-squares needed by two and draw at least that many squares in the grid. For example, if you need 48 triangle-squares, draw grid of 24 or more squares. You will get two triangle-square units from each grid square.

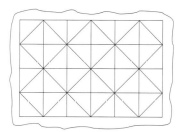

Diagram Showing All Diagonal Lines Drawn

3. Draw diagonal line through each square in grid. Draw diagonal lines in one direction, marking every other row of squares. Then, mark alternate squares with diagonal lines in opposite direction as shown. (Only one diagonal line is drawn through each square.)

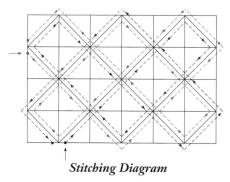

Stitching Diagram

4. If your sewing machine presser foot accurately measures a ¼" seam, use it as a guide to stitch a ¼" seam on each side of all diagonal lines. If your presser foot does not accurately measure a ¼" seam allowance, draw a stitching line ¼" on each side of all diagonal lines. Stitch along inside edge of stitching lines, since even the width of a thin line can alter size of finished triangle-squares.

First, start stitching at an outside point near top left corner of grid (blue arrow on Stitching Diagram) and stitch continuously around grid, raising presser foot and pivoting at corners. Do not worry if your stitching extends beyond outside lines of grid; this excess fabric will be trimmed. Arrows in diagram indicate starting and turning points on a sample grid. When you have returned to starting point or have stitched on one side of all diagonal lines, move to another outside point and stitch. (See red arrow in Stitching Diagram.) Check to make sure that you have stitched along each side of all diagonal lines.

Gently press stitched fabric combination to smooth stitching. If your sewing machine tension is out of adjustment or pressure on presser foot is too heavy, the stitching may have drawn-up diagonal seams slightly. If so, pull gently on each seam to relax stitching before pressing. Puckering or drawing of seams will result in distorted triangle-squares.

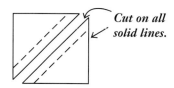

Cut on all solid lines.

5. Using rotary cutter and ruler, cut on all lines of grid to make triangle-square units, as shown.

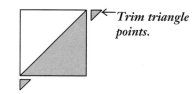

Trim triangle points.

6. Carefully press triangle-squares open, pressing seam allowances toward darker fabric. Trim little triangle points at ends of seams as shown.

Measure triangle-squares; they should measure ½" larger than square needed. For example, triangle-squares with a 3" finished size should measure 3½" square.

Bias Strip Method

With the bias strip method, contrasting strips of fabric cut on the bias are joined lengthwise and then cut into triangle-squares. (This method was developed and popularized by Marsha McCloskey and Nancy Martin of That Patchwork Place, Inc.)

Although this method is slower than the grid method, there is little variance in the size of the triangle-squares and almost no distortion of the square. It is especially useful for small triangle-squares because the seams can be pressed open before pieces are cut. However, this method is not practical for triangle-squares that finish larger than 3" to 4" because wide bias strips result in a lot of wasted fabric.

A 6" ruled square marked with squares radiating out from one corner and a diagonal line from corner to corner is the best tool for cutting triangle-squares.

If you prefer, you can make a square template that includes seam allowances, mark the squares on the fabric strips, and cut them with scissors.

1. Cut ½-yard pieces of contrasting fabrics into bias strips 1" wider than finished size of triangle-square needed. For example, cut 3"-wide strips for 2" finished-size triangle-squares.

2. Alternate colors and join strips lengthwise with ¼" seam. Press seam allowances toward darker fabric.

3. Using 6"-ruled square and rotary cutter, cut squares ¾" larger than finished triangle-square. For example, cut 2¾" squares for 2" bias triangle-squares. As you cut, keep diagonal line of ruled square along seam line.

4. Trim excess fabric of triangle-square so that it measures ½" larger than the desired finished size. For example, cut 2½" squares to finish 2" square.

5. After you have cut one set of triangle-squares along all pointed edges, reposition ruled square to cut next series of triangle-squares and trim to size.

Quick-Cutting Pieces for a Single Patchwork Block

If you are making a single block, using quick-piecing techniques that make many units may not always be practical. But you still may find it helpful to use quick-cutting methods to make the pieces that you need. Follow along as we illustrate our own "short-hand" system for making a Sawtooth Star block.

1. Make small reference drawing of your block. (See diagram of Sawtooth Star at right.)

2. Determine block grid. (See page 44 for a list of basic grids.) For example,

Sawtooth Star is a four-patch block. To make 12" finished block, each unit would be 3" square.

3. Label each different piece on your diagram and draw grain line arrows.

4. List number of each piece you will need and size to cut as shown. For example, you will need: four 3½" (1 unit + seam allowances) squares for A, and one 6½" (2 units + seam allowances) square for D.

To make triangle for C, use quick-cutting method for half-square triangles, and cut four 3⅞" squares to make eight triangles with straight of grain on legs.

To make triangles for B, use quick-cutting method for quarter-square triangles, and cut one 7¼" square to make four triangles with straight of grain on hypotenuse.

Sawtooth Star

A	Cut 4 (3½") squares.
B	Need 4 triangles. Cut 1 (7¼") square.
C	Need 8 triangles. Cut 4 (3⅞") squares.
D	Cut 1 (6½") square.

Learn To Make Four-Triangle Units While Making an Ohio Star Block

Materials:

¼ yard each of 2 fabrics
Basic quick-cutting and sewing supplies

Finished Block Size: *12" square*

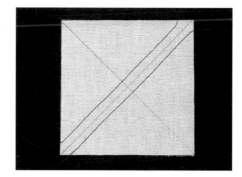

1. Cut square from each fabric. Cut squares 1¼" larger than finished measurement of four-triangle unit. For example, cut 5¼" squares to make 4" finished-size units for Ohio Star block. Since you will need four units for this block, cut two sets of contrasting squares.

2. On **wrong** sides of lighter fabric squares, draw diagonal lines from corner to corner in both directions, drawing an X.

3. With right sides facing and raw edges aligned, pair squares with contrasting squares. Machine-stitch ¼" on each side of one diagonal line only.

4. Cut on line between rows of stitching, cutting square into two triangle-squares. Press seam allowances toward darker fabric. Extend drawn diagonal line of two triangle-squares onto darker triangle so that it reaches from corner to corner.

5. With right sides of contrasting triangles facing and raw edges aligned, place triangle-square with extended diagonal line atop triangle-square without extended line. Center diagonal seam of each, butting seam allowances against each other; pin. Stitch ¼" on each side of diagonal line. Position triangle-squares so that seam allowances of top triangle-square point toward sewing machine. The sewing machine will push seams against each other, almost automatically seam-matching pieces.

Cut on diagonal line between rows of stitching, cutting square into two triangles. Press seam allowances toward darker fabrics. Each pair of triangle-squares makes two four-triangle units. If you started with 5¼" squares, units should measure 4½" square with seam allowances.

6. From one fabric, cut 4½" square for center of block. From second fabric, cut four 4½" squares for corners. Refer to block photo and arrange squares and four-triangle units in three rows; join rows.

Strip or String Patchwork

Narrow fabric strips, too narrow for use in most types of patchwork, are also called strings. In the days when all clothing was made at home, quiltmakers often cut left-over fabric scraps into narrow strips for string quilts. To-day, quilters cut their strings or strips from new yardage or from scraps leftover from other quilting projects.

Making string quilts often begins with sewing fabric strings together into strip sets. The strip sets are then cut into a variety of shapes and combined with other string pieces or single fabric pieces. In this section we'll show you some basic string-piecing concepts and how to make several string blocks.

Learn These Additional Quick-Piecing Techniques While Making a String Block from Half-Square Triangles

🏠 *making a strip set from strips of various widths* 🏠 *cutting half-square triangles from strip set*
🏠 *piecing strip-pieced units into a block*

Materials:

⅛ to ¼ yard each of 5 fabrics

Finished Block Size: *8½" square*

1. Cut various-width strips from fabrics. Sew strips lengthwise into a strip set. Press seam allowances in one direction.

For our block, we cut and sewed the following strips: 2"-wide red strip, 2½"-wide tan stripe strip, 1½"-wide brown strip, 1¼"-wide light teal strip, and 2"-wide dark teal strip.

2. Measure width of strip set, including seam allowances. Using this measurement, cut two square segments from

strip set. For example, if strip set measures 7¼", like our sample, cut squares this size. Cut each square in half diagonally into two triangles, being sure to cut both in same diagonal direction.

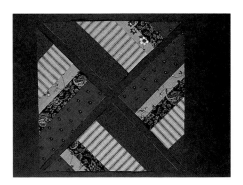

3. Arrange string-pieced triangles and sew together to make String block. Our String block measures 9" square and will finish 8½".

Learn These String-Piecing Skills While Making Three Different Blocks

🏠 cutting large triangles with hypotenuse on straight of grain from strip set
🏠 combining strip-pieced and solid triangles into a variety of blocks

Materials:

⅛ to ¼ yard each of 5 different fabrics
⅝ yard of 1 or more fabrics for plain triangles

Variation 1 of Four-Triangle Block

Variation 2 of Four-Triangle Block

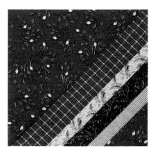

Roman Stripe Block

1. Cut strips in different widths from several different fabrics. Sew strips together lengthwise into strip set, placing wider strips to outside. Press seam allowances to one side.

For sample blocks, cut and sew: 2½"-wide medium blue strip, 1¼"-wide tan strip, 1½"-wide navy strip, 1¼"-wide gray strip, and a 2"-wide red strip.

Trim Line

Cutting Diagram

2. Trim one end of strip set at 45° angle by aligning 45° line on ruler with long edge of strip set and cutting along edge of ruler. Reposition ruler to cut large triangle, again aligning 45° line

with long edge of strip set and cut. Cut triangles along length of strip set. Half of the triangles will have one outside strip on long side; other half will have other outside strip on long side.

3. To make Variation 1 of Four-Triangle block, join two of each type of triangle. (Our sample block measures 11¾" square and will finish 11¼".)

4. To make Variation 2, substitute two solid triangles for two string-pieced triangles. To cut the solid triangles, measure length of hypotenuse of string-pieced triangles. Cut square this size; cut square diagonally in both directions forming four triangles. (We cut our triangles from a 13" tan square.) Sew two string-pieced triangles to two solid triangles to form block, as shown.

5. To make the 8½" Roman Stripe block, join a string-pieced triangle to an equal size solid triangle.

Log Cabin

The Log Cabin is one of America's all-time favorite quilt patterns, popular from the mid-1800s to the present. In this unique type of string or strip block, narrow fabric strips or logs surround a center square, which some believe represented the heart of the home. According to quilt lore, a red square symbolizes a chimney; a yellow square stands for a lantern in the window.

Virtually every type of fabric used for quiltmaking—wool, challis, silk, satin, velvet, and cotton—has found its way into Log Cabin quilts at one time or another. Log Cabin blocks containing heavy or fragile fabrics were usually constructed on a fabric foundation. The quilt tops were tied to a lining or backing at the corners of the blocks. Today, most Log Cabin quilts are made of cotton fabric and assembled and quilted in the same manner as any other type of quilt.

Log Cabin Block Variation

There are many variations of the Log Cabin pattern. They fall into one of four basic construction categories. The diagrams show the four main categories of Log Cabin blocks and the names associated with each. The numbers on the diagrams indicate the order in which the strips are sewn to the beginning square.

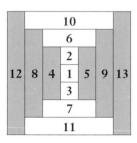

Courthouse Steps
Log Cabin Block

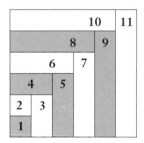

Off-Center Log Cabin Block
(Type 1)

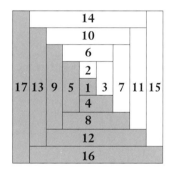

Traditional or
Spiraling Log Cabin Block

For the **Courthouse Steps** variation, add logs alternately to opposite sides of the center square. Two opposite sides of the block are usually shaded dark, and the two remaining sides are shaded light.

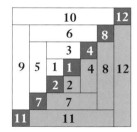

Chimneys and Cornerstones
Log Cabin Block

The **Chimneys and Cornerstones** variation has squares positioned diagonally across the block, separating the light and dark logs. To make this version, cut the logs to the length needed; stitch the squares to the logs before adding them around the center square.

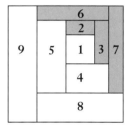

Off-Center Log Cabin Block
(Type 2)

Traditional or Spiraling Log Cabin blocks are the most common type. Build the block by adding logs around a center square in a clockwise or counter-clockwise direction. The blocks are frequently shaded in a light and dark diagonal half, as shown in the diagram.

In **off-center variations**, the beginning square is not in the middle of the block. To create a block of this type, either add strips to only two sides of the beginning square, shown as type 1; or sew narrow logs to two adjacent sides of the beginning square and wider logs to the other two sides, shown as type 2.

Learn To Assembly-Line Machine-Piece
Traditional Log Cabin Blocks

Materials:

Scraps of 8 light fabrics*
Scraps of 9 dark fabrics*

* Choose fabrics for light and dark sides of blocks. Light and dark shades of the same color can be used, such as light blue and dark blue, or use contrasting colors, such as black and red, for two halves of blocks. When using scrap fabrics in a variety of colors, such as in Log Cabin quilt shown on page 123, use definitely dark and definitely light fabrics and not too many medium shades. With dark fabric selections, include a solid red for center square.

Finished Block Size: *9" square*

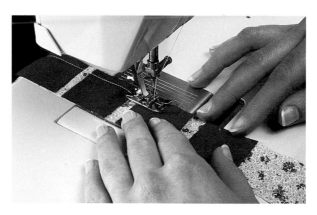

3. With right sides facing and raw edges aligned, place center square on top of light-colored strip. Stitch square to strip and sew few stitches beyond square. Lay another square on top of strip, approximately ¼" from first square. Stitch second square to strip in same manner as first. Repeat until all squares are joined to strip.

1. Cut fabrics into 1½"-wide strips for logs. If you are using full-width fabric pieces, cut strips across the fabric width. If using odd-sized scraps, cut strips on straight of grain, parallel to longest edge of fabric. If making a larger or smaller block, vary size of center square, width of strips (logs), and number of logs that surround center. Sketch block on graph paper to visualize how it will look and to calculate size each will be.

2. Cut squares from strip chosen for center. One center square is needed for each block.

4. Using rotary cutter and ruler, align ruler with raw edge of square, as shown, and cut strip even with edges of center square. Press seam allowance away from center square, taking care not to distort shape of pieces. Repeat for all squares.

5. With right sides facing and raw edges aligned, lay the two-square units atop another light-colored strip (3 in diagram on page 119). Place two-square units so that center squares (1) precede light squares (2) as you sew. Stitch two-square units to strip. Cut strip even with two-square units to form three-piece unit and press seam allowance away from center square.

6. Place three-piece units atop dark strip, so that previously sewn log of each unit (3) is sewn last. Stitch units to dark strip. Cut strip even with units to form four-piece unit, and press seam allowance away from center square.

7. In same manner, stitch four-piece units to dark strip (5). Continue in this manner, using light strips for one diagonal half and dark strips for other half, until blocks are complete. Remember to position units correctly atop strips, last log added should always be closest to you as you sew.

8. Check that all blocks are approximately same size. If using 1"-wide finished-size strips and blocks were stitched according to diagram and photo, finished blocks should measure 9½" square with seam allowances. Set aside blocks and make additional blocks in correct size to replace any inaccurate blocks.

Pre-Cutting Strips to the Length Needed Before Sewing Log Cabin Blocks

Some quilters prefer to cut each log to the length needed before sewing Log Cabin blocks. This ensures that all blocks will turn out the same size.

To determine length to cut logs, draw full-size finished block on graph paper and number pieces in piecing order. Label center square #1.

Measure length of first log (2 in traditional Log Cabin diagram). Add ½" to finished length for seam allowances; write this measurement on block drawing. Cut logs this length from strips.

Continue in this manner until all logs are pre-cut for blocks. Sew all #2 logs to #1 squares, add #3 logs, and so on until blocks are complete.

Setting Variations

Barn Raising Set

Straight Furrows Set

Streak of Lightning Set

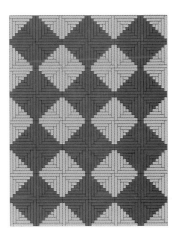

Lights and Darks Set

Traditional Log Cabin blocks, or any block variations shaded diagonally into light and dark halves, can be arranged in many ways to create interesting secondary designs when the blocks are set together. Four of the traditional settings, Barn Raising, Straight Furrows, Streak of Lightning, and Lights and Darks, are shown. Do not feel limited by these traditional settings. Try new settings before sewing blocks together by arranging blocks on the floor or making a pencil sketch. Perhaps you will invent your own, one-of-a-kind Log Cabin set.

Practice These Quick-Piecing Skills While Making *Take the Night Train* Quilt

🏠 *quick-cutting strips*   🏠 *quick-cutting squares, rectangles, and triangles*
🏠 *quick-piecing four-triangle units*   🏠 *strip-piecing*

Materials:

3¾ yards dark green fabric for sashing squares,
  borders, and bias binding
2½ yards cream fabric
1½ yards peach fabric for setting triangles
¼ yard each of 8 assorted peach print fabrics
¼ yard each of 10 assorted green print fabrics
6 yards fabric for backing
Batting

Number of Blocks and
  Finished Size: *18 blocks—12" square*
Finished Quilt Size: *approximately 77¾" x 99"*

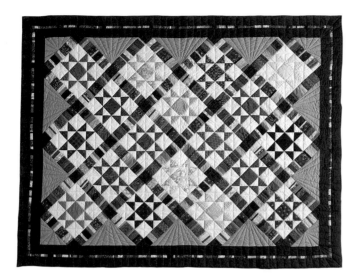

make four-triangle units and one 4½" square for block center. For strip-pieced sashing and borders, cut remainder of strips lengthwise, ranging from 1" to 2½" wide. Also cut remaining portion of each printed fabric across fabric into strips ranging from 1" to 2½" wide.

5. Make 72 four-triangle units (four for each block) from pairs of cream-and-print 5¼" squares. Units should measure 4½" and will finish 4" square.

6. Referring to photo of Ohio Star block on page 115, arrange pieces for one block. Join into three rows; join rows. Make 18 Ohio Star blocks. Blocks should measure 12½" square with seam allowances.

7. Join narrow print strips, cut in step 4, into 12½"-wide, or slightly wider, strip sets. Each strip set should contain strips of varying widths of assorted print fabrics. Press seam allowances to one side.

From strip sets, cut 48 (3½" x 12½") rectangles for sashing. Save remaining strip sets to make strip-pieced borders.

8. Referring to quilt photo and diagram, arrange blocks. Place sashing and sashing squares between blocks. Fill-in around outside and corners with setting triangles.

9. Assemble pieces in diagonal rows; join rows. Wait to trim sashing squares at ends of rows until after borders have been joined. The inner quilt top should measure approximately 64¼" x 85½", including seam allowances. (If your quilt measurement is different, adjust border lengths.)

10. Trim two green borders to quilt length, including seam allowances. Join borders to sides of quilt. Measure width of quilt, including attached borders. Cut two borders each equal to this measurement and join to top and bottom of quilt. After borders have been added, trim sashing squares around perimeter of inner quilt even with border seam line.

11. From remaining print strip sets, cut 1½"-wide segments. Measure length of quilt and piece two borders equal to quilt length from these segments. Join borders to sides of quilt. In same manner, piece borders for top and bottom. Join borders to top and bottom of quilt.

12. Trim two green borders to length for sides; join to sides of quilt. Trim two borders to length for top and bottom of quilt; join to quilt.

13. Layer backing, batting, and top; baste. Outline-quilt around pieces within each star block and along sashing and borders. Add additional quilting as desired.

14. Bind quilt with straight or French-fold bias binding.

1. From cream fabric, cut five 5¼"-wide strips across fabric; cut strips into 36 (5¼") squares to make four-triangle units. Cut nine 4½"-wide strips across fabric; cut strips into 72 (4½") squares for block corners.

2. From peach fabric, cut three 18¼" squares for setting triangles. Cut each square diagonally both ways into four triangles for total of 12 triangles. You will only need 10. To cut corner setting triangles, cut two 9⅜" squares. Cut each square in half diagonally into two triangles (four total).

3. From dark green fabric, cut eight 3½" x 95" borders. (The borders are longer than needed and will be trimmed to length when added to quilt top.) From remaining fabric, cut 31 (3½") sashing squares and approximately 10 yards of 2¼"-wide straight or bias binding.

4. From each peach and green print fabric, cut one 5¼"-wide strip across fabric. From each strip, cut two 5¼" squares to

Practice These Log Cabin Piecing Skills While Making a *Barn Raising Log Cabin* Quilt

🏠 *quick-cutting strips* 🏠 *quick-cutting squares*
🏠 *setting variations for Log Cabin quilts* 🏠 *assembly-line piecing of traditional Log Cabin*
🏠 *quick-cutting long borders*

Materials:

⅛ yard or 2 (1½"-wide strips) red for center squares

3 yards total each of light and dark fabrics*

5 yards blue stripe for borders and backing

¾ yard red print for binding

Batting, larger than 60" x 78"

*Fabrics for logs are scraps, in assorted light fabrics (tan, gold, and cream) and assorted dark fabrics (blue, red, brown, and green). You will need approximately 72 (1½"-wide) light strips and 72 (1½"-wide) dark strips. Purchase ⅛ to ¼ yard each of several colors for the scrap look.

Number of Blocks and
Finished Size: 48 blocks—9" square
Finished Quilt Size: 60" x 78"

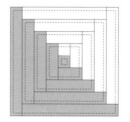 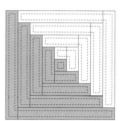

Suggested Quilting Designs for Log Cabin

1. Cut all fabrics, except blue-striped border fabric, into 1½"-wide strips for center squares and logs.

2. Cut 48 (1½") center squares from red strips.

3. Piece 48 traditional Log Cabin blocks, shading blocks diagonally in light and dark halves. Use many different fabrics in each block and vary position of fabrics.

4. Arrange blocks in eight horizontal rows of six blocks each. Join blocks in horizontal rows; join rows.

5. Measure width and length of inner quilt top, including seam allowances. (Quilt top should measure 54½" x 72½".)

6. Cut backing fabric into two 2½-yard lengths. From one length, cut four 3½"-wide borders along the length. To piece backing, sew narrow panel to wide panel.

7. Join a border to each side of quilt, mitering corners.

8. Layer backing, batting, and top; baste. Hand- or machine-quilt with fan quilting, as shown in photo, or in one of the quilting patterns below for Log Cabin blocks.

9. Cut approximately 8 yards of French-fold binding from red print and join to quilt.

First Steps in Hand Appliqué

Appliqué is the technique of sewing small pieces of fabric onto a larger background cloth. Its origins are in the humble tradition of covering a worn area of clothing with a sturdy patch. But as people began to have time and money for more than purely utilitarian enterprises, appliqué was used not just for mending but for embellishing.

First Steps in Hand Appliqué

The classic red-and-green floral appliqué quilt common in the mid- to late 1800s was often a family's best quilt—the one that stayed on the bed in the guest room or was not used at all. The great variety of such floral styles and patterns indicates that many were devised by their makers or were modified from standard patterns. (The Rose of Sharon pattern, for example, has dozens of variations.)

The remarkable Baltimore Album Quilts of the mid-nineteenth century, made by a group of Methodist ladies in Maryland, are among the finest quilts ever created. They are composed primarily of elaborate appliqué blocks, some of which must have taken scores of hours of meticulous sewing to complete. This style has come into vogue again in the 1990s.

Several appliqué designs were popular with quilters in the early twentieth century. During the Great Depression years, one of the well-known designs was Sunbonnet Sue. Other favorite patterns were butterflies, pansies, and other flowers, as well as Dresden Plate and Grandmother's Fan.

When the popularity of quiltmaking increased in the mid-1970s, women in hundreds of communities created pictorial appliqué quilts that commemorated the historic events and notable architectural structures of their areas. Some of these pictorial quilts celebrated the American Bicentennial of 1976. Many more, inspired by the Bicentennial, were made in the years that followed.

Today's quiltmakers continue to enjoy appliqué. As with any type of needlework, appliqué methods abound, and twentieth-century quilters have done their part to generate new techniques for successful appliqué. In this chapter, we include the basics of appliqué. In "Beyond Basic Appliqué," more methods are discussed for preparing and stitching appliqués, machine appliqué, and some specialized techniques.

Appliqué Basics

Pattern Formats, Making Master Patterns

Appliqué patterns in books and magazines may be presented in several ways. They may include a small diagram with a grid drawn over it, a diagram plus full-size pattern pieces, or a portion of the full-size pattern. Using master patterns ensures that the elements of a design made from symmetrical quarters or halves are positioned exactly the same way in each section of the block. For some designs, however, where symmetry is not a factor, or you are making only one block, a master pattern may not be necessary, and appliqués can be successfully placed by measuring or by eye.

To make a master pattern, cut a piece of tracing paper the finished size of the quilt block plus ½", to allow for ¼" seam allowances. You may have to tape smaller pieces of paper together to get the size you need. Use a large ruled square to make the paper square accurate. Fold the paper square in half vertically, horizontally, and diagonally both ways to create placement guidelines.

The printed pattern will probably be in one of the formats described below. Follow the instructions for each type you encounter to complete your master pattern.

Diagram Plus Full-Size Patterns

Sometimes the pattern consists of a small quilt block diagram with full-size pattern piece(s) printed nearby. The Sweetheart block pattern on page 128 and the Country Angel design on page 133 are examples of this format. Design elements may be arranged as they will be on the block, with pattern pieces connected, or pattern shapes may be scattered, with only the diagram to indicate proper arrangement.

To complete a master pattern, trace design elements onto paper square, referring to block diagram and folding paper as needed to position elements symmetrically. Darken pattern outlines with pen. Make dash marks on folded guidelines.

Small Diagram with Grid

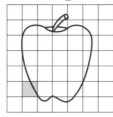

Small Diagram with Grid

Detail of Shaded Square

If a small diagram of the whole design is printed with a grid over it, you must enlarge it to full size. Information with diagram will give scale for enlargement. If enlarging information says "1 square = 1"," draw grid of 1" squares (graph paper makes this easier) and then by eye transfer line or lines in each square of diagram to corresponding square of full-size graph. Few people enjoy this tedious type of freehand enlarging, and enlarging by photocopy machines has made it generally unnecessary.

You can figure exact percentage of enlargement you need with a proportion wheel. Personnel at copy shops can show you how to enlarge a small pattern diagram to the size you need. If your original is very small, you may have to make several enlargements, enlarging various parts of the design separately and then taping them together. Generally, you can create a full-size pattern quickly at very little expense.

Trace enlarged design elements onto tracing paper square to make a master pattern and darken outlines with permanent pen. Make dash marks on folded guidelines.

Portion of the Pattern

Portion of the Pattern

Sometimes a portion of design, usually ¼ of the quilt block, is printed full-size. (See Floral Wreath block on page 136.) Trace ¼ of the design in each quadrant of tracing paper square. Darken pattern outlines with a pen and mark dash marks on folded guidelines.

Tools for Appliqué

The needle is probably the most important tool for successful hand appliqué. Use a size 11 or 12 sharp, rather than a between or quilting needle. This type of needle is what you need both for basting raw edges under on appliqués and for stitching them to the background fabric.

Always use 100% cotton fabric for appliqué work. Cotton fabric holds a crease well, enabling you to turn under edges smoothly on appliqué pieces.

Sew appliqués to background with sewing thread that matches the appliqué pieces, not the background fabric.

Learn These Basic Appliqué Skills While Making a Sweetheart Block

- 🏠 *cutting background squares*
- 🏠 *marking and cutting appliqués*
- 🏠 *positioning appliqués*
- 🏠 *making templates for appliqué patterns*
- 🏠 *preparing appliqués*
- 🏠 *appliquéing shapes*

Materials:

½ yard background fabric

⅛ yard or 1 (4") square of 4 different fabrics for hearts

Ruled square

Thread, sewing, in colors to match heart fabrics

Finished Block Size: *9" square*

1. For most appliqué patterns, you will stitch design elements to background square or block. Place ruled square on wrong side of fabric, ½" or more from raw edge or selvage, and use pencil to draw square finished size of block. Add ¼" seam allowances on all four sides of square and cut out. Mark 9" square, add seam allowances, and cut 9½" square block.

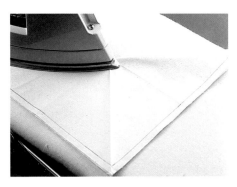

2. Fold fabric square in half vertically, horizontally, and diagonally both ways, and press lightly to make positioning guidelines.

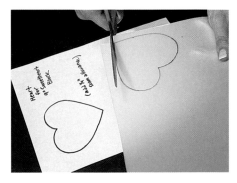

3. Make templates for appliquéing the exact finished size of each pattern piece. Seam allowances will be added when fabric pieces are cut. (Heart pattern for Sweetheart Block is on page 132.) If you are using transparent vinyl for templates, lay vinyl over full-size pattern, trace shape onto vinyl, and cut out template.

For cardboard or other nontransparent template material, trace pattern on tracing paper, glue paper to cardboard, and cut out template. (See pages 31–32 for instructions on basic template making.)

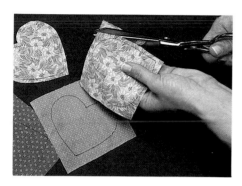

To make curved edges of appliqués smooth and bump free, use thumb and forefinger of non-needle hand to turn back seam allowance just ahead of basting. Baste each heart.

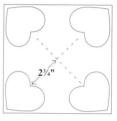

Placement Diagram

4. To mark appliqué pieces, place template on right side of fabric. Draw neatly around template with a well-sharpened pencil, holding pencil point against template edge. As you mark pieces, be sure to leave ½" or more between each shape to allow for seam allowances. Also mark at least ½" or more from raw edges or selvage. Mark heart on each fabric scrap. (See Fabric Marking Strategies, page 32.) Cut out appliqués, adding scant ¼" seam allowance. After cutting pieces, clip into seam allowances only on inside curves. The cleft of the heart, for example, must be clipped.

6. When basting into clipped corner, skip over clip with basting stitch to avoid fraying clipped threads and continue. Handle clipped areas as little as possible.

8. Refer to Placement Diagram and pin prepared appliqués in place on background square. Position hearts along diagonal guidelines with cleft 2¾" from center each way.

9. Appliqué each piece in place, using regular sewing (not quilting) thread that matches color of appliqué piece. Appliqué stitch is similar to blindstitch. Bring needle up through background fabric and barely catch folded edge of appliqué. Knot should be on wrong side of background fabric.

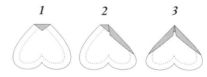

5. Use light-colored sewing thread to baste seam allowance under. Hold piece with right side facing you and turn raw edge under so that marked fold line is barely hidden. Knot basting thread. Make running or basting stitch near fold to hold seam allowance in place. (See "Basic Skills Reference Guide," pages 23 and 24, for how to make quilter's knot and basic running stitch.)

7. When basting under points such as bottom of the heart, fold point back first (1). Before reaching point with basting, squeeze fold with fingertips to set crease. Continue basting into point, turning under seam allowance preceding point (2). Put basting stitch in point; then fold back seam allowance on adjacent side and continue basting (3).

Remember:

Dark-colored basting threads, when removed, can leave lint that might show through light fabric.

10. Reinsert needle into background fabric beside folded edge where thread was first brought through and make a ⅛" stitch, bringing point of needle back up through background fabric and through folded edge of appliqué.

As thread is pulled through to complete each stitch, give it a gentle tug to keep stitches tight, but without puckering background fabric. (Background square should be same size it was before it was appliquéd.) Appliqués tend to loosen after they are stitched down, especially if quilting is done next to edges. Snug, even stitches will prevent these "floating appliqués."

11. As you begin each stitch, make sure needle enters background fabric right next to thread coming up through folded edge of appliqué. As you work around curves, use point of needle to smooth any bumps in folded edge. Lift edge of appliqué slightly and distribute fullness.

12. To end, bring needle to wrong side. To secure thread, turn work over and stitch one or two loop knots, as described in "Basic Skills Reference Guide," page 22. Stitches on back should be a neat outline of appliqué shapes. Remove basting.

Grain Line Considerations for Appliqué Pieces

For most appliqué, grain line is not as important as it is for patchwork. For shapes with curved edges, place templates on fabric at an angle, so that, as much as possible, all outer edges of shape will be on bias, which will reduce fraying of edges.

For sharp points, mark appliqué piece so that seam allowances at point are on bias. When cut on bias, threads of fabric will crisscross through appliqué shape diagonally, rather than running straight. For square or rectangular shapes, such as door or window for house design, align straight edges with straight of grain.

Practice Basic Appliqué Techniques While Making the *Sweetheart* Baby Quilt

Materials:

1 yard off-white for background squares

1 yard lavender print for border and binding

Scraps, 52 (4") squares, for hearts

1¼ yards fabric for backing

Thread in colors to match heart fabrics

Batting, low-loft, crib size

Finished Block Size: *9" square*
Finished Quilt Size: *35" x 44"*

1. From off-white, cut 12 (9½") background squares and four 4½" border corner squares.

2. From lavender print, cut four 4½"-wide borders across width of fabric for 4"-wide finished borders. (See page 110 for how to cut borders with a rotary cutter.) Set borders aside.

3. Make heart template (on page 132) and cut 52 hearts from scraps.

4. Make 12 Sweetheart blocks, following instructions for block assembly on pages 128–130.

To appliqué heart to each border corner square, first fold each square diagonally one way and lightly press to form placement line for heart. Position cleft of heart 2⅜" from raw edges of square's corner.

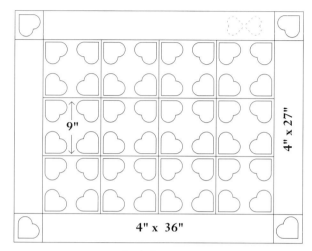

Quilt Diagram

5. Arrange blocks in four rows of three blocks each, as shown in Quilt Diagram and photo, and join blocks into rows. Join rows. (See "Basic Settings and Borders for Quilts," page 50.)

6. Measure width and length of inner quilt top, including seam allowances. If you have cut and sewn accurately, it should measure 27½" x 36½", including seam allowances. (If your actual measurements are significantly different from these, adjust border length.) Measure and trim two borders, cut in step 2, to a length of 27½", and two borders to 36½".

7. Sew 27½" borders to top and bottom of quilt top; press seams toward borders. Sew border corner square to each end of two remaining borders. Press seams toward borders. Sew borders to sides of quilt top; press seams.

8. Mark quilting designs on quilt top. (For instructions on basic marking, see pages 67–68 in "Get Ready To Quilt.") Center Four Hearts design in each Sweetheart block. Center border design in border opposite each block, as shown in Quilt Diagram.

9. Layer quilt backing, batting, and quilt top; baste. (Instructions for layering and basting are on pages 72 and 73.) Quilt marked designs. (For quilting instructions, see "The Ins and Outs of Quilting," page 76.)

10. Cut 5 yards of 2¼"-wide bias or straight-grain binding. Stitch binding to quilt, mitering corners. (For instructions, see pages 94–98 in "Finishing Your Quilts.")

Patterns for Sweetheart Baby Quilt

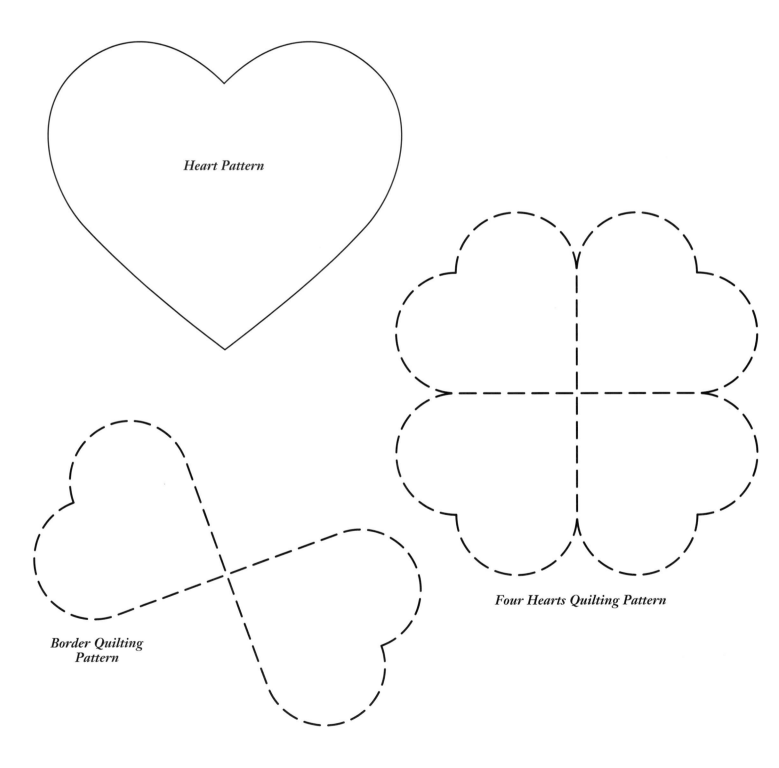

Heart Pattern

Four Hearts Quilting Pattern

Border Quilting
Pattern

Learn These Basic Appliqué Skills While Making a *Country Angel* Wall Quilt

🏠 *making compound templates*
🏠 *overlapping and layering appliqués*
🏠 *reversing templates for mirror-image pieces*
🏠 *trimming away background fabric*

Materials:

½ yard light blue for background square
½ yard beige print for setting triangles
¾ yard blue for border, binding, and hanging tabs
¼ yard blue print for dress
⅛ yard light blue print for wings
4" square brown for hair
Muslin scraps for face and hands
2½" square black for shoes
⅔ yard fabric for backing
Batting, low loft, 25" square
Cotton swab
Brown fine-point pen for permanent marking
Powdered rouge

Finished Block Size: *11" square*
Finished Quilt Size: *19½" square*

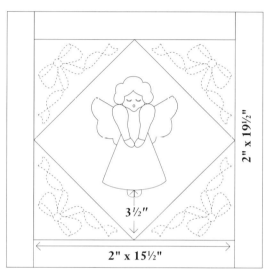

Quilt Diagram

1. From background fabric, cut one 11½" background square. Fold square diagonally one way and lightly press to form placement line.

2. Compound patterns are presented with parts connected as they will be in finished design. Make template for each pattern piece of a compound shape, such as angel's face and hair. (See page 135.) When making dress template, use dashed lines on pattern as seam line guides. Mark wing and shoe placement lines on dress template.

Connected Pattern Pieces

3. Some appliqué patterns have mirror-image elements on each side of block. Make only one template for each piece and then reverse it by turning it over to mark and cut mirror-image piece. The angel's wings, sleeves, hands, and shoes are examples of such pattern pieces where only one template needs to be made. Make templates for these pieces, using dashed lines as seam line guides for wing. Label each side of each template.

4. Using templates, mark and cut following pieces: *one dress, one sleeve, one sleeve reverse, one wing, one wing reverse, one face, one hand, one hand reverse, one shoe, one shoe reverse.*

Use fine-point marking pen to trace eyes and mouth on face. Use cotton swab and small amount of powdered rouge to add blush to angel's cheeks.

5. Elements of an appliqué design frequently overlap others, such as angel's dress that overlaps wings. Also, an appliqué shape is sometimes added on top of other, larger pieces. When preparing appliqués for overlapping pieces, do not baste under seam allowances that will be covered by piece added later. Baste back seam allowances of those edges that will not be overlapped. Clip into seam allowance at wing scallops and at curved areas of hair.

When overlapping or layering occurs, always work from background to foreground. Pin prepared appliqués in place, positioning background pieces first and then each layer in turn.

To begin, fold angel's dress in half lengthwise and lightly crease to form guideline. Align dress guideline with diagonal fold of background square. Position hem of dress approximately 3½" from bottom raw corner of square. Using placement lines, slide shoes and wings under dress. Appliqué shoes and wings and then dress to background square. When stitching underneath pieces, fold overlapping pieces back and temporarily pin out of the way. Remove basting after stitching pieces.

6. When appliqué elements in design are layered, layers of fabric may make parts of block too thick to quilt easily. To reduce bulk, trim background fabric from behind each appliqué piece, leaving ¼" seam allowance, before appliquéing next one. Also, if background fabric is darker than appliquéd piece and is likely to shadow through, trim background fabric from behind appliqué.

For example, trim away background fabric under angel's dress so that quilting around sleeves and hands will be easier. Also, since dress fabric is darker than hands fabric, trim dress fabric away from behind hands after appliquéing them, so dress fabric will not shadow through.

To trim background fabric, turn work over to wrong side after first piece has been stitched. Pinch fabrics to separate layers. Using embroidery or appliqué scissors, make small cut in background fabric. (If you layer-appliqué frequently, you may want to invest in a pair of appliqué scissors. The underneath blade is designed to prevent accidentally cutting through to top fabric.) Cut background fabric within appliquéd area, leaving ¼" seam allowance. Follow same procedure with each layered piece.

7. Pin sleeves in position and tuck hands under sleeves. Appliqué hands and then sleeves. Appliqué face before adding hair. Trim background fabric from behind pieces, leaving ¼" seam allowance, as directed above.

8. For setting triangles, draw right-angle triangle with 7¾" finished legs and add seam allowances to all three sides. (See diagram on page 135.) Make template and cut four from beige print.

Sew setting triangles to two opposite sides of angel block. Sew remaining triangles to remaining sides of block.

9. Cut two 2½" x 16" borders from blue. Sew to top and bottom. Cut two 2½" x 20" borders and sew to sides.

10. Mark ribbon bow quilting design (page 139) in setting triangles. (See pages 67–69 in "Get Ready To Quilt" on marking techniques.)

11. Cut 24" square from backing fabric. Layer backing, batting, and quilt top; baste. Outline-quilt around all appliqué elements. Quilt ribbon bow design in setting triangles.

12. Finish with bias or straight-grain binding.

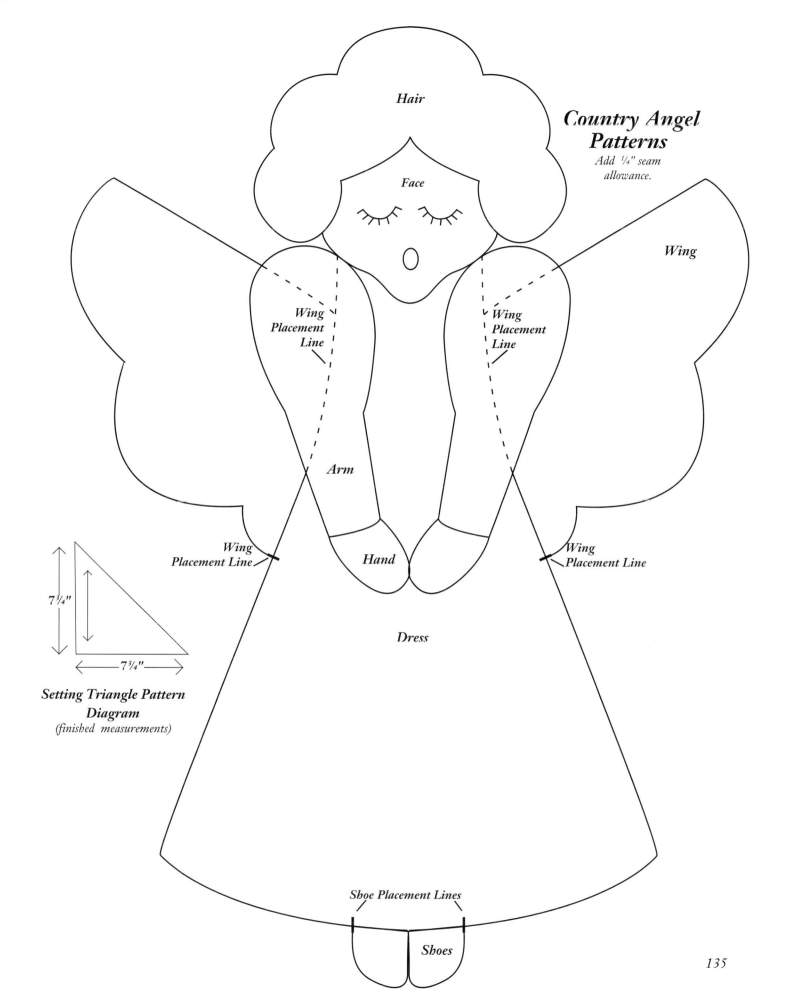

Hair

Face

Country Angel Patterns

Add ¼" seam allowance.

Wing

Wing Placement Line

Wing Placement Line

Arm

Wing Placement Line

Wing Placement Line

Hand

7¾"

7¾"

Setting Triangle Pattern Diagram
(finished measurements)

Dress

Shoe Placement Lines

Shoes

Learn These Basic Appliqué Skills While Making the *Floral Wreath* Wall Quilt

🏠 *making templates from layered patterns*
🏠 *appliquéing bias strips for vines or stems*
🏠 *marking placement lines on background fabric*
🏠 *appliquéing perfectly round circles*

Materials:

1½ yard dark red for tulip tips, outer posy, posy center, borders, backing, hanging sleeve, and binding
½ yard off-white for background square
¼ yard dark green for vine and piping
4 (3") squares dark red print for tulips
3½" square pink print for inner posy
⅛ yard green print for leaves
Batting, low-loft, 25" square
Tracing paper

Finished Block Size: *15" square*
Finished Quilt Size: *21" square*

Quilt Diagram

1. Some appliqué patterns are layered such as the posy, as shown.

Layered Patterns

Using patterns on page 138, make vinyl or cardboard templates for inner posy, outer posy, tulip, tulip tip, and leaf. Do not make templates for posy center and bias vine. Cut 15½" background square from off-white.

2. Drawing placement lines on background square enables you to position appliqué pieces precisely.

Make master pattern, tracing quarter-block pattern on each quadrant of 15½" square of tracing paper.

To mark placement lines, secure

pattern with masking tape. Fold background square diagonally both ways and crease to make positioning guidelines. Lay background square over master pattern, aligning edges and guidelines. Tape in place.

Position templates on background square, aligning them with pattern outlines. Lightly mark around templates with pencil to draw placement lines. Trace only inner line of vine.

An alternative to drawing placement lines is to lay master pattern over background fabric and place appliqués beneath it.

3. To make bias strips for circular flower vine, fold in corner of dark green fabric at a 45° angle and lightly press. Use ruler and rotary cutter to cut bias strips parallel to creased line. Make strips three times wider than desired finished stem. Cut four 1" x 7" bias strips to finish scant ⅜" wide. Always cut strips ½" longer than you will need. For straight stems and vines, cut strips on straight of grain.

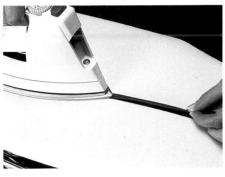

4. To prepare bias strips for appliqué, fold and steam-press each strip in thirds lengthwise. Use iron to fold over first third to wrong side of fabric. Fold over second raw edge, making sure first edge will be hidden just under fold. Turn pressed strip over and press once more on right side. (See tip box on page 141 for another way to prepare bias strip vines or stems.)

5. Baste pressed bias strips to background square, positioning inner edge of strip along placement line. Extend about ¼" of vine beyond tulip placement line to lie under overlapping tulip appliqué.

Appliqué strips in place. Since bias strips are stretchy, they curve smoothly, but this stretchiness can cause problems. When appliquéing them in curve, always stitch down inner edge of curve first to avoid unwanted buckles. The outer longer edge will stretch to lie smooth.

Encourage curved bias strip to lie flat by lightly steam-pressing it after basting.

6. Cut four tulips, four tulip tips, one outer posy, one inner posy, and twelve leaves. (See materials list and photo for fabric to use.) Prepare and appliqué pieces to background square, using techniques described on page 134 for overlapping pieces. Trim away background fabrics.

7. Because of amount of seam allowance that must be turned under, bumpy edges on circles are hard to avoid.

To achieve smooth round circles, make stiff paper template for posy center without seam allowances by drawing finished-size circle on index card or similar weight paper. Use spool or draftsman's circle for master template. Use same template to draw circle on wrong side of fabric.

8. Cut fabric circle, adding ¼" seam allowance. Run basting thread around circle, sewing halfway between drawn line and cut edge. Keep needle and thread attached.

9. Place paper template on center of wrong side of fabric circle and pull basting thread to gather fabric over paper template. Once fabric is tight, space gathers evenly and make backstitch or knot to secure thread. Cut thread.

10. Pin circle in place, pinning through paper template. Appliqué circle, stitching along folded edge. (Don't worry if you sew through paper.) Keep stitches closely spaced and pull them snug.

11. Carefully trim circle of fabric from behind appliqué circle, leaving ¼" seam allowance and exposing paper template. Pull template out through hole. Remove basting stitches. Discard template.

12. Cut four 3½" x 25" strips for borders from dark red. Following the instrutions on adding mitered borders in "Basic Settings and Borders for Quilts," page 50, mark, measure, and join borders to block.

13. Mark background quilting lines, using ruler. (See page 67 in "Get Ready To Quilt" for more information on marking designs on fabric.) The quilt shown has outline quilting around each appliqué piece and diagonal lines of background quilting 1¼" apart.

14. From dark red, cut 25" square for backing. Layer backing, batting, and quilt top; baste. Outline- and background-quilt as desired.

15. Bind quilt with piping accent and attach hanging sleeve. (Refer to "Finishing Your Quilt," on pages 99 and 101, for instructions.)

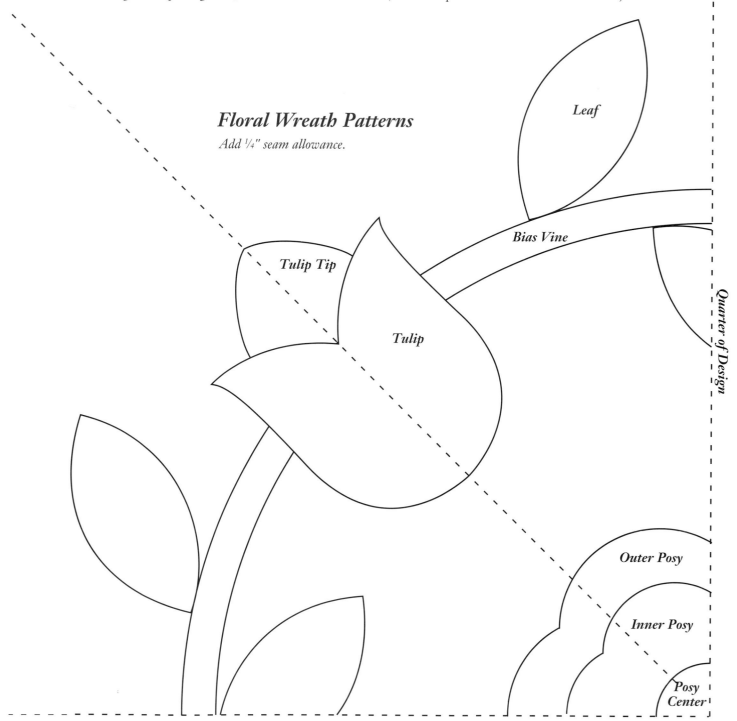

Floral Wreath Patterns

Add ¼" seam allowance.

Leaf

Bias Vine

Tulip Tip

Tulip

Quarter of Design

Outer Posy

Inner Posy

Posy Center

Quarter of Design

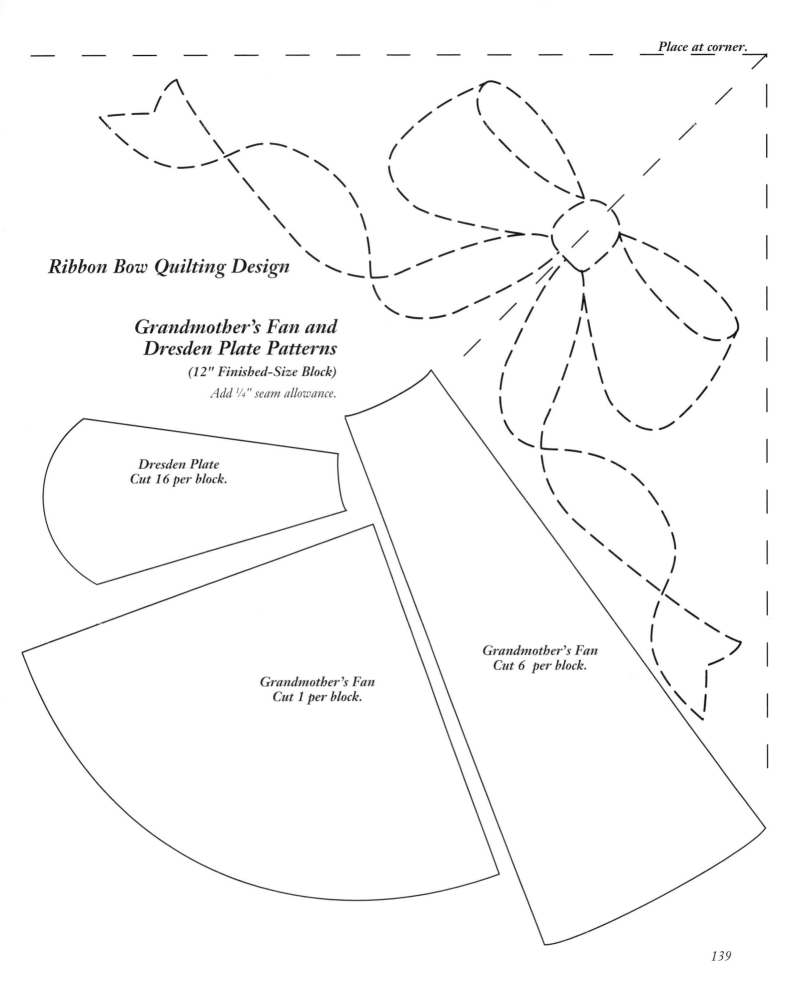

Ribbon Bow Quilting Design

**Grandmother's Fan and
Dresden Plate Patterns**

(12" Finished-Size Block)

Add ¼" seam allowance.

**Dresden Plate
Cut 16 per block.**

**Grandmother's Fan
Cut 1 per block.**

**Grandmother's Fan
Cut 6 per block.**

Blocks That Combine Patchwork and Appliqué

The Heart Basket pattern is an example of a quilt block that combines patchwork and appliqué. The basket bottom is pieced, and the heart and handle are appliquéd. (Instructions for a wall quilt using this pattern begin on page 142.) Other examples are the classic North Carolina Lily, with its pieced-diamond flowers and appliqué stems, and the Depression-era favorites, Grandmother's Fan and Dresden Plate.

Generally, you will complete the patchwork portion of such blocks first and then add the appliquéd pieces. For the Heart Basket block, baste the handle to top triangle, join the triangle to the pieced basket portion of the block, and then appliqué the handle and the heart. For the North Carolina Lily, prepare the pieced and appliquéd segments of the block separately and then sew them together. For the Grandmother's Fan and Dresden Plate blocks, piece the wedges and then appliqué them to a background block. (Patterns for Grandmother's Fan and Dresden Plate blocks are on page 139.)

Heart Basket

Grandmother's Fan   *North Carolina Lily*   *Dresden Plate*

Learn These Skills While Piecing a Combination Patchwork-Appliqué Heart Basket Block

🏠 *making a freezer-paper placement guide*   🏠 *making and appliquéing a curved basket handle*

Materials:

¼ yard dark brown print
¼ yard red-orange print
¼ yard brown-and-white check
Freezer paper, plastic-coated

Finished Block Size: *9" square*

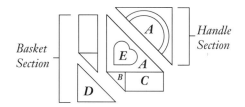

Heart Basket Block Piecing Diagram

1. Make templates for pieces A–E on page 143. From dark brown print, cut one triangle A and two triangles B. From red-orange print, cut two rectangles C, one triangle D, and one triangle A. From brown-and-white check, cut one heart (E).

2. Refer to Heart Basket Block Piecing Diagram and hand- or machine-piece basket section of block.

3. Make handle placement guide for easy symmetrical placement of basket handle. Cut freezer-paper pattern equal to finished-sized of handle section. (For Heart Basket block, this is template A.) Fold paper in half and sketch inner curve of handle on half of paper pattern.

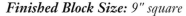

4. Flip paper over and trace drawn line to complete handle curve. Check to be sure curve fits basket section of block.

5. Cut on line to make handle placement guide. Fold red-orange triangle A in half and press lightly to form center guideline. Using wool setting and no steam, lightly press handle placement guide to background triangle, placing shiny side of paper against right side of fabric. Align fold of paper with fabric guideline, placing pattern ¼" up from raw edge.

6. Find handle length for block. (Some patterns give this information, but handle length can be found by curving measuring tape along freezer-paper handle placement guide.) Add seam allowances

plus a little extra to measurement. Choose handle width in scale with size of block. For Heart Basket block, cut a 1¼" x 9" bias strip from brown-and-white check, to finish about ⅜" wide. Press handle strip in thirds, as described in step 4 of *Floral Wreath* wall quilt (page 137) or use method in tip box at right.

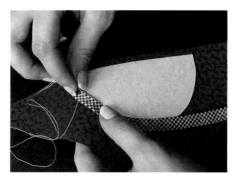

7. Baste folded strip along edge of handle placement guide, remembering that paper edge is inner curve of handle and allowing bias strip to extend beyond bottom raw edges of handle section of block. Remove paper guide.

8. Join handle section to basket section before appliquéing handle. Basting will hold handle in place adequately while joining sections. After joining, appliqué handle to block, stitching inner curve first and then outer curve. Turn block over and trim extended ends of handle even with seam allowances.

9. Fold basket in half widthwise and finger-press to make center guideline for heart. Center and pin heart so that bottom point of heart is 1½" from bottom point of pieced basket. Appliqué heart to basket bottom. Trim away fabric from behind heart if desired.

Grandmother's Method for Folding Bias

Liz's grandmother had a clever way to fold and press bias strips at the ironing board. Students always enjoy this technique when we share it during workshops. It is great for short strips used for basket handles and flower stems, as well as for longer pieces.

1. At one end of strip, fold strip in thirds for about 2" and press, as described in step 4 of *Floral Wreath* wall quilt on page 137.

2. Lay folded end of strip in center of ironing board. Insert long pin through ironing board cover, bring pin across folded strip, and reinsert it into ironing board cover on opposite side. Place second pin about 2" from first pin. Check to be sure that amount of exposed pin across strip is exactly equal to width of folded strip. (Pins should not be inserted in strip.)

3. As you gently pull folded end of strip under pins, remaining bias strip will fold itself as it is pulled under pins. As pins fold bias strip, steam-press strip, pressing newly made folds between pins. Continue gently pulling strip through until entire strip is folded and pressed.

Practice Piecing Combination Patchwork and Appliqué While Making the *Heart Basket* Wall Quilt

Materials:

1½ yards dark brown print for basket, sashing, and borders

1½ yards red-orange print for blocks, setting triangles, border corner squares, and binding

½ yard brown-and-white check for hearts, handles, and sashing squares

1¼ yards fabric for backing and hanging sleeve

Batting, low-loft, crib size

Finished Block Size: 9" square

Finished Quilt Size: approximately 39¼" square

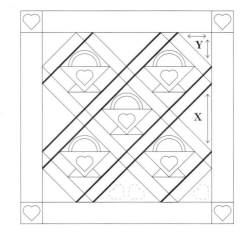

Quilt Diagram

1. From dark brown print, cut four 4½"-wide strips for borders across fabric width. Cut four 2½"-wide strips for sashing across fabric width. (These measurements include seam allowances plus extra length.) Label borders and sashing and set them aside.

2. Make right-angle setting triangle template X with 9" finished-size legs. (See pattern diagram on page 143.) Use template to mark and cut four setting triangles from red-orange print. Place template so that long side of triangle (hypotenuse) is on straight grain of fabric and add seam allowances on all three sides before cutting.

Cut template X in half to make corner setting triangle template Y. (See pattern diagram on page 143.) Cut four corner setting triangles from red-orange print. Place template so that right angle legs are parallel with grains of fabric and add seam allowances on all three sides. Cut four 4¼" border corner squares from red-orange print.

3. Make templates for pieces A–E. Use templates to mark and cut the following:
From dark brown print:
     five triangle As, ten triangle Bs
From red-orange print:
     five triangle As, ten rectangle Cs, five triangle Ds
From brown-and-white check:
     five 1¼" x 9" bias strips for handles, nine hearts (E)

4. Make five Heart Basket blocks. (See pages 140 and 141.)

5. Cut sixteen 2½" x 9½" strips for sashing from strips cut in step 1. Before cutting, make sure 9½" is actual block measurement. Adjust length of strip slightly, if necessary, keeping in mind any adjustments that you make as you sew quilt together. From brown-and-white check, cut twelve 2½" squares for sashing. (Eight squares will later be trimmed to make triangles. See step 8.)

6. Refer to Quilt Diagram and sew pieces together in diagonal rows. (Bold lines in Quilt Diagram define rows.) Join rows. Inner quilt, when set together, should measure 31¾" square, including seam allowances.

7. Trim each border to size of inner quilt. Before trimming, make sure 31¾" is actual measurement of your inner quilt. Border lengths can be adjusted slightly if necessary.

8. Appliqué heart to each border corner square. Sew borders to top and bottom of quilt. Sew border corner square to each end of remaining borders for sides of quilt and join to quilt. Completed quilt top should measure 39¼" square, including seam allowances. Trim sashing squares on outside quilt edges even with border raw edge.

9. Use heart template (E) and mark quilting designs as shown. Layer and baste backing, batting, and quilt top.

10. Bind quilt and add hanging sleeve. (See pages 96 and 101.)

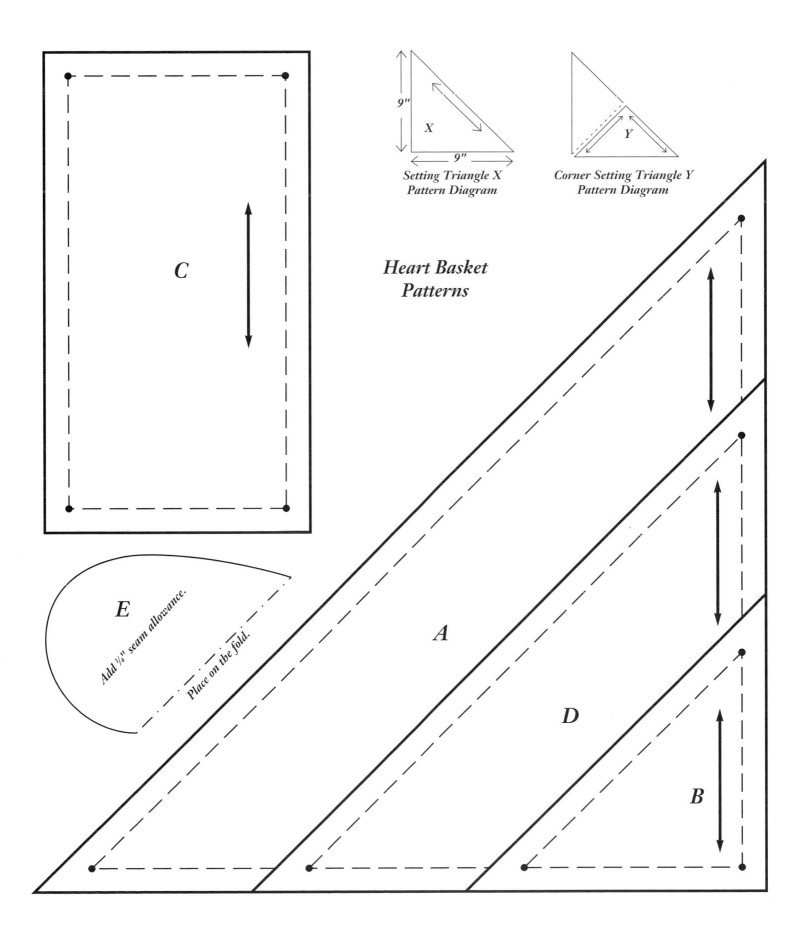

C

9"
9"
X
Setting Triangle X Pattern Diagram

Y
Corner Setting Triangle Y Pattern Diagram

Heart Basket Patterns

E
Add ¼" seam allowance.
Place on the fold.

A

D

B

Beyond Basic Patchwork

So far, we've introduced you to the basic patchwork skills that enable you to make literally hundreds of patchwork quilts. However, most quilters eventually want to try more challenging patterns, after they have mastered the fundamentals. Use the blocks and projects in this chapter to expand your patchwork skills.

Beyond Basic Patchwork

Partial Seams

Some quilt blocks that appear to require set-in pieces can be constructed easily by using a partial seam instead. Blocks of this type usually have pieces that surround a center shape and extend beyond it on one side. The partial seam creates an edge that can be sewed to other block units. After other units have been joined, the partial seam is completed.

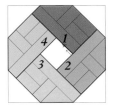

Tessellated Star   *Friendship Links*

Construction of these blocks is simplified by using the partial seam method. Units are numbered in the order in which they are to be added. The partial seam is indicated with an arrow, and a star shows its stopping point.

Learn the Partial-Seam Method While Making the Bright Hopes Block

Materials:
⅛ yard each of 5 fabrics
Rotary cutter, mat, and ruler

Finished Block Size: *6" square*

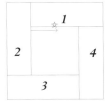

Bright Hopes Block Piecing Diagram

rectangle 1 to square with a partial seam approximately 1½" long. Finger-press seam allowances away from square.

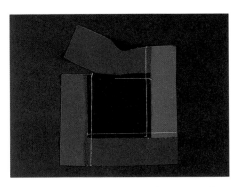

1. Cut one 3½" square from center square fabric and one 2" x 5" rectangle from each remaining fabric.

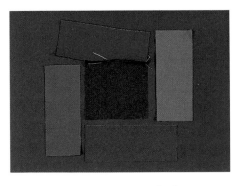

2. Refer to Bright Hopes Block Piecing Diagram and arrange pieces. Join

3. Sew rectangle 2 along edge created by first piece and center square, as shown. Sew rectangles 3 and 4 to center. Complete partial seam.

146

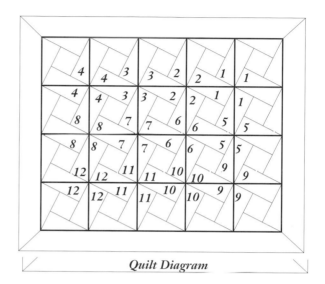

Practice the Partial-Seam Method While Making the *Tessellated Star* Wall Quilt

Materials:
*¼ yard each of 12 different fabrics**
¼ yard black cotton sateen
1½ yards black
1½ yards for backing
Rotary cutter, mat, and ruler

See Color Key with Quilt Diagram.

Number of Blocks and
Finished Size: *20—6¾" square*
Finished Quilt Size: *39¾" x 33"*

Quilt Diagram

Color Key

1. Light Gold	5. Blue	9. Light Blue
2. Dark Gold	6. Dark Blue	10. Dark Blue Green
3. Orange	7. Dark Red Purple	11. Dark Olive
4. Red	8. Light Red Purple	12. Light Olive

Tessellated Star Block Piecing Diagram

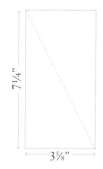

Cutting Diagram

1. Cut 20 (3½") squares from black cotton sateen.

2. From black, cut four 3½"-wide crosswise strips for the borders, and 16 (3⅝" x 7¼") rectangles.

Place all rectangles right side up on cutting mat; cut each diagonally from lower right corner to the upper left corner as shown, creating long triangles. Cut all rectangles diagonally in same direction to make 32 triangles.

3. From each colored fabric, cut two

3⅝" x 7¼" rectangles. Cut rectangles in same manner into long triangles to make four triangles from each fabric.

4. Refer to Quilt Diagram and arrange pieces in pleasing color setting. (Unnumbered pieces on diagram represent black pieces.) Stars are created at points where same colored pieces from four adjacent blocks meet.

Join pieces to make 20 blocks, using partial-seam technique shown in piecing diagram. Arrow indicates beginning and direction of first seam; star indicates stopping point for partial seam. Since outer edges of all blocks are on bias, press carefully.

5. Join blocks in four rows of five blocks each; join rows. Join borders, mitering corners.

6. Quilt lines radiating from triangle corners. Repeat pattern in borders. (See photo.)

7. Cut 2"-wide strips from star and black fabrics and make spiral binding. (See instructions for spiral binding on page 98 in "Finishing Your Quilts.") Join binding to quilt.

Freezer-Paper Templates

Cutting and piecing blocks with many different shapes as well as different numbers and shapes of pieces in adjoining rows, such as the Little House block shown below, can be simplified by using freezer-paper templates instead of traditional templates. With this method, a plastic-coated freezer-paper template is pressed onto the wrong side of each fabric piece. The freezer-paper pieces serve as cutting and stitching guides and provide accurate points for pin-matching pieces. The freezer paper also stabilizes stretchy fabrics and bias edges on angled pieces. One drawback, though, is that you will need a new freezer-paper pattern for each piece, making the method impractical when mass-producing blocks.

Learn These Piecing Skills While Making the Little House Block

🏠 *making freezer-paper templates*   🏠 *using freezer-paper templates as stitching guides*

Materials:

⅛ yard each of 5 fabrics for house

⅛ yard background fabric

Freezer paper

Rotary cutter, mat, and ruler

Finished Block Size: *6" square*

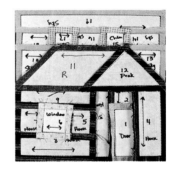

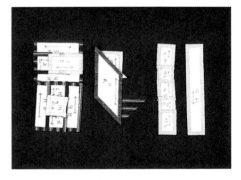

1. Trace full-size Little House patterns on page 165 onto dull side of freezer paper as shown. Label pieces. (Note: Traced house is facing in the opposite direction from finished house. It will reverse when pieces are sewn.)

2. Using a dry iron set at wool, press shiny side of freezer-paper templates onto wrong side of fabrics, spacing them at least ½" apart to allow for seam allowances. Using a rotary cutter and ruler, cut out pieces, adding ¼" seam allowances. Leave paper templates attached.

3. Refer to row labels on pattern and join pieces in numerical order to form rows. Pin-match corners as needed, and use paper edge as guide for accurate seams. Remove freezer-paper templates after joining rows.

Curved Seams

Most patchwork patterns are a composite of geometric shapes with straight edges; curved shapes generally belong to the realm of appliqué. However, a number of pieced designs, such as the blocks shown at right, do have pieces with curved edges. Each diagram includes registration marks to aid in piecing curved seams.

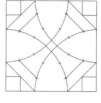
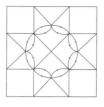
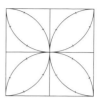

French Star   *Royal Cross*   *Orange Peel*

Make registration marks on templates and on seam lines. Pin-match seams at marks to distribute fullness.

Learn These Curved-Piecing Techniques While Making the Royal Cross Block

making templates with registration marks   *using registration marks to align edges*
sewing curved seams

Materials:
¼ yard each of 3 fabrics

Finished Block Size: *12" square*

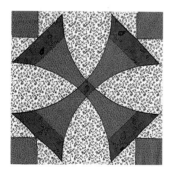

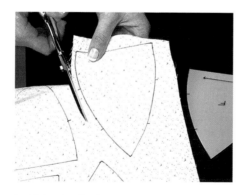

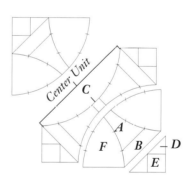

Royal Cross Block Piecing Diagram

1. Make finished-size templates of pattern pieces A–F on pages 168 and 169. Transfer registration marks on patterns. These marks match marks or seams on adjacent pieces and aid in pin-matching.

Trace around templates on wrong side of fabric and draw registration marks within seam allowances. Cut out pieces.

2. Refer to Royal Cross Block Piecing Diagram and make four AB units. Join two AB units to opposite sides of square C to form center unit. Piece four triangular DE units. Add DE units to center unit.

3. Pin-match curved side of F to curved side of AB unit, taking up only a few threads with each pin. Start at corners and registration marks. Continue pinning along seam, using enough pins to distribute fullness evenly.

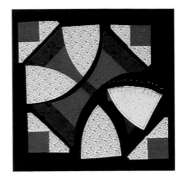

4. Stitch directly on pinned sewing line, removing pins as you come to them. Press seam allowances to one side. The gentle curve of this block does not require clipping. (On some blocks, you may need to clip into seam allowances along tight concave curves.) Attach F piece to other side of AB unit.

5. Join ABF units to sides of center unit. Add DE units to corners.

Drafting Blocks with Curved Seams

Many blocks with curved seams are based on a grid: either one of the basic grids, discussed in "Drafting Patchwork Blocks and Adding to Patchwork Skills" on page 44, or on an eight-pointed star grid. For example, the curved-seam blocks found on page 149 are based on the following grids: Royal Cross is based on a nine-patch grid, Orange Peel on a four-patch grid, and French Star on an eight-pointed star grid.

To draft a block with curved seams, draw a square equal to desired block size and sketch-in the grid. Use a ruler and compass to draw pattern pieces. Sometimes you may need to draw a larger square outside the block boundary to establish points from which to swing the compass. A ruler compass, beam compass, and yardstick compass are handy tools for drawing large circles.

Setting-In Patchwork Pieces

Some patchwork blocks, such as the Bow Tie block and the LeMoyne Star block, cannot be assembled with continuous straight seams. Pieces must be set into the openings between previously joined pieces.

Stitching must not extend into seam allowances. Illustrations below show steps for hand-piecing. (See page 151 for machine-piecing method.)

Hand-Piecing Method for Setting-In Patchwork

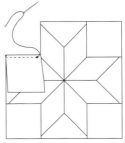

1. From outside edge, stitch into corner, stopping at corner seam line.

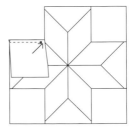

2. Backstitch at corner to strengthen corner seam and pivot.

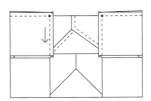

3. Align remaining sides and sew from corner to outside edge.

Learn These Set-In Machine-Piecing Techniques While Making the Magic Circle/Bow Tie Block

🏠 *making templates for set-in machine-piecing* 🏠 *assembling patchwork with set-in pieces*

Materials:

⅛ *yard each of 4 medium prints*

¼ *yard muslin*

Old sewing machine needle or other large needle

Finished Block Size: *12" square*

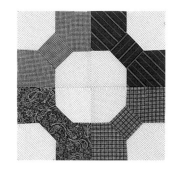

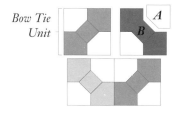

Magic Circle Block Piecing Diagram

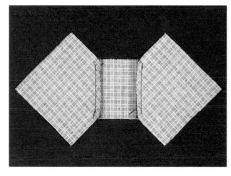

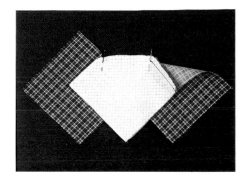

1. Make templates with seam allowances for pieces A and B on page 169. Use an old sewing machine needle to make holes in templates at corners where seam lines meet and pieces will be set-in. (Positions for holes are marked with dots on patterns.)

Mark around templates on fabric and mark match points through holes. The marked dots are guides for pin-matching and indicate the exact starting and stopping points for set-in seams.

Cut two piece As and one square B from each print; cut eight piece As from muslin. (To create a striped bow tie, cut striped piece A with long edges on bias instead of straight of grain.)

2. To make one bow tie unit, pin medium print piece A to square B, matching dots. To join pieces, start at one dot, stitch forward a few stitches, and then backstitch. Sew to next dot and backstitch. No stitching should extend into seam allowances. Join remaining piece A to opposite side of square B.

3. To set-in cream print piece A into each opening requires three separate seams. To begin, pin-match one side of cream print piece A to corresponding side of print piece A. Stitch forward from outside raw edge to inner dot, backstitching at beginning and end of seam. Remove work from machine.

Pin-match middle side of piece A to square B as shown. Stitch from dot to dot. Pin third seam; stitch from inner dot to outside raw edge. (Stitching can extend to raw edge here since no more pieces need to be set-in.) Repeat on other side of bow tie to complete section. Make four bow tie units.

4. Join bow tie units in two rows. Join rows to complete block.

Diamond Patchwork

Marking and cutting diamonds with traditional template methods is a time-consuming process. However, 45° and 60° diamonds can be cut quickly and accurately using a rotary cutter and ruler marked with 45°- and 60°- angle lines. If your ruler does not have these angles marked on it, use a 45° or 30°–60° draftsman's triangle for the correct angle.

Learn These Quick Diamond-Piecing Techniques While Making the LeMoyne Star Block

The basic eight-pointed star, also called LeMoyne Star, is the building block for a whole category of quilt patterns based on 45° diamonds.

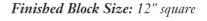 quick-cutting diamonds   stabilizing bias edges with freezer paper   piecing bias edges
making crisp diamond points at star center   setting-in pieces around star

Materials:

¼ yard each of 2 fabrics for star
¼ yard background fabric
Freezer paper
Rotary cutter and mat
Ruler with angle lines

Finished Block Size: *12" square*

For LeMoyne Star, cut strip 3" wide. Using 45°-angle line on ruler, trim end of strip.

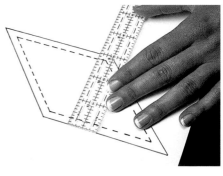

1. Measure width of diamond as shown, including ¼" seam allowances. (See page 169.)

2. From star fabric, cut strip the width of diamond, including seam allowances.

3. To cut diamonds, make cuts parallel to end at intervals equal to width of strip. For example, on 3"-wide strips, space cuts 3" apart. Check after cutting every three diamonds to maintain an accurate 45° angle; correct angle as needed. Cut four diamonds from each star fabric.

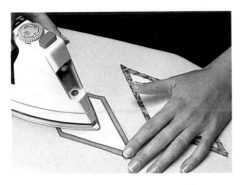

4. Make eight freezer-paper templates without seam allowances. (Hint: Paper diamonds can be quick-cut from 2½"-wide freezer-paper strips.) Center and press freezer-paper templates to fabric diamonds. Freezer paper stabilizes bias edges of fabric diamonds and establishes sewing lines. Leave paper diamonds attached until block is complete.

5. With right sides facing and paper edges aligned, pin-match diamonds in pairs. Securing beginning and end of seams by backstitching, stitch pairs along edge of paper from seam line to seam line (or dot to dot if using templates). Do not stitch past seam lines into seam allowances. Join pairs together to form two star halves.

6. Pin-match star halves. Begin at outside seam line (paper edge) and stitch length of paper edge to star center, stopping at seam line. Do not sew across star center. Repeat from opposite side to complete star piecing. Press seam allowances in one direction, either clockwise or counter-clockwise. Using tip of iron, press center seam allowances flat so that they form small star; trim excess seam allowances at star center.

7. Quick-cut four 4" squares and one 6¼" square from background fabric. Cut larger square diagonally both ways into four triangles. (Measurements include seam allowances.)

8. Set triangles into alternate openings around star first. With right sides facing and long side of triangle on outside of block, pin-match triangle tip to diamond tip and one leg of triangle to side of diamond at paper edges. Sew from outside raw edge of tips to center seam line only (paper corner), leaving inside seam allowances free. Backstitch to secure seam.

9. Pin-match adjacent leg of triangle to side of next diamond. Stitch from outside raw edge to center seam line only (paper corner). Stop and backstitch where stitching meets previous stitching.

Seam allowances should be free at center, and stitching lines should meet. Set remaining triangles into alternate openings around star.

10. Refer to steps 8 and 9 and set-in squares in same manner as triangles. Press seam allowances toward triangles and squares. Remove paper from diamonds and press.

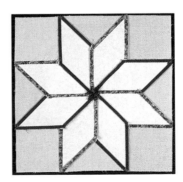

Careful Fabric Selection and Pattern Placement Can Give Your Blocks Extra Appeal

Fabrics such as stripes, plaids, and widely spaced floral designs can give otherwise ordinary blocks special appeal when you cut them carefully to take advantage of the pattern in the fabric. Study your fabrics to see if your block can be made more interesting by creative fabric design placement.

To illustrate the difference pattern placement can make, we used the same striped fabric in three different ways for the diamonds in these LeMoyne Star blocks. In the star on the left, each diamond was aligned with the same portion of the fabric pattern—the stripes run across the diamonds, giving the star a spiderweb look.

In the center star, the diamonds were cut with the same stripe running along the same side of each diamond. The star appears to swirl.

In the star on the right, the diamonds were cut with the same stripe running along the side of each diamond, but the diamond template was flipped over on four diamonds so that they are mirror images of the other four. Each diamond was then sewn to its mirror image so that the stripe formed four V-shaped patterns.

We used navy-and-white striped fabric for the Little House block on page 148. Changing the direction of the stripe on the front and side of the house helped define these areas.

In the Magic Circle block, shown on page 151, we used checked, plaid, and striped fabrics for three of the bow ties. By placing the knot template on the fabric so that it faces one direction and the bow templates on the fabric facing a different direction, we defined the knot in each tie.

 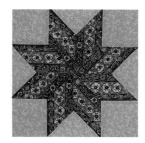 

Drafting Eight-Pointed Stars

Drafting eight-pointed stars differs from drafting many other patchwork designs. Most blocks are based on the basic equal grids discussed in "Drafting Patchwork Patterns and Adding to Patchwork Skills," page 42.

Eight-pointed stars contain 45°-angle diamonds and are based on a grid with three unequal divisions. The width of the center division is equal to the diagonal measurement of a corner square. Eight-pointed star designs are difficult to draw on graph paper because lines forming the design do not generally fall on the graph paper grid.

Two basic methods for drafting eight-pointed stars follow. Method 1 requires a compass; Method 2 involves folding tracing paper or another firm, lightweight paper.

Learn To Draft an Eight-Pointed Star by Using a Compass (Method 1)

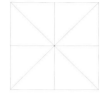

1. Draw square the size of your star. Draw lines diagonally on square from corner to corner, making an X. Mark center of each side as shown. Connect opposite points, dividing square into fourths.

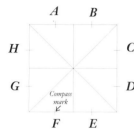

2. Place point of compass at any corner. Open compass until pencil reaches center of square. Draw arc on each side adjacent to corner. Repeat from each corner and label points as shown.

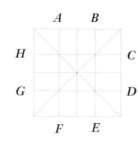

3. Connect compass points on opposite sides of square, i.e., draw lines from A to F and from B to E, etc.

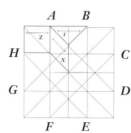

4. Draw lines from point A to D, B to G, C to F, and E to H. Identify and label diamond X, triangle Y, and square Z. Draw grain line arrows for fabric placement.

Learn To Draft an Eight-Pointed Star by Folding Paper (Method 2)

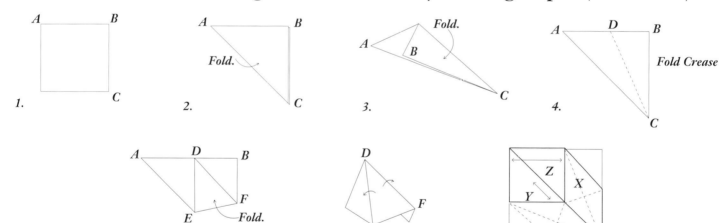

1. Draw square on tracing paper that is the size of one quadrant of your star. For example, draw a 6" square for a 12" star block. Cut out square.

2. Fold square in half diagonally; crease fold. Label points A, B, and C, as shown.

3. Fold BC side over to meet AC side and crease.

4. Open last fold and label point D. This will be the outside diamond tip.

5. Fold center point C up to point D; crease fold. Label points E and F.

6. Fold and crease along sides DE and DF.

7. Open paper. Mark fold lines, creating diamond X and square Z; label. Draw diagonal line through square Z; label triangle Y. Draw grain line arrows for fabric placement.

Eight-Pointed Star Variations

Many familiar quilt block patterns are variations of the basic eight-pointed star. Silver and Gold is created by splitting each diamond from point-to-point. Morning Star is created by dividing each diamond into four smaller diamonds. Carpenter's Wheel is created by using the same small diamond as Morning Star and smaller triangles and squares. Kaleidoscope is similar to Silver and Gold. The lines that divide the Silver and Gold diamonds form the Kaleidoscope units. The block has a triangle, rather than a square, at the block corners.

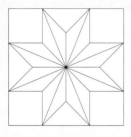

Silver and Gold

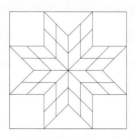

Morning Star

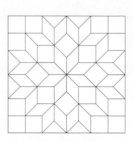

Carpenter's Wheel

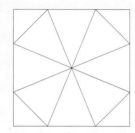

Kaleidoscope

Mathematics of Eight-Pointed Star Designs

The mathematical relationship between parts of an eight-pointed star is as follows. Assuming length of a diamond side is 1", then each square is a 1" square, and hypotenuse of triangle equals 1.41". The star block measures 3.41" square (1" + 1.41" + 1" = 3.41").

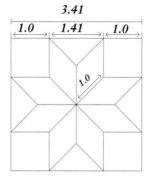

Determining finished star block size: If you know finished length of one diamond side, multiply it by 3.41" to find finished block size. Round-off numbers to nearest ⅛".

Determining finished diamond size: If you know finished block size, divide it by 3.41" to find finished length of one diamond side. Round-off numbers to nearest ⅛".

Lone Stars

Traditionally, the small diamonds for a Lone Star quilt are individually marked, cut, and then sewn into rows. Quick-cutting and quick-piecing methods make short work of this.

A Lone Star is a complex LeMoyne star; large diamonds are made up of smaller diamonds. Once the large diamonds are pieced, the star is assembled in the same manner as a LeMoyne Star.

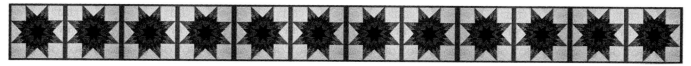

Learn To Quick-Piece Large Diamonds While Making the *Lone Star* Wall Quilt

Materials:

¼ yard black print (fabric 1)

½ yard teal print (fabric 2)

1⅜ yards rust print (fabric 3)*

¼ yard tan print (fabric 4)

¼ yard gold print (fabric 5)

¾ yard cream print

1½ yards backing fabric

Rotary cutter, mat, and ruler
    with angle guides

*Includes yardage for binding

Finished Lone Star Square: 29½"

Finished Quilt Size: *approximately*
   38½" square

1. From teal print, cut four 1½"-wide strips across fabric for inner borders.

From rust print, cut four 4"-wide strips across fabric for outer borders. Cut four 2¼"-wide strips to make binding.

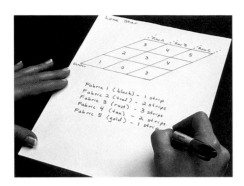

Join strips in following order: Row A: black, teal, and rust; Row B: teal, rust, and tan; Row C: rust, tan, and gold.

2. Make a working sketch of large diamond. Label rows of small diamonds alphabetically. (A working sketch is used primarily for placement of fabrics and pieces but is not necessarily drawn to scale.) Number fabrics and put numbers in each small diamond, beginning with center diamond.

Count number of times each fabric is used to determine number of strips to cut from each fabric. Make chart for each fabric, listing number of strips to cut.

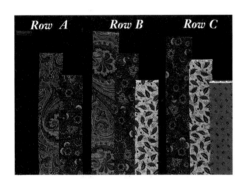

3. Cut 2½"-wide strips from diamond fabrics. Cut one from black print, two from teal print, three from rust print, two from tan print, and one from gold print.

(Note: For future quilts, if strips are wider than 3", cut additional strips to make an extra strip set in order to make eight pieced diamonds.)

Join strips lengthwise in fabric order of each large diamond row. Make strip set for each row. Offset strips by a little less than strip width as shown. Press seam allowances away from first strip in each set. Label strips sets by row.

4. Place Row A strip set right side up on cutting mat. Trim end at 45° angle, using ruler angle line. Cut eight 2½"-wide diamond segments. (Width of diamond segments is equal to width of one fabric strip.) Cut eight diamond segments for remaining rows from their respective strip sets. Label diamond segments by row.

5. To make large diamond, sew diamond segments in alphabetical order. Pin diamond segments along seams and join.

6. Since no templates were used to make these diamonds, you may find it helpful to mark ¼" sewing lines on large diamonds before assembling them into a star.

Join large diamonds into a star. Take care not to stretch bias edges while stitching. Because triangles and squares will be set into star openings, stitch from seam line to seam line; do not sew into any seam allowances.

7. One of the secrets of a successful Lone Star is cutting triangles and squares for star openings the correct size. If pieces are too large, block outside edge will ruffle and not lie flat. If pieces are too small, star center will hump up.

Custom-cut pieces to fit your star by measuring finished length of large diamond side. Measure from seam line at star opening to seam line at outer diamond tip, as shown. (The large diamond should measure approximately 8⅝".) Measure several diamonds to get an average measurement. Add ½" to this measurement for seam allowances and cut four squares this size from cream print.

To cut triangles, measure diagonally across square from raw edge to raw edge. Add ½" to measurement and cut one square this size from cream print. Cut square into four triangles by cutting diagonally from corner to corner in both directions.

8. To complete star, set triangles into alternate openings around star; then, set-in squares. (See Setting-In Patchwork Pieces on pages 150 and 151.)

9. Join each teal border to each rust border lengthwise. Sew borders to quilt top, mitering corners.

10. Outline-quilt ¼" inside seam lines of each small diamond. Quilt plume quilting pattern on page 159 in each square and triangle.

11. Bind with rust print and add hanging sleeve.

Lone Star Plume Quilting Design

Common patchwork shapes that contain 60° angles are equilateral triangles, hexagons, and diamonds such as the ones used to make Baby Blocks or a six-pointed star. Other shapes with 60° angles are variations of these basic shapes.

Special graph paper, ruled in equilateral triangles that are ¼" on a side, is available in quilt shops. Drawing these shapes with a ruler on equilateral

graph paper is the easiest method, but sometimes you may want to draw a shape with sides that are not in even ¼" increments. You can draw shapes with 60° angles in any size with the aid of a ruler and a compass. For very large shapes you will need to use a ruler compass with holes drilled in it, a beam compass, or a yardstick compass.

Drafting a Hexagon

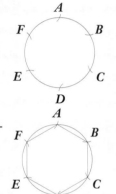

1. Draw circle with radius equal to desired length of one hexagon side. For example, to draw hexagon with 2⅛" sides, set compass radius at 2⅛". With compass at same setting, place point of compass on circle and mark at point that intersects circumference. Now put point of compass

on that mark and mark another intersecting point. Continue around circle. Label points A–F.

2. Connect adjacent points, forming hexagon as shown.

Drafting a 60° Diamond

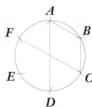

1. Draw circle and mark off six points around circumference as directed for hexagon (step 1 at left). Set compass equal to length of diamond side.

2. Connect points A and B, B and C, A and D, and C and F as shown.

Drafting an Equilateral Triangle

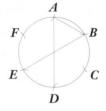

1. Draw circle and mark off six points around circumference as directed for hexagon (step 1). Set compass equal to desired length of triangle side.

2. Connect points A and B, B and E, and A and D.

English Paper-Piecing Mosaic Designs

Mosaic designs are created by putting together many pieces of the same small shape, varying the shading and colors of the small shapes. Mosaic quilts have a long history of popularity in England.

Some mosaic designs are composed of rectangles, squares, or other simple-to-sew shapes. But others are made of shapes that are more difficult to sew, especially by machine, because they cannot be joined with continuous straight seams. The use of paper templates, a method

known as English paper piecing, makes these shapes easier to join. English paper piecing is different from American patchwork because the fabric pieces are basted to paper templates before joining them and seam allowances remain open. The basted pieces are joined with a whipstitch, instead of the traditional piecing stitch. Romantic tradition suggests using old love letters for the paper templates, but our updated technique calls for plastic-coated freezer paper.

Learn These English Paper-Piecing Skills While Making the Baby Blocks Block

🏠 *making freezer-paper templates for English paper piecing*   🏠 *whipstitching pieces together*
🏠 *basting seam allowances in preparation for piecing*

Materials:
1 (4") square each from 9 fabrics*
10½" square for background
Freezer paper
Rotary cutter, mat, and ruler
Template vinyl

*Choose 3 light, 3 medium, and 3 dark.

Finished Block Size: *10" square*

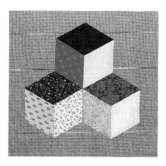

1. A freezer-paper template is needed for each fabric piece. Make finished-size diamond vinyl template. Cut strip of freezer paper wider than diamond template. (Pattern is on page 169.) Fold paper to create several layers. Mark around template on top layer as shown. Repeat to make nine paper templates.

2. Position paper templates with shiny side down on wrong side of fabric squares, aligning two diamond sides with fabric grain. With dry iron on wool setting, press paper diamonds onto squares. Use rotary cutter to cut out diamonds, adding seam allowances by extending ruler ¼" beyond paper edge.

3. Working with paper side up, fold seam allowance over paper edge. Using running stitch, baste seam allowance to wrong side, stitching through paper. Keep basting snug. To reduce bulk at sharp points, fold end of point down first; then, fold in sides.

4. With right sides facing and folded edges aligned, whipstitch two basted diamonds together, joining dark diamond to medium diamond. Pull thread

through and reinsert needle in folds next to previous stitch, looping thread over folded edges. Make tiny stitches, approximately ¹⁄₁₆" to ⅛" apart, and sew from corner to corner. Knot thread or make backstitches to secure whipstitched seam at beginning and end.

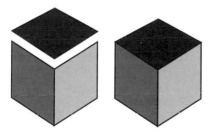

5. Set-in light diamond to form cube or baby-block unit as shown. Make three units. Join three baby-block units into stack of blocks, keeping light, medium, and dark fabrics in same relative position. Center and pin stack of blocks on background square and appliqué. Trim background fabric from behind stack of blocks, leaving ¼" seam allowance. Clip and remove basting and paper templates. Seam allowances remain open.

Long Tapered Pieces

Long tapered pieces, such as the points on the Mariner's Compass block below, present a piecing challenge. The pieces are difficult to mark because traditional finished-size templates are narrow at the point and difficult to hold in place. The narrow fabric points are also hard to pin and tend to stretch as you sew because of their bias sides. To compound the problems, accurate precision piecing is needed to maintain sharp points as the block is assembled.

The following techniques for making templates with "holding tabs" and for sewing long tapered pieces before cutting will help eliminate the above problems. The reason for a "holding tab" is that it extends the surface of the template, so that the template can be stabilized with your finger while you are marking around it. The template must be flipped so that both sides can be marked, but because the "holding tab" protects the tapered end from wear and tear, it assures that tapered pieces are accurately marked.

Learn These Skills for Piecing Long Tapered Pieces While Making a Mariner's Compass

🏠 *making templates with "holding tabs"* 🏠 *reducing number of templates by strip-piecing*
🏠 *stitching a complex design precisely*

Materials:
1 yard tan fabric
⅛ yard blue-striped print
¼ yard rust print
¼ yard gold print
½ yard brown print
⁻½ yard blue print

Finished Compass Diameter:
approximately 19"
Finished Block Size: *22¾" square*

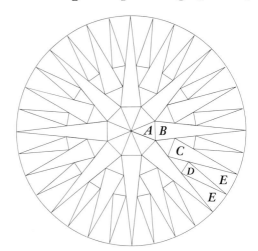

1. Make templates without seam allowances for A–E on pages 163 and 165. Include holding tabs on B, C, and D pieces to make working with tapered pieces easier. Mark dashed lines on templates C and D.

2. From gold print, cut one 2½"-wide strip across fabric. From blue print, cut one 5"-wide strip across fabric. Join strips lengthwise; press seam allowances toward wider strip.

3. Position template D on strip set so that top portion lies on gold print and bottom portion on blue print. Align dashed line on template with seam. Mark around template. (To add stitching line where holding tab is, flip template over and use other side for marking.) Mark 16, allowing ½" to ¾" between marked shapes for seam allowances.

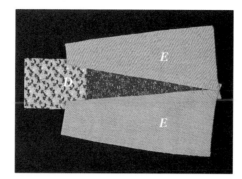

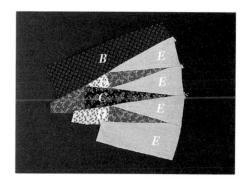

4. Cut out D pieces as rectangles as shown. For piece Cs, cut one 2½"-wide strip from blue print for top portion and one 7"-wide strip from brown print for bottom portion. Mark and cut eight piece Cs as rectangles. Mark eight piece Bs on rust print; cut out pieces as rectangles. Mark 32 wedge Es on tan; cut out pieces as rectangles. Mark and cut eight triangle As from blue-striped print, placing template in same position along striped pattern each time. Add ¼" seam allowances.

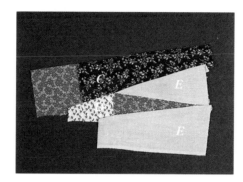

6. Join DE unit to each side of C points, using same method as explained in step 5. Make eight CDE units.

7. Join CDE unit to one side of B point. Make eight BCDE units.

8. Piece octagonal center unit by joining eight triangle As.

To add compass points to center unit, join BCDE unit to bottom of triangle A; trim excess fabric at seam line from piece B, leaving ¼" seam allowance. Join second BCDE unit to next triangle A and trim. Join BCDE units together; trim. Continue to add BCDE units to center and to each other until compass is complete.

9. From tan, cut 23¼" square for background. Fold background square in fourths and finger-press to form guidelines. Baste under seam allowances around circumference of pieced compass. Center compass and appliqué. Trim background fabric from behind compass, leaving ¼" seam allowance.

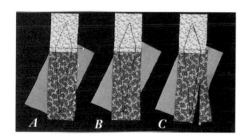

5. To make DE unit, pin wedge E to one side of D point, pin-matching seam lines (A). Sew on marked seam line, backstitching to secure stitching (B). Trim excess fabric, leaving ¼" seam allowance (C). In same manner, join wedge E to other long side of D point; trim. Make 16 DE units. (See photo above in next column.)

A
Mariner's Compass

C
Top Portion
Bottom Portion
Mariner's Compass

Holding Tab

Holding Tab

B
Mariner's Compass

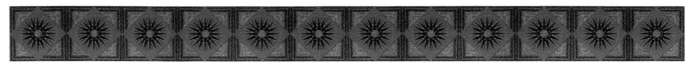

Practice Piecing Long Tapered Pieces While
Making the *Mariner's Compass Medallion* Wall Quilt

Materials:

1½ yards blue-striped print

1½ yards tan fabric*

3½ yards rust striped-border print**

¾ yard rust print

¾ yard brown print

½ yard blue print

¼ yard gold print

3 yards fabric for backing

Finished Quilt Size: 47" square

*Includes yardage for binding
**Choose print with at least 4 repeats of
each stripe across fabric width.

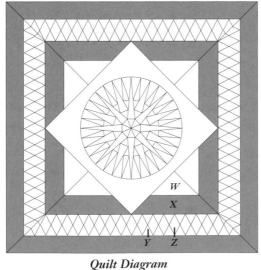

Quilt Diagram

1. Cut pieces and assemble compass. (See pages 162 and 163.)

2. From rust striped-border print, cut four 4" x 54" outer borders and eight 4" x 18" rectangles for X pieces. Measurements include seam allowances and are longer than needed. See Quilt Diagram. (Instructions for using striped-border fabrics for mitered borders are on page 203.)

3. From blue-striped print, cut eight 6½" x 11" rectangles for piece Ws, placing rectangles with long sides in same position along striped pattern each time. From remaining fabric, cut 152 triangle Ys (page 165) for pieced border, placing template in same position along striped pattern.

4. With right sides facing and raw edges aligned, center and join rectangle Ws to rectangle Xs along long edges. Refer to Triangle Diagram and draw right triangle on graph paper, as shown. (Dimensions include ¼" seam allowances.) Make triangle template and cut eight triangles from joined W and X pieces, placing bottom of triangle along edge of X rectangle. Join pairs of triangles together to form four large triangles. Join large triangles to sides of compass block.

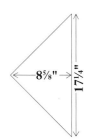

Triangle Diagram

5. Cut 36 diamond Zs (page 165) from rust print and 40 from brown print for pieced border. For each pieced border, join 38 triangle Ys (20 for outer edge and 18 for inner edge), nine rust print diamond Zs, and 10 brown print diamond Zs. Begin and end pieced border with brown print diamonds. Make four pieced borders. Join borders to each side, mitering corners.

6. Join striped-print borders to quilt, mitering corners.

7. Quilt in-the-ditch along seam lines of all compass pieces and borders. Outline-quilt ¼" inside seam lines of diamond Zs. Pick your favorite quilting pattern for the compass background.

8. Bind with French binding from tan fabric. Add hanging sleeve.

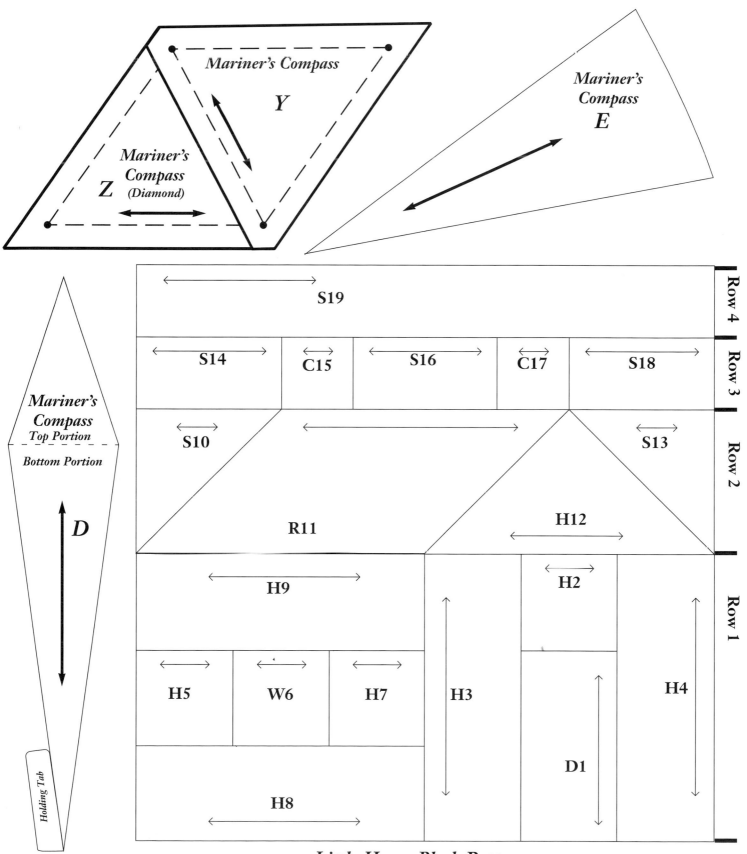

Mariner's Compass *Y*

Mariner's Compass *Z* **(Diamond)**

Mariner's Compass *E*

Mariner's Compass Top Portion

Bottom Portion

D

Holding Tab

Row 4

Row 3

Row 2

Row 1

S19

S14 C15 S16 C17 S18

S10 S13

R11 H12

H9 H2

H5 W6 H7 H3 H4

D1

H8

Little House Block Patterns

Miniature Quilts

Small quilts have a special charm, probably because they were traditionally made for children or their dolls. Some quilters make miniatures that are accurate reproductions of full-size quilts, scaled 1" to 1 foot of the original. Others who love small quilts are satisfied to simply "miniaturize" their quilts by making smaller versions that are not to scale.

The current rage for miniature quilts began in the early 1980s, with some devotees giving up life-size quilts altogether! Many find they are better at finishing small projects than large ones. Patchwork miniature quilts are the most popular, but some enthusiasts tackle appliqué miniature quilts as well.

The general guidelines in this section will help you when making either type of miniature quilt.

General Guidelines for Making Miniature Quilts

1. Choose simple blocks. The fewer the pieces and the easier the construction, the smaller you can make them.

2. If using prints, select small-scale ones so that they will be in scale with the tiny pieces.

3. Keep other quilt elements, such as the sashing, borders, and binding, in scale with the blocks.

4. For easiest sewing, machine-piece miniature patchwork quilts. Hand-piecing methods can be frustrating when working with very small pieces.

5. Use quick-cutting and quick-piecing methods where possible to avoid handling tiny pieces. These methods are explained in this chapter and in "First Steps in Quick-Cutting and Quick-Piecing," page 104. (For a specific technique that applies to small quilts, see step 1 on page 167.)

6. Correct placement of fabric grain is less important with miniature quilts than with larger ones.

7. Using ¼" seams makes measuring and stitching easy since this is the standard seam width for patchwork. If the seam allowances overwhelm the tiny patchwork pieces, either press the seams open to distribute the thickness more evenly or trim the seam allowances to ⅛" after stitching.

8. If you prefer to use ⅛" seams for miniature patchwork, use a straight-stitch presser foot and a straight-stitch throat plate so that the tiny pieces will not be drawn down into the throat plate.

9. To prevent the miniature quilt from looking too puffy, use thin batting, such as cotton, cotton-blend, or flannel, or omit batting.

10. Quilt miniature quilts in the unpieced areas such as sashing, borders, and setting squares and triangles. Quilting tiny patchwork pieces is difficult because of the seam allowances, and it usually does not show up well.

11. Finish edges on miniature quilts by binding them with narrow single-fold binding or either by bringing the quilt backing to the front or the quilt top to the back. Or, the raw edges of the quilt top and backing can be turned in and stitched together for a finish without binding. (Edge-finishing methods are discussed in "Finishing Your Quilts," page 92.)

Learn These Quiltmaking Skills While Making the *Shoo Fly* Miniature Quilt

🏠 *making small triangle-square units*   🏠 *applying general guidelines for making miniature quilts*

Materials:
½ yard blue print
⅓ yard white print
Batting, light-weight (optional)
Rotary cutter and mat
Ruler with angle lines

Number of Blocks and Finished
  Size: 12—1½" square
Finished Quilt Size: *7½" x 9½"*

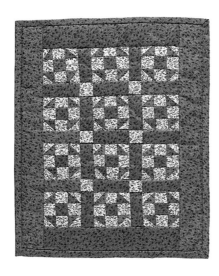

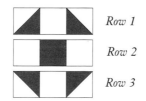

Row 1
Row 2
Row 3

Shoo Fly Block Piecing Diagram

1. For triangle-squares that finish ½" square, cut five 1" x 16" bias strips from each fabric. Pair blue strips with white strips and join lengthwise with ¼" seam. Press seams open or trim them to ⅛". (For other triangle-square sizes, the rule for obtaining strip width is to add ½" to finished size of triangle-square.)

2. Stack strip sets; trim one end at 45° angle. Cut 48 (1"-wide) segments from strips, cutting parallel to first cut. Check after cutting every three or four segments to maintain an accurate angle.

3. Align 45°-angle line on ruler along seam and measure 1" along top edge of segment as shown. Trim excess fabric. Repeat for each segment.

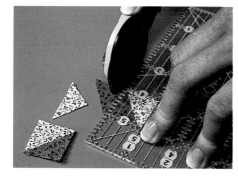

4. Turn segment and repeat on opposite side of each segment. Triangle-squares should measure exactly 1" square to finish ½" square.

5. From white print, cut 24 (1") squares. Refer to Shoo Fly Block Piecing Diagram and arrange triangle-squares and squares for rows 1 and 3; join.

6. To make row 2, cut one 1" x 15" strip from blue print and two strips from white print. Join strips lengthwise with blue print strip in center. Cut 12 (1"-wide) segments.

7. Join block rows to make 12 blocks.

8. From blue print, cut eight 1" x 2" rectangles for sashing. Alternate three blocks with sashing to form a horizontal row and join. Make four rows.

9. To make horizontal sashing rows with sashing squares, cut three 2" x 4" rectangles from blue print and two 1" x 4" rectangles from white print.

   Join strips lengthwise, placing white print strips between blue print strips. Cut three 1"-wide segments from strip set.

10. Alternate block rows with sashing rows, beginning with block row and join rows.

11. Measure quilt width (6" including seam allowances). From blue print, cut two 1½"-wide borders this length. Join borders to top and bottom of quilt.

   Measure quilt length, including top and bottom borders (10" including seam allowances). From blue print, cut two 1½"-wide borders this length. Join borders to sides of quilt.

12. From white print, cut one 10" x 12" rectangle for backing.

13. Outline-quilt on block seam lines.

14. Finish with narrow single-fold binding from blue print.

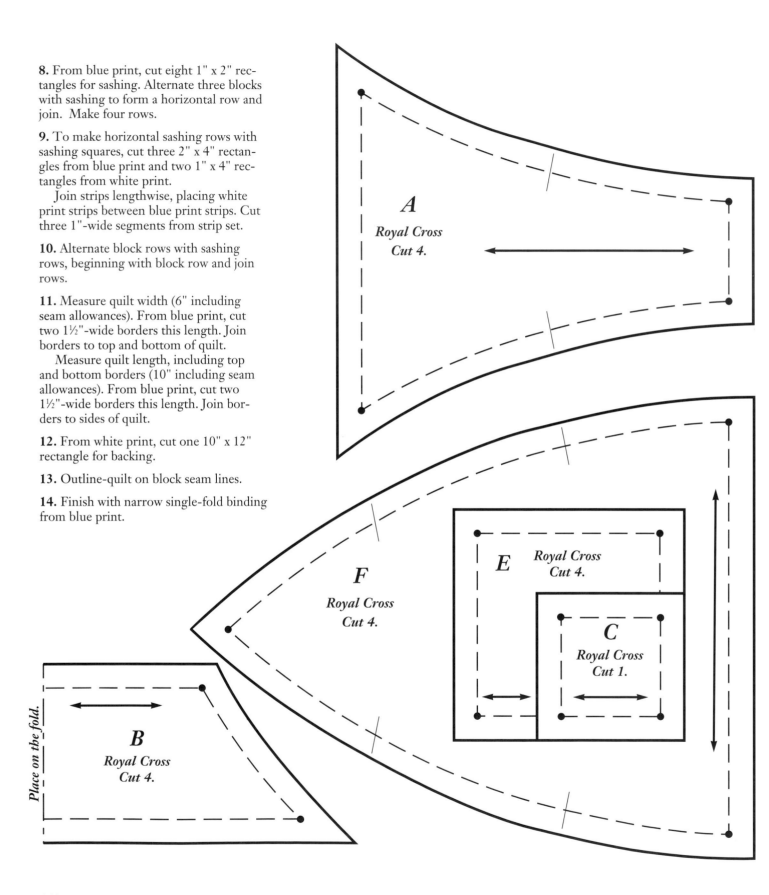

A
Royal Cross Cut 4.

F
Royal Cross Cut 4.

E
Royal Cross Cut 4.

C
Royal Cross Cut 1.

B
Royal Cross Cut 4.

Place on the fold.

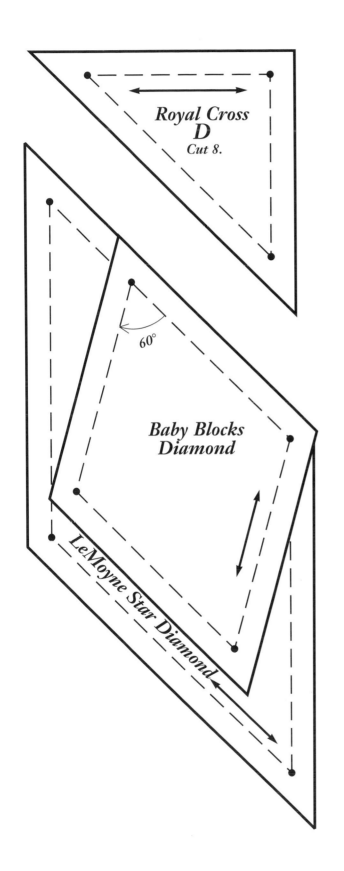

Royal Cross
D
Cut 8.

60°

Baby Blocks
Diamond

LeMoyne Star Diamond

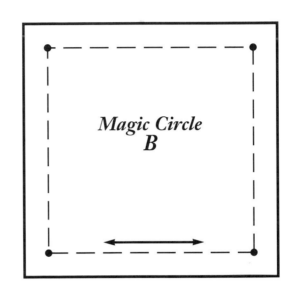

Magic Circle
B

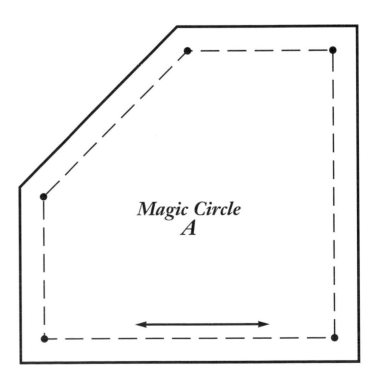

Magic Circle
A

Beyond Basic Appliqué

*I*n "First Steps in Hand Appliqué," we described basic skills that can be used to make dozens of beautiful appliqué patterns. Dedicated appliqué quiltmakers, however, have invented additional techniques to meet the challenge of more elaborate or difficult appliqué shapes or to enhance appliqué motifs. Advanced hand appliqué generally involves needle-turning, or needle-rolling, the fabric edges of appliqués under as they are stitched down, rather than basting them first.

Beyond Basic Appliqué

In this chapter, we'll introduce you to needle-turning techniques, reverse appliqué, buttonhole-stitch appliqué, and broderie perse as well as stuffed, shadow, bias, and layered-scenic appliqué. Finally, we'll outline the basic steps for machine appliqué.

Needle-Turned Appliqué

As the name implies, needle-turned appliqué involves using the point and shank of the needle to turn under the raw edges of appliqués as they are stitched to the background cloth. The advantages are that it eliminates the basting step and that shapes with tight curves, which cannot be basted under in the traditional way, become feasible for appliqué.

For needle turning, a narrower seam allowance,

approximately ⅛", is used so that appliqué pieces will lie flatter. Needle-turned appliqué is sometimes called Hawaiian appliqué, in reference to the distinctive two-fabric appliqué quilts made by the natives of the Hawaiian Islands. The large size of the single appliqué of Hawaiian quilts, the intricate tight turns, and the sharp points make basting back raw edges impractical and needle turning necessary.

Learn These Appliqué Methods While Making the Hawaiian Breadfruit Block

🏠 *cutting pattern pieces for appliqué using freezer paper (Method 1)* 🏠 *clipping narrow seam allowances*
🏠 *stitching needle-turned appliqué* 🏠 *managing appliquéd curves and points*

Materials:

14½" square yellow
14½" square white

Freezer paper
Thread to match colored fabric

***Finished Block Size:** 14" square*

1. Trace quadrant of Breadfruit pattern onto 7" square of freezer paper. (Pattern is on page 194.) Cut out paper pattern.

2. Fold yellow square in half twice to form equal quadrants and press. Press paper pattern on folded fabric, aligning right angles of paper with folds of fabric, and pin. Cut out appliqué, cutting ⅛" outside paper for seam allowance.

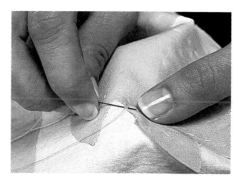

3. Fold white background square in half twice and press to form guidelines. Open out square. Remove freezer paper pattern. Position appliqué on square, aligning centers and folds, and pin in place. Hand-baste design to background, about ¼" from raw edge.

4. To prepare for needle-turned appliqué, clip seam allowance around inside or concave curves, making clips a scant ¼" apart and approximately ⅛" deep. Use scissor tips to clip straight into seam allowance. Make one clip into sharp inside points.

5. Working with point and shank of needle, as well as your fingertips, turn under raw edge of appliqué just ahead of stitching. Space stitches no more than ⅛" apart and closer on tight inside corners and curves where there is little or no seam allowance.

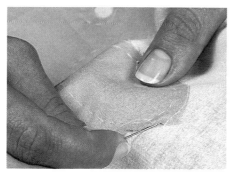

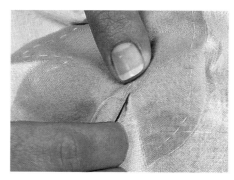

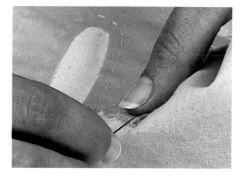

6. Outside curve: Use needle point to pick up and draw seam allowance under as shown.

Inside curve: Use needle tip and shank to "sweep" under clipped seam allowance. Once curve is formed, press it with thumb of free hand and stitch.

7. Inside point: As you approach clipped inside point (see step 4), use needle tip to grab clipped edge and fold it under. Press down with thumb. Continue stitching and stop at inside point. Use needle tip to roll under next side of point and hold down with thumb. Bring needle up at inside point, disturbing threads as little as possible, make stitch at point, and continue stitching along next side.

8. Outside point: Sew to within one stitch of point. Before making stitch on point, reposition work in hands. Turn under seam allowance on point and other side of point and flatten with thumb.

Make point stitch and continue stitching down other side.

Three Additional Preparation Methods for Hawaiian-Style Patterns
Cut-as-You-Go with Freezer-Paper-on-Top Method (Method 2)

1. Take piece of freezer paper the size of your appliqué and fold it in half twice to form equal quadrants. Open it out, with coated side down, and trace quadrant of pattern on it.

2. Refold paper. Place pins through pattern to keep folds aligned and cut out.

3. Fold fabric square in half twice to form equal quadrants and press to form guidelines. Open out freezer-paper pattern and position it on right side of fabric, coated-side down, aligning centers and folds. Using a dry iron set at wool, press pattern on fabric.

4. Place appliqué fabric square atop background square and pin. Start at any section of design and carefully cut appliqué fabric only approximately ⅛" outside freezer-paper edge for seam allowance. Cut only 2" to 3" of design at a time.

5. Use needle-turning techniques, described on previous page, and appliqué. Turn under fabric edge even with paper edge. Remove paper when all edges are appliquéd to background.

Cut-as-You-Go with Fold-Under-Line Method (Method 3)

1. Follow steps 1 through 3 above and prepare freezer-paper pattern. Press pattern to appliqué fabric square. With well-sharpened pencil, mark fold-under line on appliqué fabric by drawing along edge of paper pattern. Peel off pattern.

2. Place marked appliqué fabric square atop background square, aligning outside edges. Baste ¼" *inside* pattern outline.

3. Start at any section and carefully cut appliqué fabric only approximately ⅛" outside marked line for seam allowance. Cut only 2" to 3" of design at a time. Needle-turn appliqué, folding the fabric under along line.

Placement Lines on Background Fabric Method (Method 4)

1. Mark fold-under line on appliqué fabric square, following step 1 of Method 3 at left. Save paper pattern.

2. Press paper pattern to background fabric. With a well-sharpened pencil, mark thin placement line following paper edge. Peel off pattern.

3. Align appliqué fold-under line with placement line by pin matching at strategic points.

4. To stitch appliqué to background, use needle-turning techniques described on previous page, keeping fold-under and placement lines aligned.

Reverse Appliqué

In reverse appliqué, instead of fabric pieces being applied to a background fabric, the edges of the top fabric are cut in a design and turned to reveal an underlying fabric. The underneath fabric can be simply the background cloth, or it can be a separate underlay, like the red heart in the Heart and Hand block below.

*Ethnic examples of reverse appliqué, both involving several layers of fabric, are **Molas** (left), made by the San Blas Indians of Panama, and **Pa** ndau (right), created by the Hmong people of Southeast Asia.*

Learn to Reverse Appliqué While Making the Heart and Hand Block

Materials:

9½" square background fabric

¼ yard purple

3" square red

Freezer paper

Finished Block Size: *9" square*

1. To make pattern, draw around your hand on freezer paper. Smooth lines as needed. Draw heart outline on palm of hand pattern. Make heart template.

2. Cut out freezer paper hand. Prepare hand piece for appliquéing, using method 2, 3, or 4 (page 174). Center hand on background square and begin appliqué.

3. Mark heart on wrong side of red square. Cut it out, adding generous ¼" seam allowance. Cut out heart in appliquéd hand, leaving generous ⅛" seam allowance to inside of heart.

4. Insert red heart underlay right side up. Check position of underlay by holding block to light and pin.

5. Use needle to turn under heart seam allowance of hand piece and appliqué. Clip concave curves and heart cleft as you work. (As with all appliqué, match thread color to fabric being stitched down; in this case, the hand fabric.)

Buttonhole-Stitch Appliqué

The buttonhole, or blanket, stitch can be used to decorate appliquéd quilt blocks. This stitch was popular with Depression-era quiltmakers, who used it to appliqué butterfly patterns and character patterns such as Sunbonnet Sue and Colonial Lady. Although not as popular today, the buttonhole stitch is still sometimes used on children's quilts and to give quilts a folk art look. Buttonhole stitches, spaced so closely that they form a ridge of satin stitches, are also frequently used to appliqué the chintz cutouts of *broderie perse*.

Buttonhole stitching can be used as a substitute for appliqué blindstitches, or it can be added as an embellishment on pieces that have already been appliquéd.

Learn These Buttonhole-Stitching Techniques While Making the Heart Basket Block

🏠 *preparing appliqués for buttonhole stitching*

Materials:
¼ yard each of 2 fabrics
6" square of fabric for heart
Embroidery floss
Paper-backed fusible webbing*

*If using method 3. See step 2.

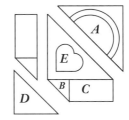

Heart Basket Block Piecing Diagram

1. Piece Heart Basket block, using patterns on page 143 in "First Steps in Hand Appliqué" and Block Piecing Diagram.

2. Prepare heart appliqué, using your choice of methods:
    Method 1: Cut out heart with ¼" seam allowances, baste under edges, and pin heart in position on basket.
    Method 2: Cut out heart with ⅛" scam allowances and needle-turn appliqué heart to basket.
    Method 3: Fuse finished-size heart to basket, using paper-backed fusible webbing. (Instructions for using webbing are in tip box on page 178.)

🏠 *making the buttonhole stitch with embroidery floss*

3. Use two or three strands of embroidery floss and buttonhole-stitch heart to basket. Space stitches ⅛" to ¼" apart if heart has already been appliquéd or fused to basket; space stitches closer if you are attaching heart to basket with buttonhole stitching.

To work buttonhole stitch, bring thread up just outside edge of appliqué. Insert needle into appliqué ⅛" to ¼" inside edge, bringing it straight out again just beyond edge of appliqué and over thread loop formed by stitch.

Broderie Perse Appliqué

Broderie perse is French for "embroidering chintz." It is a quiltmaking technique that was particularly popular in late eighteenth-century America, and it remains of interest to many quilters today. Printed motifs are cut from chintz and appliquéd to a background fabric. The method is also called "cutout chintz appliqué." Traditionally, the appliqués are realistic motifs, such as flowers, birds, and butterflies.

Fabrics for Broderie Perse

Look for richly printed fabrics with lots of different motifs or combine motifs from several fabrics. Cut out motifs and appliqué them to the background fabric by needle-turned, buttonhole-stitch, or machine appliqué. If you plan to needle-turn appliqué, make sure that the fabric is the appropriate weight and weave. Often, chintz-type prints are more readily available in decorator weights, which may be too heavy to hand-appliqué. For buttonhole or machine appliqué, the fabric can be slightly heavier.

Arrangement of Broderie Perse *Appliqués*

To create a symmetrical design using chintz cutouts, be aware that your printed fabric may not include reverses of the motifs. Achieving an illusion of symmetry may involve rotating flowers or cutting off and rearranging attached leaves to make the flowers appear to face in opposite directions. Study photos of antique *broderie perse* quilts for ways to balance your design.

Learn To *Broderie Perse* Appliqué While Making a Practice Block

Materials:

¼ yard print with motifs for appliqué
Background square several inches larger than
*   your appliqué piece*
Embroidery floss (optional)

1. Cut out motifs ⅛" outside edge of design, cutting away antennae or tendrils, very narrow stems, or other small details. (Embroider these later.)

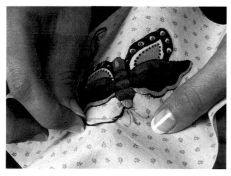

2. Needle-turn, buttonhole-stitch, or machine-appliqué motif to background square. (Fuse cutouts to background before stitching if using buttonhole stitch or machine appliqué. See tip box on next page.) Embroider details.

Using Fusible Webbing To Stablize and Position Appliqués

Using paper-backed fusible webbing, such as Wonder-Under, makes it easy to prepare appliqués for techniques like buttonhole stitching, machine-appliquéd *broderie perse*, shadow appliqué, or any other machine-appliquéd project. Available in fabric stores, the webbing is sold with manufacturer's instructions. It is applied with a warm iron.

Here's how it works:

1. Trace appliqué pattern on paper side of webbing. If design is directional, make a reverse tracing so that pattern elements will face the same way as original when ironed on. Roughly cut out webbing larger than drawn outline.

2. Place webbing side (rough side) on wrong side of appliqué fabric; press. (The paper side acts like a press cloth to protect your iron.)

3. Cut out appliqué on traced line, adding seam allowance only in areas that will underlap another piece. Peel off paper backing to expose webbing on fabric back.

4. Position appliqué, right side up, with web side against background fabric. Press to fuse.

Making Bias Strips for Very Thin Stems and Vines

For curved flower stems, vines, or basket handles with a finished width of ¼" or less, here's a method that differs from the one we described in our chapter on appliqué basics. There we advocated folding and pressing bias strips in thirds. The following method involves folding bias strips in half twice.

1. Mark a placement line on background fabric that represents outer curve of finished strip (stem or vine).

2. Cut bias strips slightly less than four times desired finished width. For example, cut 1"-wide strip for a scant ¼"-wide finished stem.

3. Fold strip in half lengthwise with wrong sides facing and raw edges aligned, and steam-press.

4. Fold pressed strip lengthwise again so that fold overlaps raw edges slightly; press. Open strip so that it is only folded in half.

5. Position raw edges of pressed strip along placement line on background fabric. Use matching thread and machine- or hand-sew strip to background, making small stitches in crease that runs down center of folded strip. Keep raw edges aligned with placement line as you sew.

6. Bring folded edge over to cover raw edges and meet marked placement line. Steam-press bias strip to help it lie flat.

7. Stitch folded edge down, using basic appliqué stitch and matching thread.

Stuffed Appliqué

Outline-quilting in-the-ditch around appliqués raises the motifs into higher relief than the background area. Sometimes, you may want to emphasize a particular appliqué element even more by adding extra stuffing. But keep in mind that loose filler may shift or wad up if the project is laundered or used heavily.

Learn These Appliqué Techniques While Making a Posy Block

🏠 *appliquéing thin stems*

Materials:

6½" background square
⅛ yard dark green
⅛ yard blue print
4" square gold
Wisps of polyester stuffing or batting

Finished Block Size: *6" square*

1. Draw placement line for outer edge of stem on background square. Follow instructions in tip box for very thin stems on page 178 and appliqué stem to square. Use leaf and outer and center posy patterns on page 138 from *Floral Wreath* and make templates. Cut two leaves and outer posy. Wait and cut posy center later. (See steps 6 and 7.) Appliqué leaves to square.

2. Appliqué posy to square, but leave ¾" to 1" section of posy edge unstitched. Select easy section, one without clefts or corners.

🏠 *stuffing appliqués from the top*

3. Insert wisps of stuffing or batting in posy opening. (A seam ripper makes a good tool for poking padding in and distributing it evenly.) Be careful not to over-stuff, which would draw block out of shape.

4. After posy is stuffed, insert large darning needle through background fabric and use point to re-arrange stuffing.

5. After shape is padded, finish appliquéing posy edge.

🏠 *stuffing circles for appliqué*

6. For circles, such as flower centers and cherries, draw placement line for finished-size circle on background fabric.

7. Cut circle with diameter twice the finished-circle size of posy center pattern. For example, for 1"-diameter finished circle, cut 2" circle.

8. Using thread that matches circle fabric, run gathering thread around circle, about ⅛" from raw edge. Keep stitches tiny and even. When you get back to starting point, pull up on thread to gather circle slightly. Tuck small amount of loose stuffing or batting into circle and pull thread again, as shown, to gather fabric around filler.

9. Backstitch to secure gathers. Do not clip thread. Position stuffed circle on posy, aligning edge with marked placement circle. Appliqué in place using still-attached thread.

Instead of hand-basting under seam allowances on individual appliqués, try these two preparation methods. Both involve using freezer paper on the wrong side of the fabric, stitching the appliqué down, and then cutting out the background fabric from behind the appliqué to remove the paper.

Method 1

1. Trace appliqué shape onto non-coated side of freezer paper and cut it out. (If design is not symmetrical, you must make a reverse tracing first.)

2. With dry iron set at wool, press coated-side of freezer-paper pattern to wrong side of appliqué fabric.

3. Cut out appliqué shape ⅛" outside paper edge for seam allowance.

4. Appliqué shape to background fabric by needle-turning seam allowance under against edge of paper. Clip inside curves and points just before stitching.

After appliquéing, cut away background fabric from behind appliqué, leaving ¼" seam allowance. Gently pull out paper pattern.

Method 2

1. Make template of shape. Also make freezer-paper template. Cut out templates.

2. Use vinyl template to mark shape on wrong side of appliqué fabric. Cut ¼" outside line for seam allowance.

3. With non-coated side of freezer-paper template against wrong side of appliqué fabric, pin shapes together, aligning paper edge with marked line. (Coated, shiny side of paper is facing out.)

4. With dry iron set on wool, use sides and tip of iron to press over and adhere seam allowance to coated side of paper. Hold iron on each section for several seconds. Be careful not to touch shiny side with iron. Clip curves and points as needed.

5. Position appliqué on background fabric. Lightly press to adhere coated side of paper to background. Stitch appliqué in place; cut background fabric from behind appliqué, leaving ¼" seam allowance. Remove paper.

Shadow Appliqué

The motifs for shadow appliqué blocks or other projects are not stitched to background fabric in the traditional way. They are cut finished size, without seam allowances, and arranged on a background fabric. Then an overlay of sheer fabric, such as organza or voile, is placed over the arranged pieces. Outline quilting along the edges of the covered motifs holds the motifs in position. Embroidered details are frequently added.

The overlaid organza or voile mutes or shadows the colored fabrics, so bright-colored appliqués are often used. We advocate using paper-backed fusible webbing to stabilize the appliqués for quilting.

Learn To Shadow Appliqué While Making the Triple Tulip Block

Materials:

9½" background square

12" square polyester organza or voile

¼ yard dark green

¼ yard dark red

⅛ yard light red

Fusible webbing

Tracing paper

Finished Block Size: 9" square

1. Fold 9" square of tracing paper in half diagonally in both directions. Make a master pattern, using leaf, tulip, and stem patterns on page 192. The straight stem is ¼" x 8½". Lay background square over master pattern and lightly draw placement lines on fabric.

2. Trace appliqué motifs on fusible webbing. Make webbing pattern for stems, leaves, and tulips. (Follow instructions in tip box on fusible webbing on page 178 to prepare shapes.)

3. Position appliqués within placement lines and fuse them to square.

4. Lay organza or voile square over appliqué block and baste around outside edge to secure top fabric and prevent fraying. Trim off excess sheer fabric.

5. Baste layers and quilt, outline-quilting appliqué elements. (If block is part of larger project, combine it with other elements before layering with batting and backing.)

Bias Appliqué

Use continuous folded bias strips for special appliqué designs such as Celtic motifs (below) or border vines. (See *Julie's Baltimore Basket* on page 189.) Bias pressing bars, made of metal or heat-resistant plastic, make the preparation of lengths of consistent-width folded bias strips easy. These bars are available at quilt shops and from mail-order suppliers and usually come in sets of three widths. Package instructions will tell you how wide to cut the fabric strip for each bar.

Learn To Bias Appliqué While Making a Celtic True Lover's Knot Block

Materials:

12½" background square
½ yard appliqué fabric
Bias bar, ⅜" wide
Tracing paper

Finished Block Size: *12" square*

1. To make master pattern, fold 12½" square of tracing paper in half vertically and horizontally. Open it out and trace quadrant of design (page 194) onto one quadrant of paper, aligning dashed lines with center folds. (Enlarge pattern before tracing.) Rotate paper and trace design in remaining quadrants. Darken pattern placement lines with marker.

2. Pin background square onto paper pattern. Working at window or light table, trace placement lines onto fabric, keeping lines light and thin.

3. Cut 1⅛"-wide bias strips from appliqué fabric to finish ⅜" wide. With wrong sides facing, fold strips in half lengthwise and machine-stitch ⅛" from raw edges.

4. Insert ⅜"-wide bias bar into sewn strip. Adjust strip so that seam is centered on one side of bar. Press seam flat. Turn bar over and press other side. Slide bar through strip until entire strip is pressed. Be careful—metal bar gets hot!

5. With seam side down, baste bias strips in place within marked placement lines, placing strips in same over/under configuration as shown in pattern quadrant. Start new bias strip at place where another strip will cover raw end.

6. Appliqué both sides of strips. On each section of design, stitch inner curves and then outer curves.

Practice Hawaiian-Style Pattern-Making Methods and Appliqué While Making the *Kathy's Hawaiian Breadfruit* Wall Quilt

Inspired by the unique quilts of Hawaii, Kathy Russi of Des Moines, Iowa, designed and appliquéd this stunning quilt.

Materials:
2¼ yards red*
1¾ yards white**
1½ yards backing fabric
Freezer paper

*Includes yardage for binding.
**The instructions below and the quilt diagram call for four separate blocks and added borders. This quilt can be made without seams, using two 44" squares (one each from red and white). Referring to Quilt Diagram, fold and press red square in quarters to make guidelines. Make freezer-paper master patterns for Breadfruit design and for border, as described in step 4 below. Use Method 3 on page 174 to mark fold-under lines, baste, cut-as-you-go, and appliqué motifs.

Finished Block Size: *14" square*
Finished Quilt Size: *42" square*

Center Side   Border   Corner
Unit   Unit   Unit

Quilt Diagram

1. Make four Breadfruit blocks. (See page 172.)

2. Arrange blocks in two rows of two blocks each and join. Join rows. (Quilt should measure 28½" square, including seam allowances.)

3. Cut four 7½"-wide borders across width of fabric, each from red and white fabrics.

4. Make full-size freezer-paper master pattern for border unit, corner unit, and center side unit. (Patterns are on page 195.) See color coding on patterns, Quilt Diagram, and Border Placement Diagram (page 195) for placement of patterns. Use master pattern and one of the appliqué methods described in this chapter to prepare borders and appliqué them.

5. Sew borders to quilt, mitering corners.

6. Layer and baste. Quilt with Hawaiian-style echo-quilting, spacing lines ⅜" apart.

7. Bind outer edges and add hanging sleeve. (See "Finishing Your Quilts," page 92.)

Layered Scenic Appliqué

The needle-turned technique for appliquéing works well for layered-appliquéd pieces used to depict landscapes in textiles. We asked nationally recognized artist Jo Diggs of Maine to design a small landscape for us to include in this chapter. The instructions below are for her own multi-layered appliqué technique. Jo generally cuts shapes freehand, but we'll tell you how to use a freezer-paper pattern, at least for your first experience with multiple layers. This method results in a bulk-free finished product that is easy to quilt.

When generating this type of design, remember that the more layers you use, the richer and more intricate the scene will be. Tips from Jo for this type of work are to use a wide range of very close color gradations, including both solids and small prints, and to generally work from the top to the bottom—a light sky to darker hills and then to a lighter foreground.

Learn These Layer-Appliqué Techniques While Making Jo's Multi-Layered Landscape

🏠 *using tracing-paper pattern as positioning guide*   🏠 *using freezer paper for layered-appliqué templates*
🏠 *trimming away excess appliqué fabric from top*

Materials:

10¼" x 11½" blue (sky and background)
⅛ yard each of 2 shades of light blue (pieces 1, 2)
⅛ yard each of 5 green prints (pieces 6, 7, 8, 16, 17, 18, 22)
⅛ yard each of 3 shades of gold (pieces 3, 4, 12)

⅛ yard each of 4 brown prints (pieces 9, 10, 13, 15)
⅛ yard each of 5 tan prints (pieces 11, 14, 19, 20, 21, 23)
⅛ yard yellow (piece 5)
⅛ yard cream print (piece 24)
¼ yard brown stripe for border

Freezer paper
Tracing paper

Finished Project Size:
9¾" x 11" (without border)

1. Make two copies of patterns (drawings) on pages 192 and 193, one on tracing paper and one on freezer paper. Draw on non-coated side of freezer paper and transfer numbers to both copies. Use tracing-paper pattern as positioning guide and freezer-paper pattern for templates. Numbers start at background and work to foreground and indicate order for appliquéing.

2. Cut out freezer-paper patterns, beginning with lowest numbers. Cut out only about six pattern pieces at a time, appliqué them, and then cut a few more.

3. Press coated side of freezer-paper pattern to right side of fabric. On edge of piece that will be stitched down (top edge), cut fabric ⅛" outside paper. (Number will be right side up.) Cut other edges ½" to 1" bigger than paper.

4. Peel freezer paper off piece 1 and position it on blue rectangle. (Lay tracing paper pattern over work to position appliqué properly.) Pin piece in place and needle-turn appliqué top edge along area that will show in finished design. Appliqué piece until line of stitching extends approximately ⅛" under piece that will overlap it. Use pins to remind yourself not to stitch too far.

5. Position and appliqué piece 2 and remaining pieces in numerical order. After each piece is appliquéd, lift up unsewn edge and trim away fabric of previous piece or pieces underneath. For example,

trim side of piece 1 along edge that is covered by piece 2. The first time you trim will be after you have stitched piece 2 in place.

6. For foreground, appliqué road piece (23) to piece 24 and then stitch layered piece to foundation to complete design.

7. Landscape is finished by matting and framing it. To prepare project for framing, add 2½"-wide brown stripe borders with mitered corners. Mount it over foam-core board. The finished-border width is 1½". (See tip box below for how to mount an appliqué piece for framing.)

Foam-Core Board Mounting for Appliqué Pictures

For mounting appliqué pictures such as the landscape on page 184, use ³⁄₁₆"-thick foam-core board (available at picture-framing shops) and stainless steel silk sewing pins. Purchase a piece of foam-core board the size you want your finished appliqué. Allow at least 1" of fabric on each side of the block to fold over to back of board.

1. Center appliqué block with right side facing you on foam-core board.

2. Fold fabric margin to back of board on each side and secure fabric with pins. Start pinning by pushing pin straight through into foam core at center of each side.

3. Continue pinning, working on each side, until pin is placed every 1" around perimeter, and appliqué is flat and smooth. Fold in one side neatly at corner and then adjacent side. Repeat for each corner.

4. On back, secure raw edges with strips of 2"-wide masking tape.

Machine Appliqué

If you love the look of appliqué quilts but lack the time and patience for handwork, machine appliqué may be the method for you. Machine appliqué is particularly appropriate for items that will get hard wear and be washed frequently, such as garments and baby quilts. Using a sewing machine to stitch down appliqué pieces is not a new idea. The appliqués on some antique quilts are machine-stitched to the background. The edges of the appliqués were first basted under; then, the motifs were straightstitched to the background next to the folded edge. The introduction of zigzag sewing machines brought about the development of new machine appliqué methods—satin-stitch machine appliqué, decorative-stitch machine appliqué, and invisible (blindstitch) machine appliqué. Below are general guidelines for these methods. Develop satin-stitch machine-appliqué skills by making the Country Angel block (page 188).

Adjusting Your Sewing Machine

Attach an open-toed presser foot to your machine. If not available, a plastic foot, blind-hem foot, or decorative-stitch foot could be used. Thread machine needle and bobbin with thread that matches the appliqué piece or nylon thread that makes the stitches practically invisible. You may want to try machine-embroidery thread which has a finer texture than regular sewing thread. Set your machine for a medium-width zigzag and a very short stitch length.

Test stitch on a scrap of medium-weight fabric. Adjust the stitch width to $1/8$" to $3/16$" wide. Adjust the stitch length so that the stitches are very close together and form a band of color but will not be so close that the fabric will not feed. Slightly loosen the top tension so the top thread is barely pulled to the wrong side. (This adjustment is usually made with the top tension because bobbin tension is hard to readjust for normal stitching.)

Satin-Stitch Machine Appliqué

Stitching appliqué pieces to a background with closely spaced zigzag stitches is called satin-stitch machine appliqué. The stitching completely covers the fabric edge and forms ridges that outline the pieces.

A small assortment of supplies is needed each time you satin-stitch machine appliqué. They are:
- quality sewing thread in colors to match appliqués
- tracing paper
- paper-backed fusible webbing
- stabilizer to support background fabric, such as freezer paper or a commercial stabilizer
- sewing machine with a zigzag stitch
- machine-appliqué presser foot that has a channel along bottom to allow ridge of satin stitches to feed through evenly. (Either a transparent foot or a foot with an open toe will allow you maximum visibility.)

Decorative-Stitch Machine Appliqué

With the advent of quality home-sewing and computerized machines, fine decorative machine stitches can be produced. Many of these can be used for machine appliqué. Stitches such as a feather stitch, outline stitch, cross-stitch, buttonhole stitching, and faggoting can be done by machine.

Invisible Machine Appliqué

Imitate the look of hand appliqué on the sewing machine by stitching appliqués in place with clear nylon thread. Most of the appliqués for *Julie's Baltimore Basket* quilt were applied this way. Prepare appliqué shapes by thread-basting under seam allowances or turning under raw edges on freezer-paper templates. (See Method 2 on page 180.) Arrange appliqués on background fabric.

Thread machine needle with clear nylon thread and either use the same thread in the bobbin or match it to the background fabric. Set the machine for a narrow-width blindstitch and a very short stitch length. Or set machine to make a narrow, fairly open, zigzag stitch.

Test your stitching by folding a fabric scrap and placing the folded edge on a scrap of background fabric. Stitch on the background fabric right next to the folded edge. Adjust the stitch width so that either blindstitch or left swing of zigzag stitch catches the edge of the fold. Adjust the stitch length so that the stitches are approximately ⅛" to ³⁄₁₆" apart. If the background fabric tends to pucker, stabilize it with plastic-coated freezer paper or commercial stabilizer before sewing. Stitch the appliqués to the background. Press the block, using only a warm iron, since the thread will melt if pressed with a hot iron.

Machine-Appliqué Strategies

The diagrams below show how to stitch around some tricky areas. The dots indicate pivot points. Stop stitching at these points. With needle in fabric, raise the presser foot and pivot the fabric. When working with shapes like those in diagrams 5 and 6, taper the stitch width before and after the pivot point.

1. Outside Curve   2. Inside Curve   3. Inside Corner   4. Outside Corner   5. Tapered Point   6. Cleft or V

Learn These Machine-Appliqué Skills While Making a Country Angel Block

🏠 preparing patterns for satin-stitched machine appliqué   🏠 layering and fusing appliqués to background
🏠 satin-stitching appliqués by machine

Materials:

11½" background square
¼ yard green plaid
⅛ yard red print
4" square muslin
6" square gold print
Machine-appliqué supplies (listed on page 186)

Finished Block Size: *11" square*

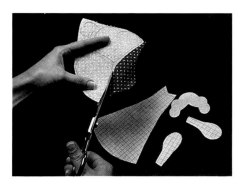

1. Trace patterns on paper for master pattern. (See page 135.) Draw dashed lines for underlap allowances on all pieces that fit under others. For a complex design such as Country Angel, fuse pieces wrong side up on pattern tracing

to assemble complete design before flipping design over and fusing it to background. Always give some thought to order in which to fuse pieces so that they will be placed correctly in finished design. In general, number pattern pieces from foreground to background, as shown.

Trace pattern pieces, including underlap allowances, onto paper side of paper-backed fusible webbing. Group pattern pieces according to fabric that they will be fused to. Roughly cut out each grouping of pattern pieces.

2. Following manufacturer's directions, fuse webbing to wrong side of appropriate fabrics and cut out pieces.

3. Remove paper backing from pieces. (Save paper backing from large pattern piece, such as angel's dress, to use as press cloth.) Use traced master pattern to position pieces. Place all pieces in numbered order on pattern with webbing side up and fabric side against pattern or other pieces.

For angel, begin by placing hair and then face on master pattern. Using paper press cloth to protect iron, fuse face to hair. Next, place arms and then hands on pattern; fuse together. Continue

adding pieces in order until entire angel is fused together. Then flip assembled design over onto square and fuse it to fabric.

4. Stabilize background fabric by ironing piece of plastic-coated freezer paper or by pinning piece of commercial stabilizer to wrong side of fabric.

Zigzag-stitch (satin-stitch) pieces to background fabric. Most of the width of the zigzag stitch should be on fabric piece. The remainder should go just beyond raw edge of piece onto background. Use thread colors to match each fabric piece. Stitch all pieces that use the same color thread at once; then, change thread color to match next fabric and stitch those pieces, and so forth. When stitching is complete, remove stabilizer from behind background fabric.

Practice Your Appliqué Skills While Making *Julie's Baltimore Basket* Wall Quilt

Julie Hart of Des Moines, Iowa, made our Baltimore-style quilt entirely by machine. The format is somewhat simpler, and the colors are lighter, than the originals. She used blindstitch; invisible machine appliqué for the basket, flowers, and outer border; machine patchwork for the sawtooth border; and free-motion machine quilting for the stippling and other designs.

Materials:
4 yards white-on-white print
1 yard pink
½ yard green
¼ yard each reds, yellows, blues, and purples for flowers

3¼ yards white for backing and binding
Tracing paper

Finished Center Block: *20½" square*
Finished Quilt Size: *52" square*

Quilt Diagram

1. From white print, cut one 21" square. Cut two 16⅞" squares for setting triangles. Cut each square in half diagonally to make four triangles. Cut two 8½" x 37" and two 8½" x 54" outer borders. From pink, cut two 1½" x 21" and two 1½" x 23"

inner borders. (All these measurements include seam allowances, and outer borders include a little extra length. Trim them to exact length when you add them to quilt top.)

2. To create basket, cut ⅞"-wide bias strips from pink. Fold strips in thirds, as described on page 137 in "First Steps in Hand Appliqué." Refer to basket pattern on page 191 for placement of strips. Trace design on background fabric, or make master pattern on tracing paper and lay it on block to position and weave strips. Prepare and appliqué basket base and rim.

3. Prepare flowers for appliquéng, using the technique of your choice. (Patterns are below and on page 191.) Arrange flowers on background square, as shown in Quilt Diagram and photo or create your own arrangement. Appliqué all pieces to square.

4. Add narrow pink borders. (Quilt should measure 23" square, including seam allowances.)

5. Join setting triangles to quilt. (Quilt should measure 32½" square, including seam allowances.)

6. For sawtooth border, make total of 68 pink-and-white 2" finished triangle-squares. (Use either of the quick-piecing methods for triangle-squares, described in "First Steps in Quick-Cutting and Quick-Piecing" on page 104, or make

template for right-angle triangle with 2" finished legs for traditional patchwork piecing.) Join sawtooth border to sides.

7. To join 8½"-wide outer borders to quilt, trim two shorter borders to size and join to top and bottom of quilt. Trim and sew the two longer borders to remaining sides.

8. For best results, make master pattern for appliquéd borders. Use photocopy machine to enlarge border repeat below. Trace placement lines on fabric or make tracing paper master pattern to lay over or under fabric to position design elements. Extend vine lines into each corner to form loop, as shown in Quilt Diagram.

9. Use 18" square of green to make 275" of 1"-wide continuous bias for vine. Fold bias strip in thirds, as described earlier, to prepare vine for appliqué. Appliqué vine, buds, leaves, and flowers on borders.

10. Layer quilt top, batting, and backing; baste. Machine-quilt.

11. Bind quilt with white print. (See "Finishing Your Quilts," page 92, for instructions on binding.)

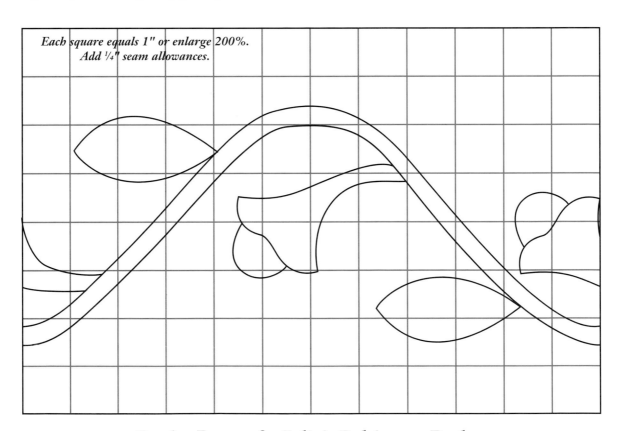

Each square equals 1" or enlarge 200%. Add ¼" seam allowances.

Border Repeat for **Julie's Baltimore Basket**
(Three repeats for each side.)

Julie's Baltimore Basket Patterns

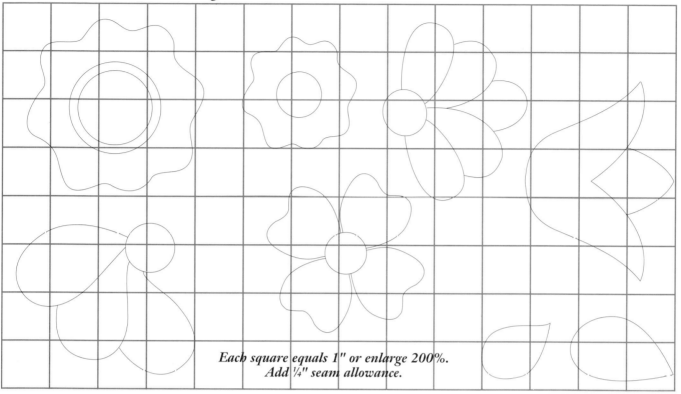

Each square equals 1" or enlarge 200%.
Add ¼" seam allowance.

Half of Design

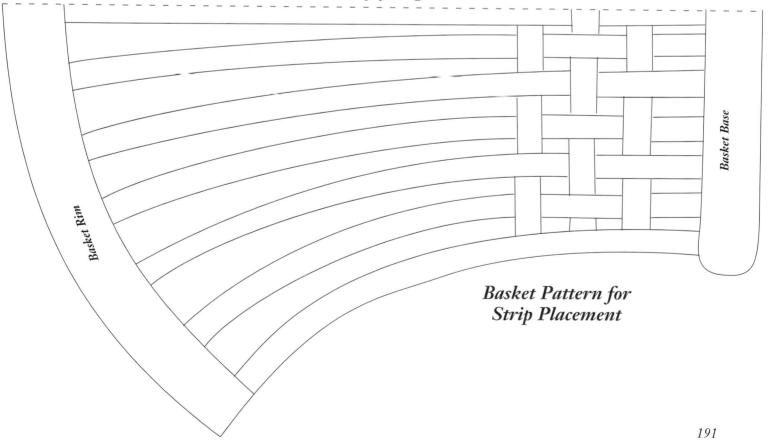

Basket Rim

Basket Base

Basket Pattern for Strip Placement

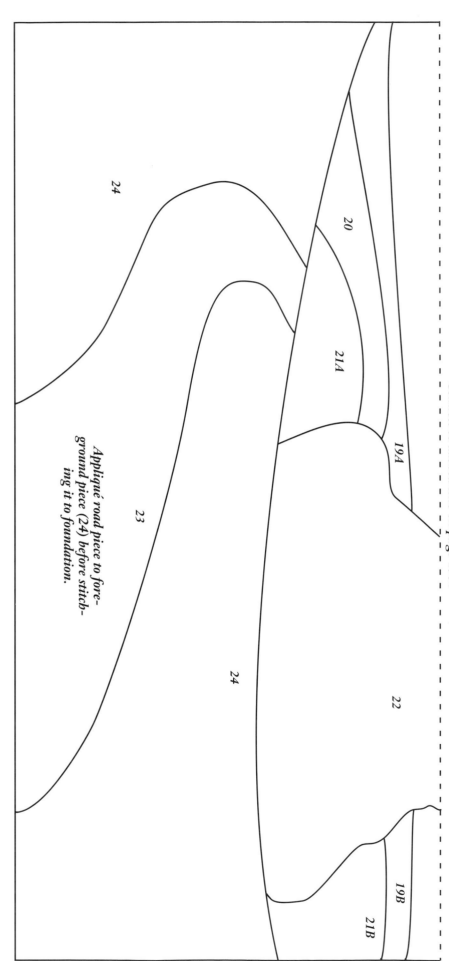

24

20

21A

19A

Applié road piece to foreground piece (24) before stitching it to foundation.

23

24

22

19B

21B

Connect to dashed line on page 193.

Triple Tulip Patterns

Add ¼" seam allowance.

Jo's Multi-Layered Landscape

(Bottom Section)

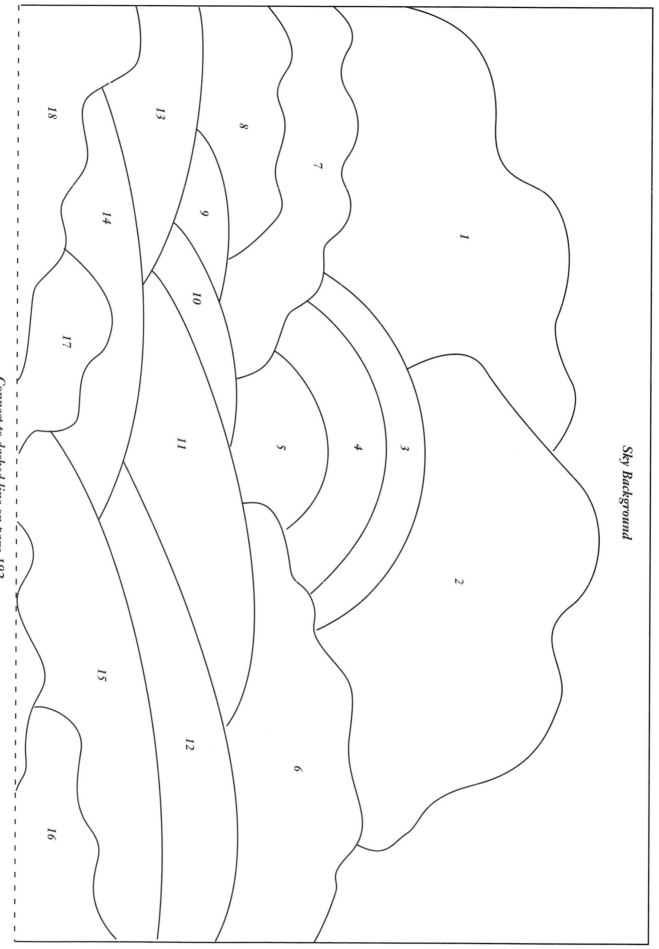

Jo's Multi-Layered Landscape
(Top Section)

Sky Background

Connect to dashed line on page 192.

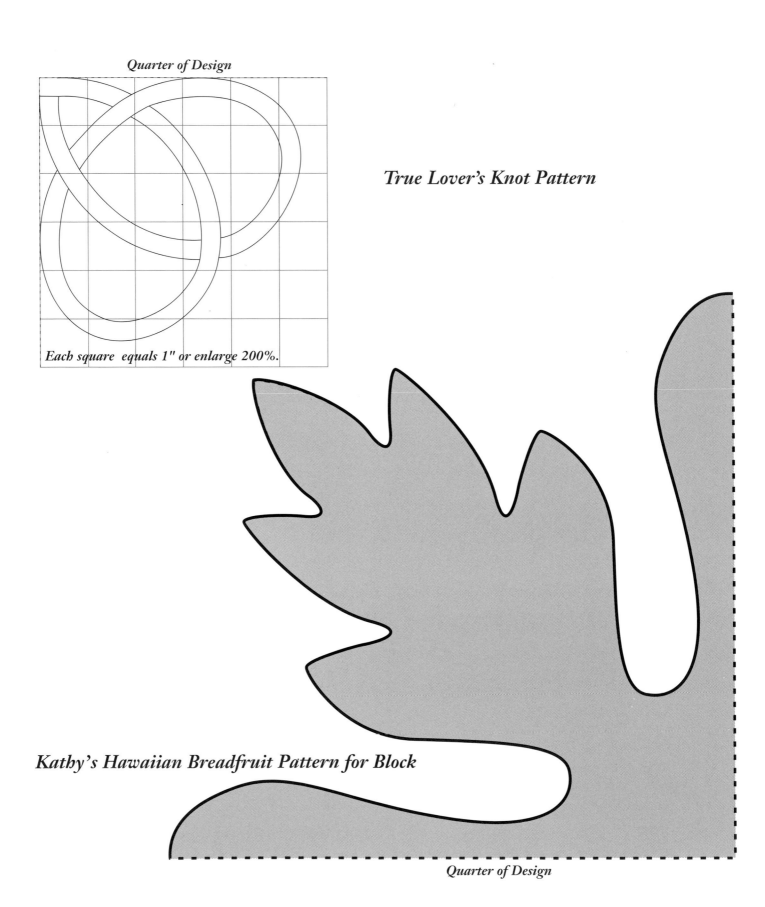

Quarter of Design

Each square equals 1" or enlarge 200%.

True Lover's Knot Pattern

Kathy's Hawaiian Breadfruit Pattern for Block

Quarter of Design

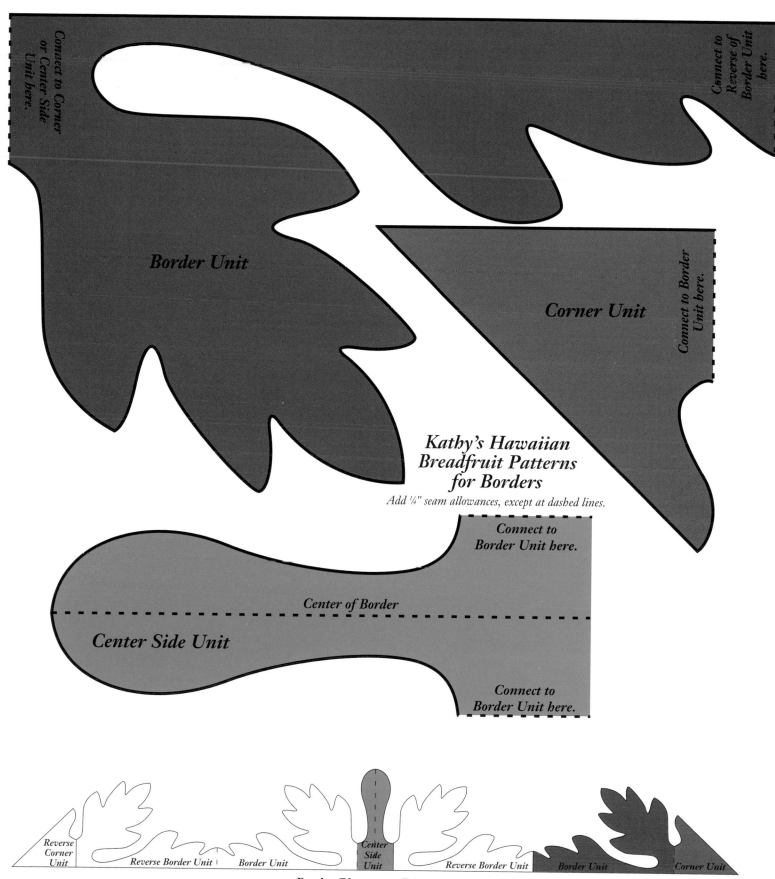

Connect to Corner or Center Side Unit here.

Connect to Reverse of Border Unit here.

Border Unit

Connect to Border Unit here.

Corner Unit

Kathy's Hawaiian Breadfruit Patterns for Borders

Add ¼" seam allowances, except at dashed lines.

Connect to Border Unit here.

Center of Border

Center Side Unit

Connect to Border Unit here.

Reverse Corner Unit

Reverse Border Unit

Border Unit

Center Side Unit

Reverse Border Unit

Border Unit

Corner Unit

Border Placement Diagram

Beyond Basic Settings and Borders

*I*n the earlier chapter "Basic Settings and Borders for Quilts," we described the simplest options for combining blocks and borders to make a quilt. In this chapter, you'll see how unique settings and customized borders often elevate a quilt to masterpiece status.

Beyond Basic Settings and Borders

This chapter takes you beyond the basic straight and diagonal sets to explore some less commonly used quilt settings. A carefully chosen quilt layout can transform otherwise ordinary blocks, such as the Nine-Patch or Sawtooth Star blocks, into an extraordinary quilt. Finally, we'll discuss ways to enhance the blocks with sashing and sashing squares.

Borders

Today's quilters tend to reserve appliqué borders for appliqué quilts and patchwork borders for patchwork quilts. Many nineteenth-century quilts, however, indicate a different philosophy, with borders that are more often a departure than a repetition of the inner quilt techniques and patterns. Also, quilters of the past apparently were not too concerned about turning all four corners of the border the same way. Many antique quilts boast four completely different corners! Study photos of pre-1900 quilts, and you will be amazed by the spontaneity of design embodied there. You can find inspiration for borders in old quilts, and then use the modern conveniences of graph paper and a calculator to customize these designs for your own quilts.

An important first step before sewing any borders to your quilt is to take accurate measurements. Find side dimensions by measuring through the quilt center, not along the edges, since they may have stretched. Or figure what the dimensions should be mathematically, based on the size of the pieces used. Borders should fit the sides of your quilt. And think of the corners as separate units, even though they may have been cut as part of the borders.

Appliqué Borders

Appliqué borders on floral quilts usually reflect the floral motifs of the blocks that make up the inner quilt. Flowers and leaves may be unconnected or arranged along undulating or interwoven vines. Swag borders with bows, flowers, or other connecting motifs are another popular style.

When designing an appliqué border, begin by dividing the border lengths into sections of equal size or repeats. If the quilt is square, you will need only one repeat. If the quilt is rectangular, you may need one repeat for the width and another for the length. (Follow the instructions in the tip box, Determining Repeat Units for Curved Border Designs, on the next page to establish repeat units for an appliqué border.)

Some of the most popular appliqué border designs are based on either a continuous flowing vine or a swag motif. (See next page.) Both types are based on repeat units. Once you have established the repeat units, the next step is to draw a curve that fits within the repeat length and plan a compatible corner. (Follow the instructions in the tip box, Drawing Repeat Curves, on page 200.)

When you complete the border design to your satisfaction, make templates and prepare appliqués as for other appliqué projects. For some designs, appliqué the borders before you sew them to the quilt; for continuous curve designs, sew the borders to the quilt before appliquéing.

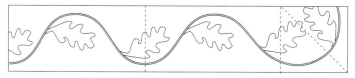

For a flowing vine border, as shown, position vine along the undulating repeat curve. Experiment with arrangements of design elements such as leaves or flowers on a piece of tracing paper with an undulating curve drawn on it. In a similar manner, plan a compatible corner design.

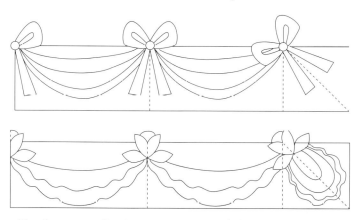

To plan a swag border, experiment with design possibilities on a piece of tracing paper with the basic swag curve drawn on it. The appliqués in your blocks may also suggest variations to these basic borders.

Determining Repeat Units for Curved Border Designs

Follow the steps below to figure a repeat-unit length for an undulating curved border design. This method works for flowing vine appliqué designs, undulating curved border quilting designs, and cable quilting designs.

1. Multiply finished border width times 2 (12" x 2 = 24") to determine approximate repeat-unit length.

2. Ignore corner for now. Treat it as a separate design unit (a square) even if you want design to flow continuously around the quilt. Divide approximate repeat-unit length into inner quilt length (90" ÷ 24" = 3.75) and into inner quilt width (66" ÷ 24" = 2.75).

To find number of repeats for each border, round-off fractions to nearest whole number. Since 3.75 will round-off to 4, the sample quilt will have four repeats along length; 2.75 rounds-off to 3 so the sample quilt will have three repeats along width.

3. To determine the exact size of repeats, divide number of repeats into inner quilt dimensions (90" ÷ 4 repeats = 22½" and 66" ÷ 3 repeats = 22"). Side borders will have four 22½" repeats, and top and bottom borders will have three 22" repeats.

If repeats seem too dissimilar, try multiplying border width times 3 instead of 2. (See step 1.)

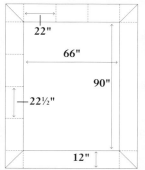

Length Repeat:
12" x 22½"

Width Repeat:
12" x 22"

Finished quilt is 90" x 114".

Drawing Repeat Curves

To design curved-border motifs, cut a rectangle from tracing paper equal to repeat-unit length and border width.

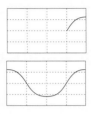

Undulating Curve. Fold rectangle in fourths vertically and horizontally to form drawing guidelines. Draw gentle curve in upper right portion; then fold paper to trace curve onto other sections of paper. Use this basic undulating curve to plan flowing appliqué or border quilting designs.

Cable Designs. Fold same rectangle for undulating curve in half lengthwise and trace undulating curve, drawn in first step, on it.

Swag Borders or Scalloped Edges. To create curve for swag borders or scalloped edges, fold rectangle in half widthwise. Draw curve on one half; trace curve onto other half for swag line from which other lines can be drawn.

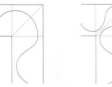
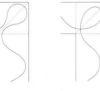

C Corner	*Horseshoe Corner*	*Looped Corner*	*Cable Corner*

Border Corners. To work out corner motif that will combine with the rest of the border, cut piece of tracing paper the size of finished corner square. Fold square in half diagonally and draw curve; then, trace curve onto other half. When working with corner design, remember that the repeats may be slightly different for quilt length and width. Therefore, you may need to "fudge" the corner design slightly to make it meet. These diagrams show some corners that work well with curved-border designs.

Pieced Borders

Pieced borders are patchwork units joined into strips. The patchwork units may be based on squares, triangle-squares, diamonds, or other geometric shapes. On pages 202 and 203 are diagrams of some common pieced borders that are our personal favorites.

Choose a pieced border for your quilt that is compatible with the patchwork shapes used in the inner quilt. For the *Snowball* quilt on page 205, we chose pieced borders based on squares.

You can look to old quilts for inspiration, or you can design your own pieced border. Begin by looking for elements within the patchwork blocks that will create an interesting design when joined in a long strip. If the block is a fairly simple one, you may want to repeat a smaller version of it in the border strip.

Each patchwork unit in a pieced border is based on a repeat unit. For the borders to fit, the quilt dimensions must be evenly divisible by the repeat unit measurement. For example, if your quilt measures 80" square, you could use a pieced border with 2"-, 2½"-, 4"-, 5"-, 8"-, or 10"-long repeat units.

To maintain pleasing proportions in your quilt and to make planning pieced borders easier, keep other quilt elements, such as sashing, mathematically compatible with the repeat unit you have chosen.

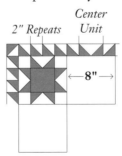

2" Repeats   *Center Unit*

←— 8" —→

Straight-Set Quilts. Figuring repeat units for straight-set quilts is easiest if you use a border repeat unit measurement equal to the drafting-grid division of the block or a multiple of the grid division. (Drafting-grid divisions are explained on pages 44 through 46 in "Drafting Patchwork Blocks and Adding to Patchwork Skills.")

The 8" Sawtooth Star block shown above is a Four-Patch block; each drafting grid division is 2". The Sawtooth border is based on 2" repeat units sewn to a quilt with straight-set blocks. Since the repeat units are equal to the grid division of the blocks, border seams line up with the seams that the join blocks.

Diagonally Set Quilts.

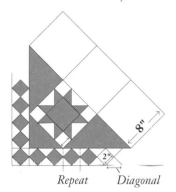

Repeat   Diagonal

Pieced borders for diagonally set quilts are easiest to plan if you use a repeat-unit length equal to the diagonal measurement of a drafting-grid division of the block or a multiple of this. Each repeat unit for the diagonally set quilt shown is equal to the diagonal measurement of the 2" grid division.

Choosing a border that lends itself to diagonally set quilts also simplifies planning. Look for borders that have the long side of triangles to the outside of the border. In this pieced border, each triangle has legs (short sides) equal to the drafting-grid division of the blocks (2"). Since the blocks are Four-Patch blocks, the long side of each triangle is equal to one-fourth of the diagonal measurement of the blocks.

Spacer Borders.

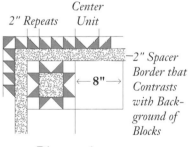

2" Repeats — *Center Unit* — *2" Spacer Border that Contrasts with Background of Blocks*

Diagram 1

Spacer borders are plain borders that separate pieced borders from the main body of the quilt. Spacer borders can be single borders, as shown in Diagrams 1 and 2, or multiple borders, as shown in Diagram 3. If the border repeat-unit measurement is based on the drafting grid of the patchwork blocks, use a spacer border width that is the same dimension as the repeat unit, as shown in Diagrams 1 and 2, or a multiple of the repeat unit, as shown in Diagram 3.

If the border repeat-unit measurement is not mathematically compatible with the dimensions of the quilt, use spacer borders to increase the size of the quilt so that the repeat unit divides evenly into the quilt dimensions. You

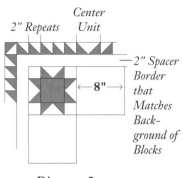

2" Repeats — *Center Unit* — *2" Spacer Border that Matches Background of Blocks*

Diagram 2

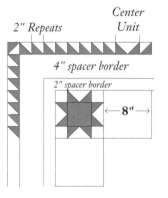

2" Repeats — *Center Unit* — *4" spacer border* — *2" spacer border*

Diagram 3

may need to use one width of spacer borders on the quilt sides and a different width on the top and bottom of the quilt to achieve the quilt size you need. Cutting uneven-width spacer borders from fabric that matches the background of the blocks will make the difference in border widths less noticeable.

Using a spacer border between the quilt and the pieced border defines the quilt and border areas. A spacer border made from fabric that contrasts with the background fabric of the blocks accentuates the separation, as shown in Diagram 1. Borders made from fabric that matches the background of the blocks makes both designs appear to float, as shown in Diagram 2.

Directional Borders.

Some patchwork borders flow in a particular direction. (See page 202.) The diamonds in the spiral border and the triangles in the Goose Chase border move counter-clockwise. The Sawtooth borders are also directional. Small dark triangles move either to the left or to the right side of the border.

Since you will want the borders to look the same on all four sides of the quilt and turn the corners smoothly, advance planning is especially necessary for directional borders. For some borders, such as the spiral border, sew a border to each side of the quilt and then to the top and bottom to keep the border flowing around the quilt.

Using this approach for the Goose Chase border would not result in pleasing corners. The best approach for this type of directional border is to plan a special corner unit that is compatible with the borders.

Some directional borders, such as the Shaded-Triangles border and Sawtooth borders, are easiest to turn at the corners if the border changes direction at the center of the quilt sides. Use a specially designed center unit that is two repeat units long, as seen in the Shaded-Triangles border, to change the direction of the border. Because of the special center unit, an even number of total border repeats should be used on each side of the center unit.

Directional Pieced Borders

Spiral Border

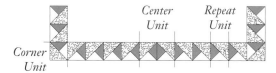

Shaded-Triangles Border

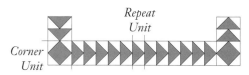

**Goose Chase Border with
Border Corner Squares**

**Goose Chase Border with Corners
that Don't Turn Smoothly**

Borders Based on Squares

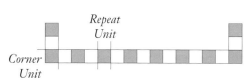

Alternating Square Border

Checkerboard Border

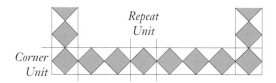

Squares on Point Border

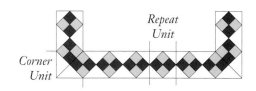

Squares on Point Border Variation

Borders Based on Triangle-Squares

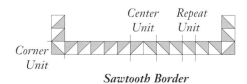

Sawtooth Border

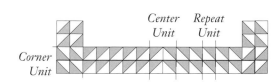

Double Sawtooth Border

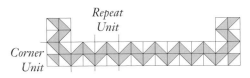

Zigzag Border

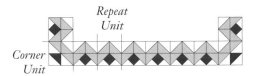

Zigzag Border Variation

Diamond Borders

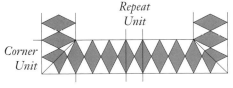

Diamond Border

Piecing Unit

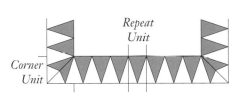

Dogtooth Border

Piecing Unit

Using Border Prints and Striped Fabrics for Mitered Borders

Large-scale striped fabrics with or without additional printed motifs, sometimes called border-printed fabrics, make effective borders for some quilts—the elaborately printed stripes form decorative frames. Borders cut from these fabrics look best when the prints and stripes are matched at the seams, and the corner seams are mitered. The *Mariner's Compass Medallion* wall quilt, shown on page 209, features borders cut from border-print fabric.

Matching border stripes and prints at the corners of a square quilt is relatively simple: Place borders of the same width on each side with the printed motif centered. Accomplishing attractive border-print corners on a rectangular quilt is more challenging. Follow these instructions for success:

1. Measure quilt and write down dimensions for width and length. Mark center point on each side with a pin. Cut print/stripe borders approximately 10" longer than you would normally cut mitered borders.

2. Choose a printed motif on border and center it on long sides of quilt. Determine needed border length by measuring from each side of center motif to quilt ends. Draw end point and a 45° angle line on

border, as described in mitering instructions in "Basic Settings and Borders for Quilts," page 50. Repeat for other side border. Sew borders to sides of quilt, matching center and end points. Press under border ends along marked diagonal lines but wait to trim off excess fabric.

3. Working on a flat surface, center and lay a border along top edge of quilt and position border ends under side borders. Take up or pull fabric at center of top border until you arrive at a pleasing design at quilt corners. Make sure you are pulling up equal amounts from each end of fabric strip so that corners will match. Mark end points of corners on inner edge of border. Fold a pleat or several small pleats in border to take up excess fabric; stitch pleats and trim, leaving ¼" seam allowances. (Disruption of design caused by stitching pleats will be less noticeable than corners that don't match.) Repeat for bottom border.

4. Measure borders to be sure they are correct length. Stitch borders to top and bottom of quilt, matching centers and corner points. Miter corner seams.

Diagonal Sets

Floating the blocks, zigzag, and big corners are all variations of the basic diagonal set. These quilt layouts require setting triangles and, in some cases, setting squares to fill in around and between the blocks. (You may find it helpful to review instructions on cutting setting triangles and squares for diagonal sets on pages 54 and 55.)

Floating the Blocks

The corners of the outer blocks in this Nine-Patch quilt do not reach to the edges of the border. Blocks appear to float on the background because the setting triangles are larger than ordinarily necessary and they overlap.

To quick-cut oversized setting triangles, measure one block diagonally from corner to corner. Cut squares that are at least 2" to 3" larger than this diagonal measurement. Cut each square diagonally from corner to corner in both directions to make four setting triangles.

To quick-cut oversized corner triangles, divide diagonal measurement of block in half. Cut two squares at least 2" to 3" larger than this measurement. Cut each square in half to make two triangles. These triangles will have the two short sides on straight of grain.

Sew blocks and setting triangles together in diagonal rows. Determine how much you want the quilt to float, and trim excess setting and corner triangles acordingly, allowing ¼" for seam allowances. Setting triangles will not finish as triangles but rather as irregular polygons.

Zigzag Set

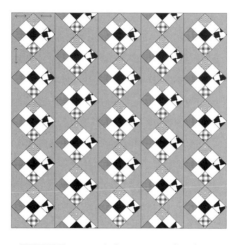

Row Assembly Diagram

Other names for the zigzag set are Picket Fence and Streak of Lightning. Blocks are set on point and arranged in vertical rows with large and small setting triangles. Rows that begin and end with full blocks alternate with rows that begin and end with half blocks. Offsetting blocks makes the setting triangles form a zigzag path between blocks. Choose blocks that work well as half blocks.

To set blocks, cut large setting triangles with long sides on straight of grain and small setting triangles with short sides on straight of grain. (See Row Assembly Diagram above.) Sew them together in vertical rows. For rows that begin and end with half blocks, use full blocks at ends of rows and trim them after rows are assembled.

Big Corners Set

An alternative to the traditional arrangement of diagonally set blocks is one that results in extra-large triangles at quilt corners. These can either be cut as large triangles (upper left in diagram) or pieced from two side setting triangles (upper right in diagram).

Strip or Bar Sets

The blocks in strip- or bar-set quilts are usually arranged in vertical, rather than horizontal, rows. The rows are separated by sashing that defines the rows. Designs, such as the *Tree Everlasting* quilt and the Flying Geese pattern shown, depend on a bar set for their identity. Quilt blocks, such as those in the Nine-Patch quilt shown, can also be set in a bar set.

To set quilt blocks in this manner, arrange them on point in vertical rows like the full-block rows in a zigzag set quilt. All rows begin and end with full blocks.

Tree Everlasting

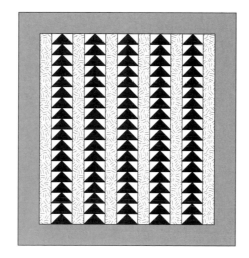

Flying Geese

Nine-Patch Strippy

Two Block Sets

Interesting quilts can be created by alternating patchwork blocks with other patchwork blocks, rather than with solid squares. The two blocks interact with each other to create secondary designs. Irish Chain and Snowball are two familiar quilt patterns of this type.

Irish Chain

Snowball

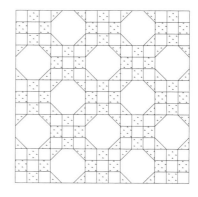

Piecing Alternate Blocks from Triangles

Other two-block quilt settings are created by alternating the main blocks with simple patchwork blocks made of either two or four contrasting triangles joined into squares.

Nine-Patch blocks, alternated with two-triangle blocks, form a Barn Raising setting. To keep set symmetrical, have an even number of blocks in the horizontal and vertical rows.

Two-Triangle Alternate Blocks. Use traditional Log Cabin setting variations by alternating blocks with blocks made from one light and one dark triangle.

Nine-Patch blocks, alternated with two-triangle blocks, form a Straight Furrow setting.

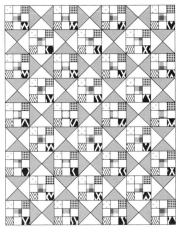

Four Triangle or Hourglass

Four-Triangle Alternate Blocks. Four triangles sewn together form a setting block that combines well with many different blocks to create a special setting. Two different fabrics or a variety of fabrics can be used for the triangles. When light and dark triangles are adjacent to one another, these simple blocks are sometimes called Hourglass.

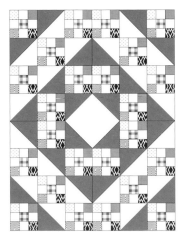

Barn Raising

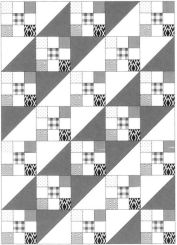

Straight Furrow

Integrating Two Different Blocks

Distinctive designs can be made by alternating blocks of two different patterns and integrating them through careful fabric placement. When choosing blocks to integrate, look for blocks that have compatible joining points. Usually these blocks will be in the same pattern-drafting category. For example, the two blocks shown are four-patch blocks that can be drafted on a 16-square grid.

To plan this type of quilt, make a line drawing of the two blocks. Then, draw at least a nine-block arrangement of the two blocks, switching positions of the blocks from row to row. Experiment with shading to make blocks flow into each other and lose their identity as separate blocks.

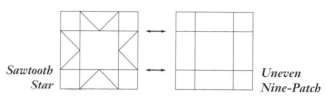

Sawtooth Star   *Uneven Nine-Patch*

Look for blocks with joining points (see arrows).

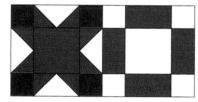

Shading Blocks. This choice of values does not take advantage of integration possibilities, as shown.

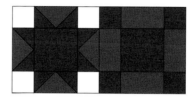

Here the value placement allows the blocks to flow into each other, as shown.

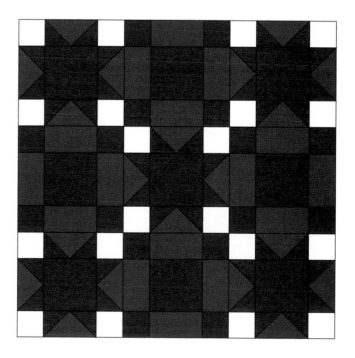

Creative Use of Fabric and Color

Arrange fabrics and colors creatively to make a distinctive quilt that is viewed more as a whole than as an arrangement of blocks.

Robbing-Peter-to-Pay-Paul Set

Alternating the same patchwork block in opposite or positive-negative colorations gives the impression that the leftover pieces from one block have been used for piecing the other block. These are often called Robbing-Peter-to-Pay-Paul quilts and are usually made from just two fabrics.

Breaking-Out-of-the-Block Set

Because they are pieced individually, we often think of blocks as separate units, without considering the design possibilities we can create if we place the blocks next to each other and shade the quilt as a whole. The stars appear in the *Tessellated Stars* wall quilt, shown on page 147, because of the different fabric arrangement from block to block.

To explore this kind of option, make a line drawing of your quilt without any shading. You will need at least a two-by-two or three-by-three block layout to see the design possibilities. Make several copies of the quilt drawing. Look for the shapes that flow into other shapes or that create interesting secondary designs. Use colored pencils to define the areas and experiment with the design possibilities.

The shaded diagrams that follow show an original block, Shoo Fly Star, with all blocks shaded identically and with the quilt shaded as a whole.

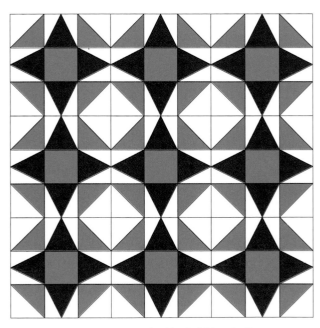

Shoo Fly Star Blocks Shaded Identically

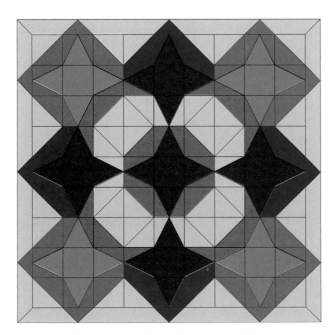

Shoo Fly Star Quilt Shaded as a Whole

Allover Sets

One-patch quilts and single-block quilts do not require a set because they are not pieced in the block format.

One-Patch Quilts

One-patch quilts repeat the same shape, such as a hexagon, diamond, or square, for the entire quilt. *Diamond Jubliee*, shown below, is an example of a one-patch quilt.

Single-Block Quilts

Some quilts are one large block, rather than several smaller blocks arranged in a set. The *Lone Star* wall quilt, shown below, is an example of a single-block quilt.

Medallion Quilt

An allover quilt set that deserves mention is the medallion format, also called framed center, framed medallion, and central medallion. These terms all refer to a quilt that has a central motif surrounded by multiple borders. The borders may be one piece, appliquéd, pieced, or a combination of techniques. The *Mariner's*

Compass Medallion wall quilt at left combines a central patchwork design, striped borders, and a patchwork border. (Instructions for quilt are on page 164.) *Julie's Baltimore Basket*, on page 189, features a basket of flowers as the central motif, a sawtooth patchwork border, and a flowing appliqué vine outer border.

Square Format

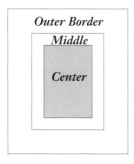

Rectangular Format

Most medallion quilts consist of three main design areas: a center section, a middle section, and an outer (border) section. (See diagrams.) The three sections should be in pleasing proportion to each other.

The center section contains the important central motif and the area surrounding it. The size of this section is generally one fourth the size of the top of the bed. For a wall quilt, the size of the center section is approximately one fourth of the total area of the combined center and middle sections.

The center of a medallion is a good place to use a complex, relatively difficult pattern since you only have to make one block. Patchwork designs such as Lone Star and Mariner's Compass are good choices for a central motif. They are complex enough to hold your attention, and the pointed edges draw the eye outward toward the rest of the quilt.

The middle section is the area between the center and the outer border sections. On a rectangular bed quilt, this section fills out the quilt to the edge of the mattress.

The outer (border) section of a medallion gives the quilt a sense of completeness. On a bed quilt, this section drops over the sides.

A working diagram is essential for a medallion quilt. The information and diagrams that follow will give you guidelines for designing a medallion quilt.

If you want to make a rectangular quilt but are beginning with a square block, elongate the quilt in the center section where it will be less noticeable than in the middle or outer sections. One way to do this is to begin with a square block and add a triangle to each side to set the

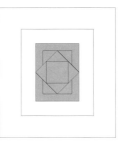

Whole Quilt

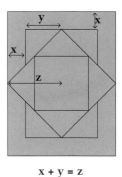

x + y = z

Medallion

Working Diagrams for a Medallion Quilt

square on point. (See Working Diagrams for a Medallion Quilt.) Then measure diagonally from corner to corner across the large square on point. (One half of this measurement is Z.)

Decide how much longer you want the center to be; one half of this amount is X. Subtract X from Z to determine Y; cut four triangles that have legs Y-inches long and sew them to the center. Cut borders that are X inches wide and sew them to the center. The center section will then be two times X longer than it is wide.

In a successful medallion quilt, all of the various elements of the quilt should appear to be a natural part of the design. This is called unity. Unity is achieved through repetition of colors, fabrics, design elements, and borders. In other words, each fabric, design element, and border should be used at least two or more times in your quilt. Work from the center section outward, repeating the fabrics and shapes used in the center.

Unity of color is established in the *Mariner's Compass Medallion* wall quilt on page 209 by maintaining a rust-and-blue color scheme and repeatedly using the various border fabrics. Unity of design is established by the Dogtooth border pattern that repeats the diamond shapes in the central Mariner's Compass.

Sashing Variations

Unpieced sashing and sashing squares, such as those shown, separate and define the individual blocks, but in a rather ordinary way. Piecing the sashing squares, sashing, or both adds a little variety to your setting.

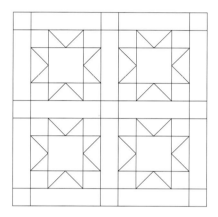

*Plain Sashing and
Sashing Squares*

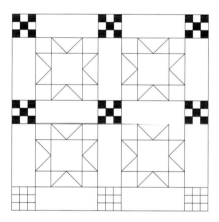

*Use a simple block such as Nine-Patch
for sashing squares.*

Pieced Sashing Squares

Draw attention and add interest to sashing squares by replacing them with either a block unit such as Square-within-a-Square, or with simple patchwork blocks, such as Nine-Patch or Shoo Fly.

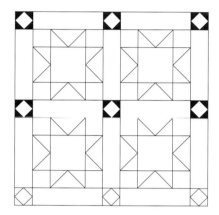

*Square-within-a-Square
Sashing Squares*

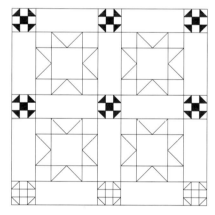

*Use a simple block such as Shoo Fly
for sashing squares.*

Pieced Sashing

Piecing sashing and shading unpieced sashing squares to coordinate with sections of sashing create interesting secondary designs.

Piecing Both Sashing and Sashing Squares

A number of options are available when both the sashing and sashing squares are pieced.

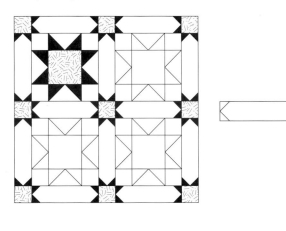

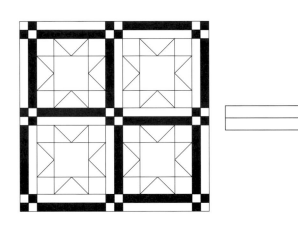

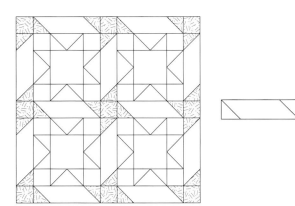

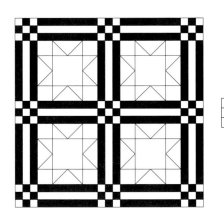

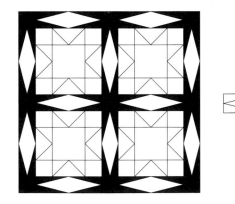

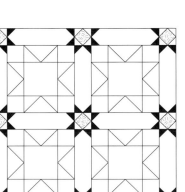

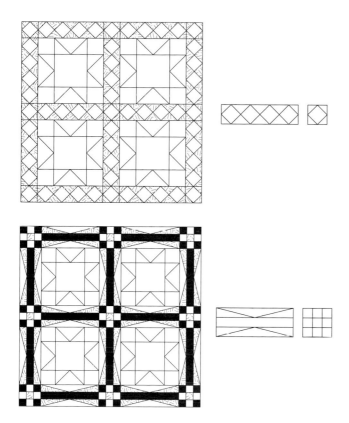

Using a Block as Sashing

Simple pieced blocks, such as Attic Windows and Bright Hopes, can be used for sashing. A search through quilt pattern books should lead you to other blocks that can be employed in this manner.

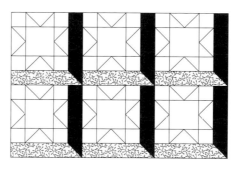

Attic Windows as Sashing

Attic Windows Block

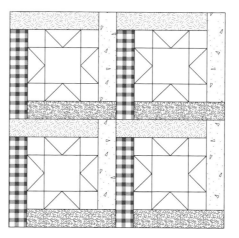

Bright Hopes as Sashing

Bright Hopes Block

Garden Maze Set. Garden Maze is a distinctive quilt setting with pieced sashing. Although there are several ways to create this special setting, the simplest method we have found is shown below. First frame the blocks with narrow strips. Then set them together with pieced sashing that is twice as wide as the narrow framing strips.

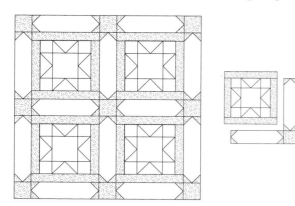

Etcetera Techniques

*O*ver the years, quilters have used their fabrics in ways other than traditional patchwork and appliqué to create coverlets and other items. Often these are not true quilts since they are not quilted. At county or state fairs, such projects are frequently labeled novelty quilts. We have had fun with these techniques ourselves and know many quilters enjoy them, whether they use them in large or in small projects.

Etcetera Techniques

Folded-Star Patchwork

In the late 1970s, when we were novice quilters, the folded star, also called LaGrange Trivet, was one of the mini-fads that came along. At that time, we loved making small items we could give as gifts, and the folded star was perfect for that. We have set them into tote bags and into the backs of vests.

The instructions that follow are for an easy trivet, 5"–6"-diameter, to use as a table accessory. Use 100% cotton for easy pressing and select fabrics that contrast well so that the radiating stars will be distinct.

Learn the Folded-Star Technique While Making a Folded-Star Trivet

Materials:

¼ yard each of 4 fabrics: 2 light and 2 dark

9" square muslin

Fusible webbing (optional)

1. Cut four 4" squares from light fabric for center star. Cut one 8"-diameter circle from muslin for foundation. (When making a folded star, always choose a fabric for foundation that does not contrast with center fabric.) Cut eight 4" squares from each of remaining three fabrics.

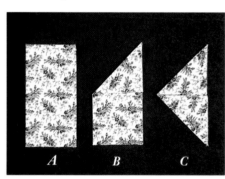

2. Press each square in half with wrong sides facing (A); then, fold top corners in to meet at center of bottom edge to make a triangle with all raw edges at bottom (B and C).

3. Fold foundation circle in fourths and press lightly to form guidelines. Open circle and work with foundation right side up. Position first four triangles so that points meet at center, with folds facing up. Align folded sides of triangles with fold guidelines. Pin triangles in place, or use small pieces of fusible webbing to hold triangles in position. (Follow manufacturer's instructions for pressing webbing to fabric and removing protective paper.)

4. Open folded flaps on one triangle and stitch on fold lines to secure it to base. Repeat for remaining three triangles.

5. Add second row in two sets of four triangles. Place first set of four triangles so that each top point is ½" from center of foundation. Center line (where flaps meet) should be directly over line where two center triagles meet. Stitch in place as in step 4

6. Place second set of four triangles, so that top point of each is also ½" from center, but center lines where flaps meet are directly over center lines of center triangles. Stitch.

7. Add third and fourth rows in same manner, with top points in each row ½" out from top points of previous row.

8. Cut an 8"-diameter backing circle and a 2" x 30" strip of bias for binding from one of the four fabrics. Pin star to backing. Sew binding to top edge of trivet with a ½"-wide seam. Trim excess fabric. Turn bias to back and hand-finish.

Make Smaller Folded Stars for Tree Ornaments

Small folded stars make wonderful Christmas decorations. Use a 5"-diameter base and 2½" squares, and space rows ¼" apart.

Pleated Patchwork

During the Victorian era, scraps of silk, satin, brocade, and lightweight wool were popular fabrics to use for Log Cabin and patchwork Pineapple blocks. Because these fabrics were either fragile, slippery, or stretchy, the blocks were usually pieced on a muslin foundation square. Sometimes, to give these blocks extra dimension, the fabric strips were pleated along the seams. Quilts pieced on a foundation were usually not quilted because of the extra thickness of the foundation. They were simply lined, without any batting, and tied.

Learn These Pleated-Patchwork Skills While Making a Pleated Pineapple Block

🏠 *adapting a pattern for pleated patchwork*
🏠 *transferring pattern to foundation fabric*

🏠 *cutting fabric strips for pleating*
🏠 *piecing a block on a foundation square*

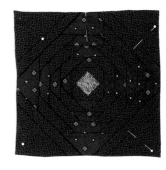

Materials:

⅛ yard green print
¼ yard red print
⅛ yard gold print
9" square muslin*
Tracing paper
Iron-on transfer pen or pencil

Some brands of transfer pens work best on polyester/cotton blends; therefore, refer to pen instructions before purchasing fabric for foundation square.

Finished Block Size: 6" square

1. Trace Pineapple pattern (on page 219) onto tracing paper and complete design. (To adapt your own block drawing for pleated patchwork, place tracing paper over full-size block drawing and draw lines ¼" outside all pattern lines to serve as guides for placement of strips. Your resulting tracing paper pattern will be ½" larger than finished size of block to allow for seam allowances.)

2. Using transfer pen, prepare tracing-paper pattern to use as transfer. Transfer block pattern onto muslin square.

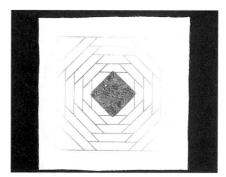

3. Measure center square (1⅞") and cut piece of gold fabric this size for center. Pin square within guidelines on the center of foundation.

To determine width to cut patchwork strips, measure width of strips on pattern (½") and add 1" to allow for seam allowances and pleating. Cut two 1½"-wide strips each from red and green prints, cutting across fabric width.

4. With right sides facing and raw edges aligned, sew red print strip to center square through all layers.

5. Open strip and align raw edge with guideline on foundation and pin. This will form small pleat along seam. Repeat and sew strip to opposite side of center square.

6. Trim ends of strips along guidelines; hold scissors at angle with strip folded against blades and cut. Sew red strips to other two sides of the center square and trim. This completes first round of patchwork.

7. For second round, sew green strips around center in similar manner.

Use red strips for third round of patchwork. Continue alternating colors for rounds of patchwork until all strip locations on foundation are covered with strips.

8. To cut strips for corners, measure corner width on pattern (1¼"). Add 1" for seam allowances and pleating. Cut 2¼"-wide strip from red print.

9. With right sides facing, sew strip to block corners. Form pleat by matching corner markings and trim. When block is complete, trim excess foundation fabric.

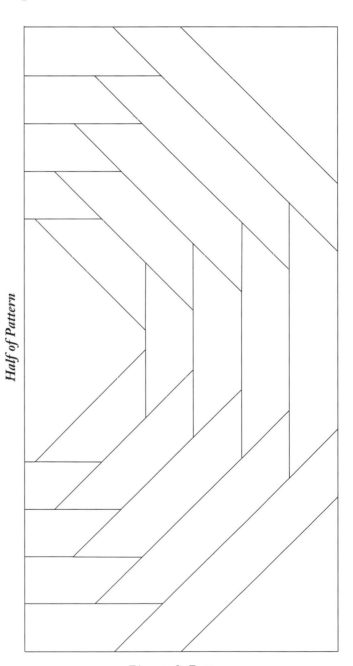

Half of Pattern

Pineapple Pattern

Seminole Patchwork

Deep in the Florida Everglades, the Seminole Indians originated quick-piecing methods to create colorful bands of patchwork to decorate their clothing. They favored solid-colored fabrics, usually in bold, clear colors, arranged in contrasting placements.

The techniques for sewing Seminole patchwork are similar to those used for other quick-piecing methods. Most designs begin with a strip set that is cut into segments. The segments are usually cut either perpendicular to the long edge of the strip set or at a 45° angle. The segments are then sewn together in an offset position to form a long band. Long fabric strips, called edging strips, finish off the edges of the band.

Bands of Seminole patchwork can be used to embellish clothing or to decorate household accessories, such as place mats and towels.

Learn Seminole Patchwork Techniques While Making Sample Bands of Four Basic Designs

Designs 1 and 2 were created from rectangular segments cut perpendicular to long edges of beginning strip set. Designs 3 and 4 were created from angled segments.

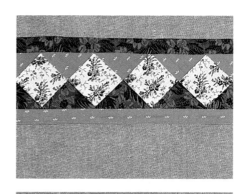

Design 1

Design 2

Materials:
*½ yard each of 3 different fabrics
Rotary cutter, mat, and ruler*

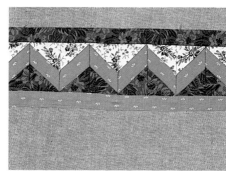

Design 3

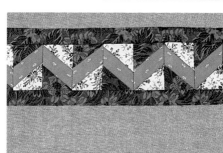

Design 4

Assembly of Designs 1 and 2

1. Determine placement of fabrics in design. For center middle squares, cut one 1¾"-wide strip. Cut one 2"-wide strip from each of the two remaining fabrics.

2. Join strips lengthwise, placing narrower strip in center. Press seam allowances either away from center or to one side.

3. Fold strip set in half widthwise with right sides facing. Cutting through both layers, cut 1¾"-wide segments, perpendicular to long edges of strip set. Divide segments into two groups of ten, one group for Design 1 and one for Design 2.

4. To make Design 1, join 10 segments together into a long strip, offsetting them as shown and matching seams. Sew pairs of segments together; then, stitch pairs to pairs until all pieces are joined. The band will finish approximately 16" long. If you prefer, join all 20 segments into same design to make a longer band that will finish approximately 33" long.

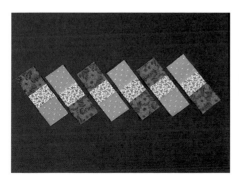

5. To make Design 2, turn every other segment so that colors alternate as shown. Join together as above.

Assembly of Designs 3 and 4

1. Determine placement of fabrics in each design. For center strip, cut two 1"-wide strips. Cut two 1½"-wide strips from each of the remaining two fabrics.

2. Make two identical strip sets by sewing together groups of three strips, placing narrower strip in center. Press seam allowances either away from center or to one side.

3. Place strip sets with right sides facing and with fabrics matching. Cutting through both layers, trim one end at 45° angle. Cut 1½" wide segments, checking to be sure that you are maintaining a 45° angle. Cut nine pairs of segments for Design 3 and nine for Design 4.

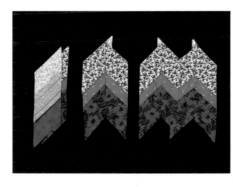

4. To make Design 3, sew pairs of segments together as shown; then, stitch pairs together. Band will finish approximately 18" long. If you prefer, join all 18 pairs into same design to make a longer band that will finish approximately 36" long.

5. To make Design 4, turn every other segment so that colors alternate as shown. Join together as above.

Adding Edging Strips to Bands

Cut 1½"-wide strips across fabric width for edging strips. Press each strip in half lengthwise with wrong sides facing. On right side of Seminole band, mark positioning line for edging strip ¼" outside of proposed sewing line. Align raw edges of edging strip with positioning line. Sew edging strip to band, taking a ¼"-wide seam.

Trim excess patchwork band even with raw edges of edging strip as shown. Press edging strip away from band. Repeat on opposite side. To attach band to finish item, such as place mat, machine-topstitch along outer edge of edging strips.

Sashiko Quilting

Sashiko is a form of Japanese stitchery similar to quilting but more decorative than functional. It is worked with contrasting heavy cotton thread in long running stitches, approximately five stitches per inch, through one or two layers of solid-colored cloth with no batting.

Typical Sashiko designs reflect traditional Japanese motifs, such as family crests and religious symbols, and elements in nature, such as waves, flowers, leaves, and tortoise shells.

Learn These Sashiko-Quilting Techniques While Making Sashiko Napkins

🏠 *transferring Sashiko designs on fabric*   🏠 *beginning and ending threads*   🏠 *stitching*

Materials:

4 solid-colored napkins*
Contrasting heavy cotton thread**
Dressmaker's tracing paper
Crewel needle
Tracing paper

Finished Design Size: *3" square*

*Choose napkins in a medium- to heavyweight fabric with a moderately loose weave, or make your own napkins from chambray, lightweight denim, linen, homespun, or other similar fabric.
**If special Sashiko thread is not available, use embroidery floss, pearl cotton, or cotton crochet thread. Select a thread size that is suitable for your fabric; the thread should be heavy enough to lie on top of the fabric and show up well but not be so coarse that it distorts the fabric weave.

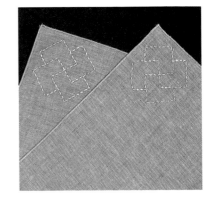

1. Trace Sashiko pattern onto plain tracing paper. The Hiragumi Manji Tsunagi or Flattened Pinwheel design is similar to the American patchwork pattern called Card Trick. Using dressmaker's tracing paper and a dull pencil, transfer design onto one corner of each napkin.

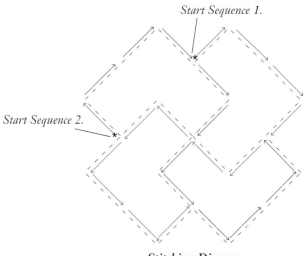

Stitching Diagram

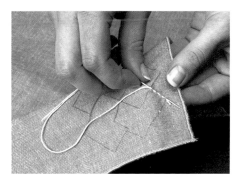

2. Stitch pattern in two steps. Stars on Stitching Diagram indicate the starting points, and arrows indicate direction of stitching.

To secure beginning of thread, insert needle approximately ½" ahead of starting point and make three running stitches, moving toward starting point. Leave short thread tail on top of fabric. Turn needle direction and stitch back over these stitches. Clip thread tail close to fabric after stitches are made.

3. Sashiko stitching is done in continuous lines by loading needle with most or all stitches in one straight section before pulling needle through fabric. Do not pull thread too tightly since some cotton threads will shrink.

A stitch gauge of five to seven stitches per inch is appropriate for most threads and fabrics. Try to keep stitches equal in size to each other and make stitches approximately twice as long as space between them.

4. To end thread, stitch back over last three stitches. Clip thread close to fabric.

Sashiko Stitching Pattern

Crazy Quilting

Crazy quilts are patchwork quilts pieced from odd-shaped pieces of fabric stitched onto a foundation in a seemingly random manner. Although sometimes not apparent at first glance, most crazy quilts are actually small blocks that are joined together.

From 1870 to 1900, crazy quilts reached their peak of popularity. The Victorian crazy quilts created during this period were often made of fancy dressmaking fabrics such as silk, taffeta, brocade, and velvet. The irregular-shaped pieces were stitched to a muslin foundation and embellished with decorative embroidery stitches that showcased the maker's needlework skills. Most Victorian crazy quilts are not true quilts, because they are not actually quilted. The tops are backed and tied at block corners. Crazy quilts are primarily decorative, rather than functional. Most of the delicate fabrics are not washable, and the quilts are not warm because they do not include batting. Above is an example

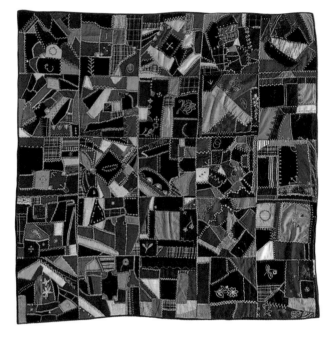

of a typical Victorian crazy quilt.

Wool crazy quilts were the poor but functional cousins of fancy Victorian crazy quilts. They were generally pieced from woolen scraps from men's or women's suits and coats. The individual fabric pieces were often larger than on the fancy quilts. They were sparsely decorated with yarn, which was added more to secure the pieces than to embellish the quilt.

Another variation of crazy quilts, known as crumb quilts, save-all quilts, or piece-as-piece-can quilts, evolved from the popular Victorian crazy quilts. Made from humble, everyday cotton fabrics, these quilts were seldom decorated with embroidery. The tops were almost always layered with batting and backing and quilted. Sometimes the entire surface was made from odd-shaped scraps; in other cases, portions of a traditional patchwork block, such as the diamonds for a LeMoyne Star, were pieced in this manner.

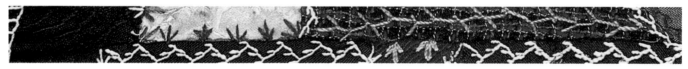

Learn Quilt-as-You-Go Crazy-Quilting Techniques While Making a Sample Rectangle*

Materials:

¼ yard each of several coordinating fabrics

1 (10" x 13") rectangle muslin

1 (10" x 13") rectangle fusible polyester fleece

Embroidery floss in various colors (optional)

Thread in various colors for machine embroidery (optional)

Finished Project Size: 10" x 13"

1. To prepare quilt-as-you-go patchwork foundation, fuse fleece to wrong side of muslin rectangle. (If you do not want to use fleece [batting], omit it and work directly on the foundation fabric.)

From one fabric, cut an odd-shaped piece with straight sides. Center wrong side of piece atop fleece and pin in place. (The right side of piece should be facing you.)

Cut an odd-shaped piece from different fabric. With right sides facing, pin it atop first piece, aligning raw edges along one side. Stitch through all layers, taking ¼" seam. (This joins the pieces and quilts them at the same time.)

2. Open out top (second) piece. Trim pieces so that they are in proportion to each other and have straight sides.

Trim successive pieces so that they are in proportion to first piece.

3. Pin third piece atop first and second pieces and stitch. Trim third piece so edges are in a straight line with first two pieces.

4. In this manner, continue to add patchwork pieces to cover entire foundation. If you accidentally create an L-shaped opening or curved edge that you cannot easily stitch piece to, appliqué piece by hand over open area; then, continue adding pieces as previously described.

5. If you desire, hand- or machine-embroider along seams to embellish piece. Consult general sewing or embroidery book for instructions for decorative hand stitches. The following hand-embroidery stitches are commonly used individually or in combination on crazy quilts: buttonhole, herringbone, chevron, feather, cross, star, fern, and French knot.

Sample can be used for making a baby bib (instructions follow) or a decorative pillow. Use washable fabrics if making baby bib.

Crazy-Quilt Baby Bib

Materials:

1 (10" x 13") crazy-quilted rectangle made from washable fabrics

1 (10" x 13") rectangle for bib lining

45" double-fold purchased bias tape for ties

Finished Bib Size: 9½" x 12½"

1. Fold crazy-quilted rectangle in half lengthwise and cut out small neck opening at center top (approximately 4" in diameter). Round-off rectangle corners.

2. With right sides facing and raw edges aligned, pin bib top to lining rectangle. Stitch top to lining along bib perimeter with a ¼" seam, leaving neck area open. Trim excess lining even with bib and clip around curves. Turn bib right side out through neck opening.

3. Mark center of length of bias tape. Open out folded tape. Match center of opened-out tape to center of bib neck opening. With right sides facing, pin tape along neck opening, aligning crease in tape with ¼" seam line on neck. Excess tape will extend at both ends of neck opening to form ties. Stitch tape to neck opening, stitching along tape fold and through top and lining.

4. Trim excess fabric along neck opening even with edge of tape. Fold tape over raw edges and pin to bib lining. Beginning at one end of tape, topstitch folded edges of tie together. Continue stitching along neck opening to opposite end of tie. If necessary, trim ends of bias ties, so that they are the same length.

Yo-Yo Patchwork

The origins of yo-yo patchwork are unknown, but, judging from the fabrics used in older examples we have seen, the technique has been popular at least since the 1930s. Other names for these novel little fabric circles are powder puffs, pucker puffs, bonbons, and rosettes.

Because the gathered circles (yo-yos) have open spaces between them when joined, yo-yo patchwork is always displayed over an undercloth or spread. Our project, a yo-yo topper for a table, uses 361 (2") yo-yos. Whole coverlets can require over 1,000 yo-yos!

Learn To Make Yo-Yos While Making a Trip-Around-the-World Yo-Yo Topper

Materials:

¾ yard each of 9 fabrics

Quilting thread to match fabrics

Template vinyl or freezer paper

Finished Topper Size:
approximately 40" square

Finished Diameter of 1 Yo-Yo: 2"

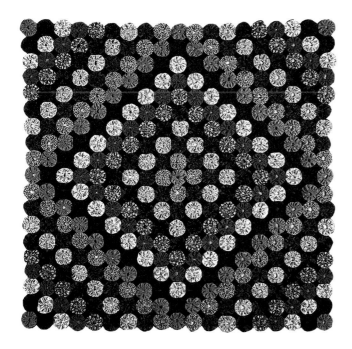

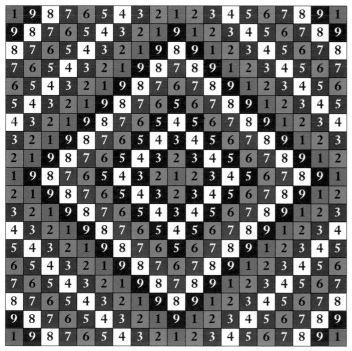

Setting Diagram: Numbers in Setting Diagram represent the nine fabrics.

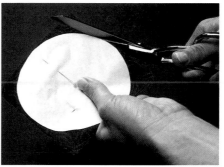

1. Cut 41 (4½") squares from each fabric. Make a 4½"-diameter circle template from vinyl or freezer paper. Cut squares into circles. To cut multiple circles, use template to mark one square; then, stack several squares and cut. Or, press freezer-paper circle to square, stack, and cut. (Freezer-paper template can be re-used.)

2. Turn raw edge of circle ¼" to wrong side and take small running stitches around edge. Use quilting thread or other strong thread that will not break when gathered.

3. Pull thread to gather circle with right side of fabric facing out. Make a knot to hold circle closed. (The gathered side is the front.)

4. Join yo-yos by placing two together front to front. Using thread that blends with fabrics, whipstitch them together on one side. Join yo-yos into rows, and then join rows as shown in Setting Diagram.

Cathedral Window Patchwork

Cathedral Window is a novelty patchwork technique that seems to have been invented in this century. Traditionally, muslin is combined with colored insert squares in an interlocking fashion to make a coverlet. The inserts can be all one fabric or various fabrics. Since Cathedral Window spreads are extremely heavy, we think of them as decorative, rather than utilitarian, items.

Follow the instructions below to make Cathedral Window units that can be used to make a coverlet, or combine a few into a smaller project, such as the child's pinafore, shown on page 229. Or use Cathedral Window units as borders for place mats or a table runner.

Learn To Make Cathedral Window Units

Materials:

4 (7¼") squares muslin

4 (2") squares insert fabric

Finished Unit Size: *3¼" square*

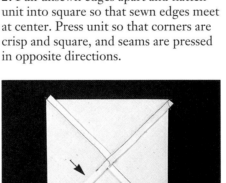

2. Pull unsewn edges apart and flatten unit into square so that sewn edges meet at center. Press unit so that corners are crisp and square, and seams are pressed in opposite directions.

4. Turn square right side out through openings and press flat. Unit will be approximately 4¾" square.

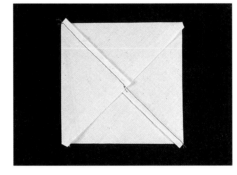

1. Fold a muslin square in half and press. Stitch ¼" seam across each short end.

3. Sew remaining raw edges together with ¼" seam, from corner to just past center seam. Then sew from opposite corner just far enough to leave 1" opening. (See arrow.)

5. Working with seam side of unit facing up, fold each corner to center and press fold to form guidelines. Repeat steps to make three more units.

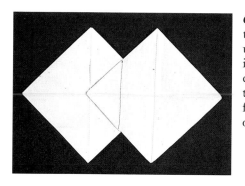

6. Place two units together, with the unseamed sides facing, aligning corners carefully. Stitch them together on folded guidelines in order to make rows.

7. Join rows together in same manner. Once rows are joined, hand-tack loose corners at center of each unit.

A

8. Place insert over seam that joins units (A).

B

9. Roll folded muslin edges over raw edges of insert and blind-stitch in place, sewing through all layers (B). Taper muslin edges at corners. Repeat with remaining inserts to complete design.

Purchase a pinafore pattern and personalize it with your own Cathedral Window panel.

Make a rectangle of Cathedral Windows (see page 228) larger than the finished-size of garment bodice. Using the garment bodice pattern, cut rectangle to pattern size. Continue by following the instructions for the garment pattern, lining bodice.

Evaluating and Exhibiting Your Work

As teachers, we encourage our students to satisfy themselves first in their quiltmaking. For most of them, quilting is a hobby, a pastime, something they do because it gives them pleasure. Do not lose sight of that fact. And if you decide to enter shows and competitions, do it for fun and for what you will learn.

Evaluating and Exhibiting Your Work

Exhibiting Your Work

Quilt shows give you an opportunity to compare your work with that of others. Events that are exhibitions only offer a great way to share your finished projects with other people without the pressure of competing, and attending a show where your quilt is on display is fun.

At a judged show, especially one with money prizes, the atmosphere is a bit different. A judge or a team of judges determines which quilt in each category is best. They also choose the Best of Show, the quilt that excels all the others in both design and workmanship.

Most quilters, once they take the plunge and exhibit their work, find it beneficial, if only to give them a deadline for actually finishing something to show! If you do decide to compete, take the time to prepare your quilt, as well as your attitude, for competition.

Preparing for Competition

Prepare Quilt. The most important thing you can do is read the contest rules carefully and comply with them to the letter. If you overlook the stated size and other requirements, judges have every right to eliminate your entry. Observe the registration and shipping deadlines, and do not wait until the last minute.

Submit Quality Photographs or Slides. In a juried quilt show, quilts to be exhibited or judged are selected in advance from photos or slides (transparencies). Show officials often ask for a detail shot as well as an overall photo. Label the slides according to show rules and send the specified number. Send slides that show your quilt to its best advantage. Poor slides may keep your quilt out of the running.

Use a camera that will produce a clear, sharp, properly exposed slide. A 35-mm camera with adjustable focus, shutter speed, and lens openings usually gives good results. Choose daylight slide film with a relatively slow speed, such as an ASA or ISO number 64, 125, or 200, rather than the faster films with higher speeds that produce grainy, less clear pictures.

Photographing outdoors on a calm, sunny morning or in early evening will give a good result. As a rule, natural lighting will generally give you the most accurate color reproduction. Choose a nondistracting background and try to position the quilt so that it is side-lit from a 45° angle. (Sun is at your side.) The side lighting will cast soft shadows and, therefore, show quilting details. If you are working indoors, be sure your quilt is within the distance limits of your flash; otherwise, the slides will be under-exposed.

Expose plenty of film and bracket the exposure, i.e., take photos at the f-stop indicated by your light meter and also at lower and higher f-stop settings. Professional photographers shoot lots of film to ensure getting at least one good picture. To be safe, shoot an entire 24- or 36-exposure roll of the quilt and details.

Clean Quilt. Make sure your quilt is clean. Look it over carefully and check that it is free of lint, threads, and pet hairs. Many judges feel that a dirty quilt entered in a show is an insult to them and the show.

Sign Quilt. Sign your quilt and also include your address and phone number, so that your quilt can be returned to you even if it is separated from the entry forms or the identification tag placed on it at the show. (See Signing Your Quilt on page 102.)

Prepare Yourself. Try not to entertain the notion that your life depends on winning a quilt contest. Be a good sport when you compete. Maintain perspective when you enter your work.

Understand the Judging Process. Judging quilts is a difficult task. Recognized experts with strong personal feelings about color, design, and workmanship make every effort to examine the entries objectively. Some judges have studied and been certified as judges by respected organizations. Others are deemed qualified because of having won significant awards or other recognition in the quilt world.

When your quilt is returned to you, you will often receive an evaluation form or critique that can help you assess your strengths and weaknesses.

Guidelines for Shipping

Have Adequate Insurance Coverage. See the following chapter for a discussion on quilt appraisal and insurance. Often your homeowner's insurance, even with a special quilt rider, does not cover quilts during shipping. You must buy extra coverage.

Pack and Address Properly. When you fold your quilt to box it, you can prevent hard creases from forming by crumpling acid-free tissue paper and stuffing it along the folds. Place the folded quilt in a cotton pillowcase and then in a plastic bag. Always use a sturdy corrugated cardboard box that is a little larger than the folded bundle. If you want your quilt returned in the same carton, write your name and address on an inside flap.

Before closing the box, lay a piece of cardboard on top of the bundle to protect the quilt or double-box it in case a sharp packing knife is used to open the box. Include a self-addressed postcard in the box so that show personnel can let you know your quilt arrived safely, or request acknowledgment of delivery from the shipper. Use plenty of strong tape to secure the box.

When addressing the package, avoid using the word "quilt." The rising value of quilts has received a lot of publicity in recent years, and thefts sometimes occur. Since a box addressed to "Hometown Quilt Show" makes its contents obvious, address your box to a person, whenever possible. If the shipper requires a listing of the contents, "custom bedcovering" is a handy phrase to use. It elevates your quilt beyond a blanket, but does not raise the red flag that the word "quilt" might.

Quilt Show Etiquette

Among quilters, respect for quilts comes with the territory. But when quilts are put on display for the general public, it is a good idea for the group holding the show to try to educate show attendees about what they can and cannot do in the exhibition hall. Here are some guidelines to consider when you display quilts. You and your quilt group may want to post show rules at the door of the show room or print up a list of "dos and don'ts." In addition to the areas of concern is the question of photography. Some show organizers do not allow flash photography, feeling that the accumulated extra light of many exposures may damage the quilt. Other shows allow electronic flash.

Example of Quilt Show Rules

1. Please do not touch the quilts. Even clean hands contain oils and acids that can harm textile fibers. Ask a "white-gloved attendant" to turn the quilt corner if you wish to see the back.
2. Please do not bring food or drink into the show.
3. Please, no smoking. Quilts absorb smoke fumes that may be harmful to the fibers.
4. Please keep children by your side. We encourage you to bring them, because they love quilts, too. But uncontrolled children may damage a quilt or distract viewers.
5. Please keep your comments about the quilts respectful. The maker may be standing nearby!
6. Please respect the judges' decisions. Their closer inspection of a particular quilt may have revealed workmanship that kept it from a ribbon status.

Collecting, Displaying, and Caring for Quilts

We who populate the quilt world feel that owning quilts is a serious responsibility. If we are fortunate enough to possess family quilts, we are intent on preserving them as a legacy for our own descendants. If we collect old, anonymous quilts, we often feel we are saving them from destruction. The quilts we make ourselves are also near to our hearts. Many quilters will admit that, after their family and friends, they cherish their quilts.

Collecting, Displaying, and Caring for Quilts

In this chapter, we offer a few ideas on collecting quilts, guidelines for safe display of quilts in your home—how to store, care for, and repair quilts—and some advice on insurance and appraisal.

Guidelines for Collecting

If you are interested in collecting quilts, here are some guidelines dealers and collectors have passed on to us.

1. Buy only quilts you like. That way, if values go down, you will still own pieces you enjoy. The quilts you collect should be intrinsically valuable to you.

2. Buy the best quality you can afford.

3. Educate yourself about quilt patterns and styles so that you can recognize common and uncommon quilts and spot areas in which a quilt may have been repaired.

4. Examine a quilt thoroughly before purchasing it.

5. Display and store quilts properly and have them appraised and insured.

Displaying Quilts

Display quilts, old or new, with thought both to preserving and enjoying them. All textiles are sensitive to light, temperature change, chemicals, dust, dirt, body oils, perfume, and smoke. A quilt, like any textile, has an estimated life expectancy. Depending on the care you provide, you can extend or shorten that life expectancy. Decorating magazines offer lots of ideas for quilt display, many of which aren't good for quilts! A few years ago, the quilt world was in an uproar when a magazine ran a photo of children jumping on an antique bed covered by a gorgeous quilt!

Display Environment

Ideal conditions for quilts include 50% humidity and 60° to 70° temperatures. Such an environment is hard to maintain in the home, but sensible use of a humidifier, a dehumidifier, air conditioning, and heat can help. Comfortable conditions for you are also good for quilts.

All light damages quilts, especially sunlight and fluorescent light, which contain ultraviolet rays. Keep quilts out of direct sunlight. To reduce light damage, apply polyester film to window panes, regulate sunlight with shades, filter fluorescent light with sleeves available from suppliers, and keep incandescent (hot) light 10 to 12 feet away from your quilt.

Choose low-traffic areas to display quilts, where people won't touch or brush against them. Also keep quilts away from windy areas. Choose locations relatively free from unpleasant odors, harmful grease, and moisture. Kitchens and bathrooms are not kind to quilts.

Of course, when handling quilts, be sure your hands are clean. Serious collectors wear clean, white cotton gloves, especially when touching rare or fragile textiles.

Wall Display

Hanging a quilt on the wall for display exposes it to lots of light, so consider rotating several quilts throughout the year so that each quilt can have a rest period.

In "Finishing Your Quilts," page 92, we described methods for sewing hanging sleeves to quilts. The purpose of a sleeve is to distribute the weight of a quilt evenly. Our instructions are for double sleeves that keep the rod or dowel from touching the quilt directly. If a quilt does not hang flat and straight, consider adding a second sleeve at the bottom of the quilt and inserting a second rod to add weight to that end. Hanging sleeves at opposite ends will also enable you to rotate the quilt to keep light distribution even.

A wooden dowel, a length of lattice stripping, PVC pipe, or a curtain rod can be inserted in the hanging sleeve to support the quilt. The rod should be slightly shorter than the width of the quilt but longer than the sleeve. Thus, the part of the rod that extends beyond the sleeve will be hidden and can be supported by nails or hooks fixed in the wall. If your support rod is unfinished wood, coat it with polyurethane sealant before using it. The sealant protects the quilt from the potentially harmful acidity of the wood.

An alternative to hanging a quilt by a sleeve is a type of wall rack currently advertised in home decorating and quilting magazines. These decorative racks feature non-damaging clamps designed for hanging textiles.

Other Ways to Display Quilts

Stack quilts on shelves in a cupboard. Line the shelves with acid-free tissue paper (see Storing Quilts, below) or seal the wood with polyurethane to put a barrier between your quilts and the acidity of the wood. Cupboard doors can be closed part of the time to protect the quilts from light.

Place quilts on quilt racks. Because of the current popularity of quilts in home decorating, many furniture stores sell free-standing floor racks that will hold several folded quilts. Place the rack out of direct light and refold quilts every few months so that light exposure is uniform. Also, be sure the wood hanging bars are sealed as above or cover them with acid-free tissue paper.

Place quilts on other furniture. Display quilts folded over the back of a sofa, on a trunk at the foot of a bed, in an antique cradle, and, of course, on the bed itself. If you want to use a quilt as a tablecloth, cover it with a clear plastic drop cloth from a hardware or paint supply store.

Storing Quilts

The first time we were involved in a local quilt show was in the late 1970s. Our club borrowed quilts from people throughout the community. They pulled 100-year-old quilts out of their closets, and the quilts were generally in mint condition. Most of them had been stored with other linens, wrapped in sheets, or folded in pillowcases. The people had taken a common sense approach to protecting their quilts, and it was successful.

The ideal way to store a quilt is spread flat, so that no creases develop. If you have a spare bedroom that can remain darkened, keep your quilts stacked flat on the bed and rotate them from time to time.

If space permits, rolling quilts on cardboard carpet tubes is the next best approach. Cover the tube with sheets of acid-free tissue paper (sources listed on page 239) or several layers of pre-washed muslin to protect the quilt from the acid in the cardboard. Roll the quilt loosely on the tube, with the pattern side toward the inside, and tie it in place with muslin strips.

Most people do not have room for either of these storage methods and must store quilts folded. When folding, place crumpled rolls of acid-free tissue paper or cotton muslin inside the folds to soften them. Then, wrap the folded quilt in an old cotton sheet, pre-washed muslin, or a pillowcase. Place the folded quilts on closet shelves, no more than two deep, if possible. You can also purchase acid-free boxes for individual storage. Check quilts periodically for damage and refold quilts every three to six months. Change the acid-free tissue paper every three years.

Since quilts need to "breathe," do not store them in plastic, because it closes out air and traps moisture. Nor should you store quilts in cedar chests unless the quilts are wrapped in cotton first, since the highly acid wood can cause brown spots on the quilt.

Insects can also damage your quilts. To protect against them, use dried artemesia (southernwood), a natural pesticide. Make a bug discourager by crumbling the dried leaves of this plant and placing them in a cloth sack. Keep the sack in the quilt storage area but do not let it touch the quilt.

Repairing Quilts

A fragile or damaged quilt that is of special historic or artistic value should be put in the hands of professional restorers or conservators. Many people, however, have older quilts that fall into the "utility" category and would like to make a few repairs themselves. Be aware, however, that anything new you do to an old quilt will probably lessen its value, even though you may prolong its life. A wise approach to such repair is to make only repairs that can be removed in such a way that the quilt can be returned to its pre-repair condition.

Use 100% cotton thread to carefully mend loose seams or re-attach loosened appliqué pieces. If pieces of fabric on the quilt are missing or worn, hand-sew patches of silk tulle or netting over the areas to prevent further damage. If you can find antique fabrics from the quilt's era or similar new fabrics, cover the worn pieces by carefully appliquéing replacement patches onto them. If you have a quilt that is in good condition except for the binding, re-bind it with fabric in keeping with the other fabrics in the quilt. You may have to remove the old binding first. Since this goes against the repair philosophy described above, weigh your options carefully.

Cleaning Quilts

"Wash-o-mania" is a disease that affects most American households. Be aware that washing, no matter how carefully done, contributes to the fading and wearing of fabrics. Clean your quilts with caution, taking into consideration the age and condition of the quilt. If an old quilt absolutely must be cleaned, use the wet cleaning method described below.

The best way to clean quilts at home is by vacuuming them, front and back, with a small hand vacuum cleaner that has a brush attachment. Spread the quilt out flat on tables that have been pushed together. Cover the quilt with nylon net and tape the net to the underside of the tables. Then vacuum on low power, using long strokes from one end of the quilt to the other.

Another way to spruce up quilts is by airing them outdoors. Cover the clothesline with clean towels so that when you hang the quilt over the line, it won't develop a hard crease. Hang the quilt over several lines if possible. Cover the quilt with a clean cotton sheet to protect it from ultraviolet sun rays and passing birds. If your clothesline is high enough and your quilt small enough, hang it without folding, using plastic clothespins spaced every four inches.

Washing or Wet Cleaning

Although quilt conservators might not approve, we wash new quilts that we have made in the washing machine and sometimes dry them in the dryer. Because of our teaching and lecturing, our quilts are handled frequently, so we wash them carefully every few years. We use Orvus WA Paste (about ⅛ cup) and wash them in a front-loading machine with cold water. (The agitator in a top-loading machine may harm the quilt.) We prefer to dry a quilt spread flat between two sheets, preferably outdoors in the shade, or dry it in a dryer set for low or no heat. Many quilters plan to wash their quilts the moment they finish them—they use cotton batts and like the crimped, old-fashioned look that washing after quilting imparts.

Wet cleaning is actually the conservator's term for washing. This type of cleaning at home, using the bathtub, is a difficult process that can take an entire day. Professional conservators have large shallow troughs at standing height that enable them to keep the quilt open.

Before undertaking wet cleaning, evaluate the condition of the quilt to be sure it is still strongly constructed. Be aware that many stains on old quilts will not come off with any type of cleaning. Make stabilizing repairs before cleaning. (See Repairing Quilts, page 237.) Also, dye-test fabrics to make sure colors will not bleed. To dye-test, use a soft clean cloth and room-temperature water. Wet the cloth and press it against one fabric to see if dye comes off. Then follow the same procedure but this time use a small amount of one of the safe detergents mentioned below on the cloth. If no color comes off, you may proceed with wet cleaning.

Choose a day that is clear and dry so that you can dry the quilt outdoors. Have an old blanket or mattress pad ready to receive the quilt. Make sure your tub is clean and rinsed free of other soaps. Use a clean cotton blanket as a cradle to support the quilt in the water during tub washing.

Steps for Washing an Antique Quilt

1. If water is hard, purchase distilled, de-ionized, filtered, or soft water. Fill bathtub or trough to a depth of 6" to 8". First rinse quilt in clear water without soap. Lower quilt into clear, tepid water. If color bleeding occurs, despite pre-testing, remove quilt as quickly as possible and dry. (See step 4.)

2. Gently rock quilt back and forth in cradle to remove surface dirt. Without taking quilt out of the bath, pull plug and drain dirty water away. If quilt appears clean, remove quilt from tub as described in step 4.

3. If quilt is not clean and it passed soap pre-test, dilute ½ ounce of non-ionic detergent, such as Orvus WA Paste (Igepal) or ½ ounce of a mild detergent, such as Ivory, in one gallon of water. Add diluted detergent to bath and gently repeat washing process. Rinse quilt six to eight times to remove all soap or detergent.

4. While quilt is in tub, use towels to gently wick excess water from body of quilt. (Never remove it from tub when it is heavy with water.) Do not squeeze or wring quilt. Lift it from tub with cradle and carry it to prepared drying area.

5. Spread quilt on pad and cover it with a white cotton sheet. Turn quilt every hour or so. Because of ground moisture, quilt may not dry completely. Finish drying process by hanging quilt on a clothesline, as described in Cleaning Quilts, page 238, for airing quilts. Do not fold or store quilt until it is completely dry.

Insurance and Appraisal for Quilts

Because each quilt is unique, if one is lost, damaged beyond repair, or stolen, it cannot be replaced. An insurance settlement enables you to purchase a replacement quilt of similar age and style or pays for the materials and time to make another.

Check with the agent who handles your homeowner's insurance policy to make sure you have adequate coverage. Usually, the agency will write a fine arts floater to cover full replacement value of the quilt. Make sure you understand the conditions of your coverage and get the agent to put all terms you agree upon in writing.

Most companies will not accept self-appraisals, but a sales receipt is proof of cost. Keep receipts for quilts you purchase. The best way to obtain adequate coverage and ensure a headache-free claim in the event of loss or damage is to have your quilts appraised by a certified quilt appraiser. For a list of certified appraisers, send an SASE to American Quilter's Society Appraiser List, Box 3290, Paducah, KY 42002-3290.

Sources for Quilt Conservation Supplies

American Quilter's Society
Box 3290
Paducah, KY 42002-3290

Conservation Materials Ltd.
1165 Marietta Way
Sparks, NV 89431

C & L Enterprises
Box 289
Quincy, IL 62306

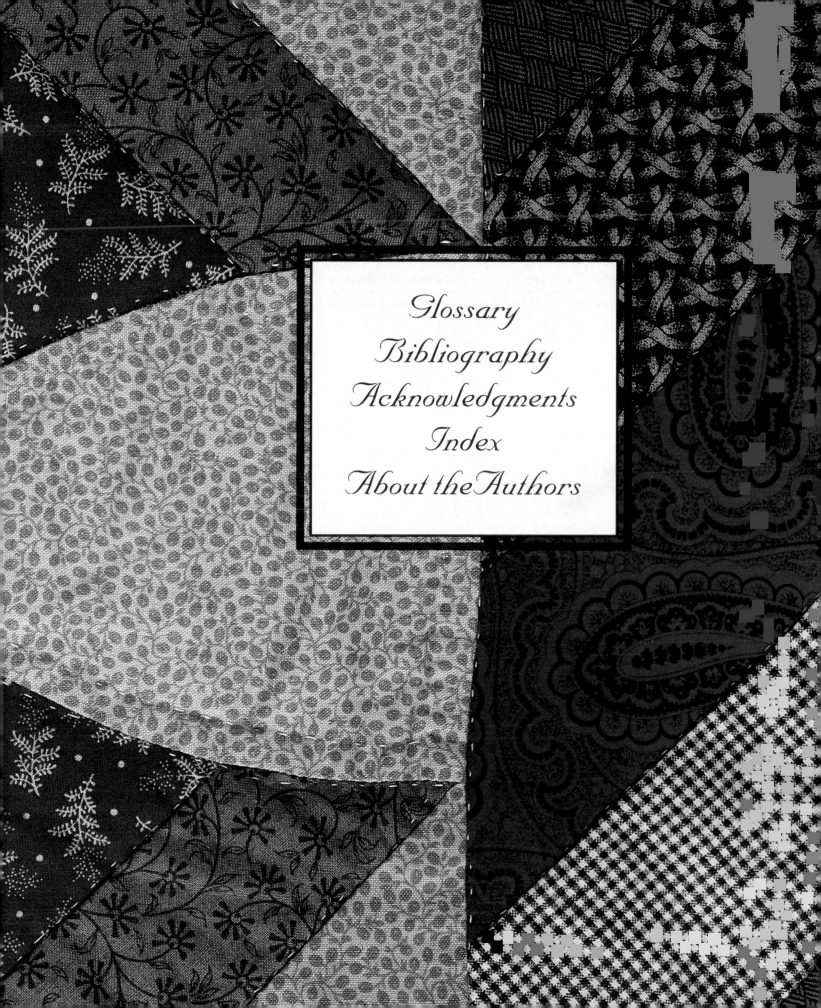

Glossary

Bibliography

Acknowledgments

Index

About the Authors

Glossary of Quilting Terms

Accent piping. A narrow flange, either plain or corded, that is usually inserted between the quilt border and binding and is made from a contrasting fabric. It can also be inserted between the inner quilt and border.

Acid-free paper. A material used for storage of quilts. It has a life expectancy of three years. Acid-free boxes, which protect for a longer period of time, are available.

Adhesive template. A reusable quilting guide that adheres to the quilt top, eliminating the marking step. The quilting follows along the edge of the template, and then template is removed.

Album quilt. A quilt in which each block is different. Some are friendship projects, in which each friend makes and signs a block with ink or embroidery. A sampler quilt by one maker can also be referred to as an album quilt.

Allover quilting. Stitching that does not follow the pieced or appliquéd pattern lines. For example, a grid of squares or diamonds may be quilted over the entire quilt.

Allover set. One-patch quilts and single-block quilts pieced in one unit.

Alternate plain block set. A block arrangement in which pieced or appliquéd blocks are alternated with plain (print or solid-colored) blocks (setting squares) in a straight or diagonal set.

Amish quilt. A quilt made by the Amish (a Mennonite sect) prior to 1940, typically of dark, solid colors and relatively simple patterns. "Amish" is also used to describe any quilt made in the style and colors of the original Amish quilts.

Appliqué. The process of sewing small pieces of fabric onto a larger piece of fabric by hand or machine.

Appliqué or bandage shears. A fabric-cutting instrument with a protruding lip that prevents accidental cutting of wrong fabric when trimming fabric from behind appliqué pieces.

Appliqué stitch. A handstitch, also called blindstitch or slip-stitch, used to secure the folded edge of fabric (appliqué) to the foundation fabric. It is also used to hand-finish the quilt binding. (See pages 23 and 130 for illustrations.)

Assembly line piecing. Piecing identical units of several blocks at the same time, instead of piecing each unit and completing one block at a time.

Background fabric. The foundation material on which appliqués are sewn.

Background quilting. Stitching that appears to run behind or underneath a main motif, whether the motif is a larger quilting design or an appliquéd piece.

Backing. The fabric used as the bottom layer (back) of the quilt.

Backstitch. A machine-stitch in reverse over previous stitches to strengthen the beginning or end of a seam. Or, handstitching taken over two or more stitches.

Backstitch loop knot. A knot that is used to end the thread for most handsewing, except hand quilting.

Baltimore-style appliqué. Appliqué patterns depicting flora and fauna, baskets, people, and architectural structures. This style originated with a group of Methodist ladies in Maryland during the mid-nineteenth century.

Basting (safety pin). The process of joining the layers of a quilt together with safety pins.

Basting (thread). The process of joining layers of fabric or the layers of a quilt with long hand stitches before quilting to keep them from shifting. It is also used to turn-under seam allowances of appliqués before stitching them in place.

Batting (batt). The fiber used as the filler between two pieces of fabric to form a quilt to provide warmth. It can be cotton, polyester, cotton-poyester blend, wool, or silk. A piece of batting for a quilt is called a batt.

Batting, glazed and bonded. Batting which is treated by a manufacturing process that stablizes the loose fibers of a batt and retards fiber migration. A glazed batt is coated on both sides with resin. A bonded batt is sprayed with resin.

Batting loft. The thickness of a batt.

Batting, needlepunched. Batting with fibers stabilized by a machine with barbed needles that pound the batt, twisting and tangling the fibers together.

Bearding. A problem associated with synthetic batts. The loose fibers of a batt tend to work their way out or migrate through the spaces between threads of woven cloth and come to rest on the quilt top, instead of breaking off. As more fibers migrate, they join and twist, forming little balls or pills.

Beeswax. The substance that is rubbed on quilting thread to stiffen, strengthen, and reduce tangling when quilting.

Between. A short needle used for quilting. The higher the number, the shorter the needle.

Bias. The diagonal grain in relation to the lengthwise and crosswise grains of a woven fabric. The true bias is at a 45° angle to the selvages. It is the direction in which the fabric has the most stretch or give.

Bias appliqué. An appliqué design that uses curved strips of bias-cut fabric. (See Celtic appliqué.)

Bias binding. The strips of fabric that are cut on the bias, joined into a single strip, and used to cover the edges and batting of a quilt. (See Binding.)

Bias-strip method for making triangle-squares. The technique in which contrasting bias strips of fabric are joined lengthwise and then cut into triangle-squares, using a 6" ruled square and a rotary cutter.

Big corners set. A block arrangement in which extra-large triangles are placed at the quilt corners in a diagonal set.

Binding. The straight-grain or bias strips of fabric used to cover the raw edges and batting of a quilt. Binding is also the term used to refer to the technique of finishing the quilt edges.

Binding, continuous bias. The fabric strips used for binding that are cut on the bias and joined to form one long strip.

Binding, double or French. A fabric strip folded lengthwise (doubled) and used to cover the raw edges and batting of a quilt.

Binding, single. A one-layer fabric strip used to cover the raw edges and batting of the quilt.

Binding, spiral. A continous fabric strip made from different-colored strips that are cut on the bias and used to cover the raw edges and batting of the quilt.

Bleeding. The loss of dye when water is applied to fabric.

Blindstitch. See Appliqué stitch.

Block. The design unit of a quilt top. Usually square, it can be made of patchwork, appliqué, or a combination.

Block-to-block set. A block arrangement without sashing, set straight or on the diagonal.

Block units. The small pieced sections or subdivisions of a block. (See Triangle-squares.)

Border. A strip of fabric or pieced strip of fabric joined to the edges of the inner quilt and used to frame it.

Border corner square. The square that is joined to the end of a border and positioned at the corner of the quilt.

Breaking-out-of-the-block set. A block arrangement in which identically-pieced blocks are placed in a block-to-block set but color selections for blocks cause the quilt to appear to be in an allover set.

Broderie perse. A French phrase meaning "embroidering chintz." Printed motifs are cut from chintz and appliquéd to a background fabric.

Butted corner seam. See Squared corner seam.

Buttonhole or blanket stitch. A hand stitch used to secure pieces in decorative hand appliqué and some *broderie perse* appliqué, and to embellish the folded edges of fabric pieces in crazy quilting.

Buttonhole-stitch appliqué. A type of appliqué in which pieces are stitched to a background fabric with a buttonhole stitch. If the stitches are close together, they become satin stitches. (See Satin stitch and Zigzag stitch.)

Cable quilting. A quilting design that resembles a rope with twisted or intertwining lines for quilting.

Calico. A medium-weight printed fabric that is popular in quilt-making because of its plain weave and small repeating designs.

Cathedral window. A novelty technique that involves placing and centering a colored fabric square on a folded and stitched muslin square.

Celtic or bias appliqué. An appliqué technique using consistent-width, folded bias strips to produce complex, curved geometric designs, like those made in eighth- to tenth-century Ireland.

Center-outward block construction method. A method for piecing of a block by beginning with the center unit and building outward.

Chain piecing. A technique for joining several fabric pairs in a chain by feeding them through the machine one after the other without lifting the presser foot or cutting threads between pairs.

Charm quilt. A patchwork quilt, usually one-patch, made of many different fabrics, no two exactly alike.

Chintz. A cotton fabric with a chemically applied glazed finish. The glazing may wash or wear off with time. It is also called polished cotton.

Chintz quilt. An early type of quilt made from chintz fabrics. Chintz appliqué work is known as *broderie perse*.

Clamshell edging. Curved "pockets" or semicircles of fabric sewn to the edge of the quilt for a novelty finish, instead of binding. The clamshells are placed either side by side or overlapping.

Clip. A small cut to ease fabric and to make it lie flat made perpendicular to the seam allowance edge and up to, but not touching, the seam line.

Color contrast in printed fabrics. The degree of color difference between the printed motifs and the background color. Printed fabrics range from small-scale, monochromatic, low-contrast fabrics to bold, multicolor, high-contrast fabrics.

Color shade. The darker value of a hue, made by adding black to a pure color. Navy is a shade of blue, and maroon is a shade of red.

Color tint. The lighter value of a hue, such as clear pastels, made by adding white to the color. Pink is a tint of red, peach a tint of orange, and lavender a tint of purple or violet.

Color tone. A dulled, grayed value of a hue formed by mixing pure colors with gray. Tan, beige, taupe, and dusty rose are examples of tones.

Color value. The lightness or darkness of a hue or color. We often make reference to three shades (light, medium, and dark) of a color when we are really referring to three values.

Color wheel. A circular arrangement of the 12 basic colors.

Combination block. A block that is composed of both appliqué and patchwork pieces.

Comforter. A bed covering that has a thick filler and is tied instead of quilted. (See Tied quilt.)

Compound patterns. Patterns that are presented with the parts connected as they will be in the finished design.

Concave curve. A curve that is rounded inward like the inside of a bowl.

Convex curve. A curve that is rounded outward like the outside of a circle.

Cool color. A calming and soothing color that tends to recede in relation to other colors. Examples: blue and green.

Corded or Italian quilting. A type of relief quilting that involves inserting a length of yarn or cording into a quilted channel. Though corded quilting originated in England, it was popularized by the Italians.

Corner triangle. A triangle that fills in at the corner of a diagonal-set quilt.

Coverlet. A woven bedspread that is sometimes quilted or made of heavy material.

Crazy patchwork (and quilt). The irregular-shaped pieces stitched to a muslin foundation in a seemingly random manner. Pieces are embellished with hand embroidery that showcases the needlework skills, and the quilt is not usually quilted.

Crib quilt. A small quilt often made for a baby or a small child.

Cross-hatching. A network of parallel quilting lines that run in two directions, forming either a grid of squares or of diamonds.

Crosswise grain. The threads in fabric that are perpendicular to the selvages. The crosswise grain has a little more stretch than the lengthwise grain.

Cut-as-you-go with fold-under-line appliqué method. A method in which appliqué fabric is marked with the appliqué pattern. The appliqué fabric is cut just before the piece is appliquéd to the background fabric.

Cut-as-you-go with freezer-paper-on-top appliqué method. A method in which a freezer-paper appliqué pattern is used as a stitching guide for needle-turned appliquéing a piece to the background fabric. The appliqué fabric is cut just before the piece is appliquéd to the background fabric.

Cutting line. The line on which a shape is cut out of the fabric.

Darning presser foot. A sewing machine attachment designed for use when the feed dogs are either lowered or covered, allowing the fabric to be guided and moved freely during free-motion machine quilting.

Diagonal-bar block construction method. A method for piecing blocks by joining triangle units to the opposite sides of a rectangle (diagonal bar) that runs from corner to corner of the block. The diagonal bar may be pieced or solid. If pieced, complete piecing of the diagonal bar before adding triangle units.

Diagonal-bar unit. A pieced square that is formed when two triangles are joined to opposite sides of a rectangle (bar unit).

Diagonal basting stitch. See Tailor's padding stitch.

Diagonal set. A block arrangement in which the sides of the blocks run at a 45° angle to the quilt sides.

Directional borders. Patchwork borders that flow in a particular direction.

Directional prints. Fabrics printed with distinct up-and-down motifs. (Striped fabric is an example.)

Easing. The process of adjusting the length of one fabric edge to match the unequal length of another fabric edge while stitching the pieces together.

Echo quilting. A type of outline quilting most often used on appliqué quilts. The appliqué motif is first quilted in-the-ditch. The next line of quilting is parallel to the first, approximately ¼" away, the third line the same distance away, and so on. Echo stippling uses the stipple quilting stitch in the same way.

Edge finishing. Any of several techniques that encase or embellish the edges of the quilt. (See Binding; Clamshell edging; Edges, self-finished; Prairie points; and Ruffled edging.)

Edges, self-finished. The process of turning under the quilt's raw edges and blindstitching the folded edges together. There is no separate binding.

Embroidery. The process of forming decorative designs with thread or yarn on fabric by hand or machine.

English paper piecing. A method of hand piecing in which fabric shapes are basted over paper templates and whipstitched together along their fabric edges.

Even-feed or walking foot. A sewing machine presser foot attachment for machine quilting that moves the top fabric through the machine at the same rate that the feed dogs move the bottom fabric.

Fabric, right side and wrong side. The front or top of the fabric is the right side. Printed fabrics and fabrics with a finish, such as chintz, have a definite right side and wrong side.

Fancies. A general quilting name for elaborate quilting designs.

Fat eighth. A 9" x 22" fabric piece.

Fat quarter. An 18" x 22" fabric piece.

Feather quilting. See Fancies.

Finger-pressing. A technique for forming guidelines for appliquéing or making seam allowances lie flat by pinching fabric between your fingers or smoothing a seam with your fingernail to form a temporary crease.

Finished size. The measurement or dimensions of a completed block or quilt without seam allowances.

Floating the blocks. A block arrangement in which the corners of the outer blocks do not reach the edges of the border, making the blocks appear to float.

Folded-star patchwork. A technique using squares of fabric folded into triangles, layered to form a star, and stitched to a background fabric.

Foundation fabric. A base piece of fabric onto which smaller fabric pieces are stitched.

Four-patch block. A block with two, four, or multiples of four units per row.

Four-triangle or Hourglass alternate block set. A block arrangement in which four triangles are sewn together to form a setting block (square) that alternates with the patchwork block. These blocks are sometimes called Hourglass blocks when light and dark triangles are adjacent to one another.

Four-triangle block construction method. A method for piecing blocks with seams that run diagonally through the block (corner to corner) in both directions. Four-triangle units are made first, and then the units are joined to complete the block.

Four-triangle unit. A pieced square that is formed by joining four triangles at their short sides.

Freedom quilt. A quilt made for a young man and presented to him upon reaching 21 years of age.

Free-motion machine quilting. The process of quilting curved and intricate designs by machine.

Freezer-paper appliqué. A technique in which freezer-paper patterns are used as seam line guides for turning under seam allowances on appliqué pieces.

Friendship quilt. A quilt made as a group project for one member of the group, with each participant making and signing a block or more for the top.

Fusible webbing. A man-made material treated with a

heat-activated adhesive that fuses fabric pieces together when pressed with a warm iron.

Goose-Chase unit. A pieced rectangle that is formed by sewing two smaller right triangles to the short sides of a larger right triangle that is twice the size of the smaller triangle.

Grain. The lengthwise and crosswise threads of a woven fabric. Lengthwise grain (parallel to the selvage) is the most stable or least stretchy fabric grain.

Grain line. An arrow or line printed on a pattern that indicates the proper alignment of the pattern on the grain of the fabric.

Grid. A network of uniformly spaced horizontal and vertical lines, used in reducing or enlarging patterns to scale. It is also a type of background quilting. (See Cross-hatching.)

Grid method for making triangle-squares. A method in which two fabrics are placed with right sides facing, a grid of squares is marked on the top fabric, diagonal lines are marked through the squares, and diagonal seams are sewn. Stitched fabrics are cut apart on all solid lines to form triangle-squares.

Hand-quilting stitch. A small running stitch that is made through all three layers of a quilt. (See page 79 for illustrations.)

Hanging sleeve. A tube of fabric sewn to the top edge of the quilt back through which a hanging rod can be inserted.

Hanging tabs. Small loops of folded fabric sewn to the top edge of the quilt through which a decorative rod can be inserted.

Hawaiian appliqué. A type of needle-turned appliqué, constructed by folding a single piece of cloth into fourths, cutting the design, and then appliquéing it to a background fabric.

Homespun. A loosely woven fabric, usually of wool or linen, hand-loomed from hand-spun yarns.

Hue. The name of the color that distinguishes one color from another, such as blue, green, etc.

Inner quilt top. The central area of a quilt without borders.

In-the-ditch quilting. A type of outline quilting that is done alongside a seam or an appliqué edge. No marking is needed for this type of quilting.

Invisible machine appliqué. The use of nylon thread, a narrow-width blind hemstitch, and a very short stitch length to stitch a fabric piece to a background fabric.

Ironing. The process of moving an iron across fabric to smooth and flatten it. Yardage is ironed before being marked and pieced. However, patchwork is pressed. (See Pressing.)

Lap quilting. The process of quilting blocks or sections of a quilt before assembling them.

Lattice strips. See Sashing.

Layered appliqué. The process of stitching appliqué pieces over one another. The pieces are appliquéd to the background fabric and to each other, working from background to foreground.

Layering. The process of spreading out and aligning the backing, batting, and top of a quilt before basting them together in preparation for quilting.

Lengthwise grain (warp threads). The fabric threads that run parallel to the selvages. Fabrics are most stable and have the least give on the lengthwise grain.

Light box. An apparatus used to enable quilters to see through dark fabrics so that they can trace patterns and designs from a paper pattern.

Linsey-woolsey quilt. A quilt constructed of a top layer of glazed wool, a batting of wool, and a bottom layer of linen.

Log Cabin. A quilt pattern in which narrow fabric strips or logs surround a center square to form a block.

Long half. A 22" x 36" piece of fabric.

Machine appliqué. A process of machine sewing appliqué pieces to the background fabric.

Masterpiece quilt. A quilt made by an accomplished quilter to show off his or her skills. Such a quilt is rarely (or never) used and may be passed down in a family along with other heirlooms.

Matching point. The place at which seam lines meet, most often at corners, represented by dots on pattern pieces.

Meander quilting. Random lines of stitching that usually do not cross each other.

Medallion quilt. A quilt with a central motif as the focal point, surrounded by multiple borders.

Memory quilt. A quilt made from clothing of a deceased person, usually a family member.

Miniature quilt. A small-scaled reproduction of a full-size quilt.

Mitered seam. A 45°-angle seam that is most often used when joining borders at corners.

Mola. A type of reverse appliqué that originated with the San Blas Indians of Panama.

Muslin. A plain-woven cotton fabric of medium weight. Unbleached muslin is naturally off-white and has small brown flecks. Bleached muslin is white.

Needle marking. A traditional method for marking a quilting design on a quilt top. The quiltmaker follows around the edge of the template with a darning needle, making a faint line.

Needle-turned appliqué. A method of hand appliqué in which the point and shank of the needle are used to fold under the raw edges of appliqués as they are stitched to the background fabric.

Needles. See Betweens and Sharps.

Needling. The process of inserting the needle through the layers when hand quilting. Fabrics and batting are sometimes described in terms of ease or difficulty of needling.

Nine-patch block. A block composed of nine units, joined in three rows of three units each.

On point. A block arrangement in which a block is placed with its corners up and down and to the sides. (See Diagonal set.)

One-patch quilt. A quilt in which the same shape, such as a hexagon, diamond, or square, is repeated.

One-way design. A print in which all the motifs, such as trees, are oriented in the same direction, creating a distinct up and down impression.

Opaque projector. A projector that enlarges patterns.

Outline quilting. Stitching that follows the outline of the patchwork or appliqué pattern.

Overcasting stitch. See Whipstitch.

Pa ndau (pronounced "pond ouw"). A type of reverse appliqué that originated with the Hmong people of Southeast Asia.

Partial piecing. A technique in which a partial seam is used to eliminate setting in a piece.

Patch. An individual fabric shape joined with other patches to make a block or a quilt.

Patchwork. The network of small pieces of fabric sewn together to form a larger piece. Creating patchwork is called piecing.

Patchwork quilt. A quilt with a top made of fabric pieces joined together to form one piece (patchwork). The patchwork may be organized in block units or an overall design.

Pattern. The printed outline for the fabric piece.

Pattern, double-line. A pattern with seam allowances marked.

Pattern, single-line. A pattern that is the finished size and does not include seam allowances. The line delineating the piece is the stitching line.

Pattern drafting. The process of drawing a pattern accurately to a specific size.

Pearl cotton. A silky-appearing cotton thread used for embroidering and tying quilts.

Permanent press. A fabric finish in which a memory is built into the fiber to reduce wrinkling.

Pieced border. A long strip of fabric of patchwork units to be joined to the inner quilt.

Piecing. A process of sewing together pieces of fabric by hand or machine to make patchwork.

Piecing diagram. A schematic guide for assembly of a patchwork block.

Piecing stitch. A stitch used to hand-piece patchwork.

Pillow tuck. The part of the quilt that will be folded underneath the bed pillow.

Pin-basting. A technique for temporarily holding fabric pieces together with pins, instead of thread.

Pin-matching. A technique for aligning the seam lines of two fabric pieces for accuracy by inserting a pin through matchpoints, marked at the beginning and end of seam lines.

Placement line. A guideline for the positioning of fabric pieces.

Pleated patchwork. A strip of fabric is aligned with a patchwork pattern and stitched to a muslin foundation square. The strip is then folded to form a pleat. Additional strips are stitched to the foundation, overlapping and covering the stitching of the previous strips.

Pouncing. A traditional method for marking quilting designs. Small holes are poked through the lines of a cardboard or paper pattern; then, powdered cinnamon or cornstarch is dusted through the holes.

Prairie points. Folded fabric triangles used as an edge finish.

Presser foot. The part of a sewing machine that holds the fabric flat against the throat plate during stitching.

Pressing. A lifting and lowering motion of the iron used to set seams and to remove wrinkles without stretching or distorting the fabric. Press, rather than iron, all seams when finished.

Prewashing fabric. The process of rinsing fabric in hot water with or without detergent to shrink it and remove sizing before cutting and piecing. After drying, steam-iron fabric.

Primary colors. The three basic colors (red, yellow, and blue) that can be combined to create the other colors on a 12-part color wheel.

Quarter-inch quilting. A type of outline quilting that is done ¼" from seams to avoid stitching through seam allowances.

Quick-cutting. The process that eliminates the steps of marking around templates and cutting pieces individually with shears. The fabric is cut into strips and pieces with a rotary cutter.

Quick-piecing. The method for machine-sewing pieces of fabric together for patchwork before they are cut into specific shapes, instead of cutting and sewing small pieces individually.

Quilt. A bedcover made of two pieces of fabric with some kind of filler between them.

Quilt back. The wrong side of a quilt.

Quilt top. The upper layer or right side of a quilt.

Quilter's knot. A knot used for most hand-sewing tasks, including quilting, appliqué, and piecing. (See page 23.)

Quilting. The small running stitches that hold the three layers of a quilt together.

Quilting design. The pattern of the stitching used to hold the layers of a quilt together.

Quilting frame. A large free-standing floor apparatus made from wood or plastic pipe that holds the layers of a quilt together during quilting.

Quilting guide bar. A sewing machine attachment that helps to space rows of straight stitching more evenly.

Quilting hoop. A small circular or oval apparatus that is used to hold the layers of a quilt together during quilting.

Quilting stencil. A firm one-piece guide that contains the quilting designs in a cutout format. A marking tool is inserted through the cutout to transfer the quilting design onto the quilt.

Quilting template. A solid, firm pattern of one quilting motif.

Quilting thread. A cotton or cotton-covered polyester thread, heavier than ordinary sewing thread, used for hand quilting.

Raw edge. The unfinished cut side of fabric.

Reverse appliqué. The technique of turning under the edges of one fabric to reveal an underlying fabric.

Reverse pattern. The mirror image of a pattern.

Right side. See Fabric, right side and wrong side.

Robbing-Peter-to-Pay-Paul quilt. A quilt in which the same patchwork block is changed by alternating colorations, opposite or positive-negative. It gives the impression that the leftover pieces from one block have been used to piece another block. The blocks are usually made from just two fabrics.

Rotary cutter and mat. The rotary cutter is a fabric cutting tool with a circular blade that cuts through several layers of fabric at once. It is best used with a thick, clear plastic ruler as a cutting guide. A cutting mat is essential to protect the work surface and preserve the blade's sharpness.

Ruching. A fabric strip that has been tucked and gathered before being appliquéd to the background fabric.

Ruffled edging. A fabric strip that has been gathered and sewn to the quilt edges for a novelty finish.

Running stitch. A handstitch used to sew pieces together temporarily and to baste turned-under seam allowances for hand appliqué. (See page 24 for illustrations.)

Sampler quilt. A quilt constructed of a collection of blocks in different patterns, usually with no pattern repeated. Blocks may be the same or different sizes.

Sashiko. A form of Japanese stitchery similar to quilting.

Sashing. The fabric that separates the blocks, framing them and making the quilt larger. There are two basic kinds of sashing: continuous and sashing with squares.

Sashing, continuous. An unseamed piece of fabric running the full length or width of the quilt between block rows. Perpendicular to the continuous sashing, short sashing is inserted to separate the blocks within each row.

Sashing, pieced. A patchwork strip of fabric inserted between the blocks.

Sashing with squares. An unseamed or patchwork strip of fabric (the length of the block) used between blocks and set with squares at block intersections. Squares may be solid or pieced.

Satin stitch. A closely spaced, side-by-side stitch, done by hand or machine, that resembles satin.

Scale. The size of one element relative to another.

Scrap quilt. A quilt, usually patchwork, made of many, instead of a few, different fabrics, often leftover from other projects.

Seam. The meeting of two pieces of fabric held together with stitching.

Seam allowance. The margin of fabric between the seam and the raw edge.

Seam line. The guideline that stitching follows.

Secondary color. A color created by mixing equal amounts of two primary colors.

Selvage. The lengthwise finished edge on each side of fabric.

Seminole patchwork. A type of strip piecing originated by the Seminole Indians, that uses strips of fabric joined lengthwise to form a strip set. The strip set is cut at intervals across seam lines to form segments, and the segments are rearranged and sewn together to form patchwork patterns.

Set or setting. The organization of the various design elements in a quilt top.

Setting-in. The process of stitching pieces into the openings between previously joined pieces.

Setting square. The plain block used between patchwork or appliquéd blocks in an alternate plain block set.

Setting triangle. A triangle used to fill in the space between blocks along the sides of a diagonal-set quilt. (Also called half-block setting triangle.)

Shade. The darker value of a hue, made by adding black to a pure color. Navy is a shade of blue.

Shadow appliqué. A technique in which motifs for appliqué are cut to the finished size and arranged on a background fabric.

Then an overlay of sheer fabric, such as organza or voile, is placed over the arranged pieces. Hand quilting along the edges of the motifs holds the pieces in position.

Sharps. General, all-purpose sewing needles that are most frequently used in appliquéing, patchwork piecing, and basting.

Signature document. A label, usually attached to the quilt backing, that includes the basic information about the quilt, such as the quiltmaker's name and the date and place the quilt was completed.

Single-block quilt. A quilt design in which one large block makes up the entire top.

Slipstitch. See Appliqué stitch.

Soap slivers or soapstone pencils. Tools which make marks that show up well on dark fabrics.

Square knot. The knot made of two reverse half-knots and used most frequently to tie a quilt. (See page 23 for illustration.)

Squared or butted corner seam. A seam that is made when one border is stitched past another at a 90° angle. The seam runs parallel to the sides of the quilt. Bindings may also be finished with this seam. (Compare Mitered seam.)

Square-within-a-square unit. A pieced square formed by joining the hypotenuse edges of four triangles to the sides of a diagonally set or on-point square.

Squaring-off end of fabric. The process of trimming one end of the fabric so that it is perpendicular to the adjacent side.

Stained-glass appliqué. A technique in which black bias strips are blindstitched over the raw edges of fabric pieces which are basted on a fabric foundation to duplicate the look of the leading in stained-glass windows.

Stenciling. The process of using a stencil to mark or paint a motif on the quilt top fabric. The motif may be a solid design used to embellish patchwork, or it may be in an outline format to make lines for quilting.

Stippling. Very closely stitched background quilting that can be done by hand or machine to create surface texture. This dense quilting flattens the background, which results in raising the motif it surrounds.

Straight of grain. See Grain.

Straight set. A block arrangement in which the sides of the blocks run parallel to the sides of the quilt.

Strip or bar set. A block arrangement in which blocks are in vertical, instead of horizontal, rows. The rows are separated by sashing that define the rows.

Strip or string patchwork. A type of patchwork in which many narrow fabric strips, traditionally called strings, are randomly joined together into strip sets. The strip sets are then cut into a variety of shapes and combined with other strip-pieced or solid shapes to make a quilt top.

Strip-piecing. A technique in which strips of fabric are cut and joined lengthwise to form a strip set (panel) of fabric strips that resemble striped fabric. The strip set is cut at intervals across seam lines to form segments. Joining these segments to form block units is also called strip-piecing.

Strip set. A panel of two or more strips joined lengthwise to form one piece.

Tailor's chalk pencil. A marker used to transfer a quilting design onto a quilt. The marks rub off as the quilt is stitched.

Tailor's padding stitch. A stitch used to baste together the layers of a quilt.

Tall-triangle unit. A pieced square formed by joining two small triangles to the sides of a large triangle.

Template. A firm pattern, usually made from vinyl (plastic) or posterboard, used as a guide for marking and transferring patchwork or appliqué shapes onto fabric. Templates may be finished-size or include seam allowances.

Thimble. A metal or leather finger shield to protect the finger from needle pricking during stitching. For hand quilting, a thimble with indentations on top is recommended to guide the needle and prevent it from slipping.

Thread basting. See Basting.

Tied quilt. A type of quilt in which yarn or thread ties are used to secure layers of the quilt, instead of quilting stitches. Ties may be on the front or on the back. The process is also called tufting. A tied quilt is also called a comforter or a tufted quilt.

Trapunto. A quilting technique that raises the quilting design in relief by stuffing from behind.

Trapunto needle. A 6" needle with a blunt point and large eye, used for inserting yarn through the quilt backing and pulling it through the areas for stuffing.

Traveling. A method for moving the quilting needle from one point to another through the batting.

Triangle-squares. A pieced square formed by joining two triangles at their hypotenuses.

Tufted quilt. See Tied quilt.

Tufting. See Tied quilt.

Two-bar unit. A pieced square or rectangle formed by joining two rectangles at their long sides.

Two-block set. A block arrangement in which one type of patchwork block is alternated with another type of patchwork block, often resulting in an interesting secondary design. Popular two-block sets are Irish Chain and Snowball.

Two-triangle alternate block set. A block arrangement in which blocks are alternated with blocks made from light and dark triangles. The Barn Raising set is an example.

Two-way fabric designs. A print in which half of the motifs are oriented in one direction, and the remainder are oriented in the opposite direction.

Unit-row construction method. A method for piecing a block in which the small block units are joined into rows and then the rows are joined.

Utility quilt. A quilt made for everyday use, generally in a simple pattern involving no elaborate sewing skills.

Walking foot. See Even-feed foot.

Warm color. A visually stimulating and exciting color that tends to advance in relation to other colors. Examples: yellows, oranges, and reds.

Warp. The threads that run the length of a woven fabric.

Weft. The threads that run across a woven fabric.

Whipstitch. An overcasting stitch used most often to join pieces in the English paper-piecing method.

Whole-cloth quilt. A quilt made from one large piece of fabric, usually a solid color, that is quilted only. Neither patchwork nor appliqué is used to decorate the quilt top.

Wrong side. See Fabric, right side and wrong side.

Yardage. An amount of fabric, measured in yards.

Yarn needle. A long, thick needle with a blunt point and a big eye, used in tying quilts and executing trapunto.

Yo-yo patchwork. A novelty technique in which fabric circles are gathered and flattened to form rosettes or yo-yos. The yo-yos can be individually stitched to a block but are most often tacked together at their folded edges.

Zigzag set. A block arrangement in which blocks are set on point and arranged in vertical rows with large and small setting triangles. Rows that begin and end with full blocks alternate with rows that begin and end with half blocks. This set is also known as Picket Fence and Streak of Lightning.

Zigzag stitch. A side-to-side machine stitch that is used to cover the raw edges of appliqués and join them to a background fabric. The width of the stitch can vary from $1/16$" to $3/8$". The length of the stitch can be spaced so closely that the side-to-side threads touch and form satin stitches.

Bibliography

Beyer, Jinny. *The Art and Technique of Creating Medallion Quilts*. McLean, VA: EPM Publications, 1982.

Beyer, Jinny. *Patchwork Patterns*. McLean, VA: EPM Publications, Inc., 1979.

Beyer, Jinny. *The Quilter's Album of Blocks and Borders*. McLean VA: EPM Publications, Inc., 1980.

Birren, Faber. *Creative Color*. West Chester, PA: Schiffler Publishing, Ltd., 1987.

Brackman, Barbara. *An Encyclopedia of Pieced Quilt Patterns*. Lawrence, KS: Prairie Flower Publishing, 1984.

Brackman, Barbara. *Clues in the Calico*. McLean, VA: EPM Publications, Inc., 1989.

Bradkin, Cheryl Greider. *The Seminole Patchwork Book*. Atlanta, GA: Yours Truly, Inc., 1980.

Bullard, Lacy Folmar, and Betty Jo Shiell. *Chintz Quilts: Unfading Glory*. Tallahassee, FL: Serendipity Publishers, 1983.

Colby, Averil. *Patchwork*. London: B.T. Batsford Ltd.; Newton Center, MA: Charles T. Branford Co., 1958.

Colby, Averil. *Quilting*. New York: Charles Scribner's Sons, 1971.

Flynn, John. "Dots and Dashes, Quilting Experiments in the Art of Stippling." *Threads* (June/July, 1991):38-39.

Fons, Marianne. *Fine Feathers*. Lafayette, CA: C & T Publishing, 1988.

Fons, Marianne, and Elizabeth Porter. *Classic Quilted Vests*. Atlanta, GA: Yours Truly, Inc., 1982.

Haders, Phyllis. *The Warner Collector's Guide to American Quilts*. New York: The Main Street Press, 1981.

Hargrave, Harriet. *Heirloom Machine Quilting*. Westminster, CA, Burdette Publications, 1987.

Hargrave, Harriet. *Heirloom Machine Quilting*. Lafayette, CA: C & T Publishing, 1990.

Haywood, Dixie. *The Contemporary Crazy Quilt Project Book*. New York: Crown Publishers, Inc., 1977.

Holstein, Jonathan. *The Pieced Quilt, An American Design Tradition*. Greenwich, CT: NY Graphic Society, Ltd. , 1973.

"How to Make a Quilt, Easy Lessons for Beginners. Lesson No. 6A: Choosing Fillers and Linings." *Quilter's Newsletter Magazine* (November–December, 1984): 23.

Hughes, Trudie. *Template-free Quiltmaking*. Bothell, WA: That Patchwork Place, 1986.

Itten, Johannes. *The Elements of Color*. New York: Van Nostrand Reinhold Company, 1970.

Katzenberg, Dena S. *Baltimore Album Quilts*. Baltimore: The Baltimore Museum of Art, 1983.

Leman, Bonnie, and Judy Martin. *Taking the Math Out of Making Patchwork Quilts*. Wheatridge, CO: Moon Over the Mountain Publishing Company, 1981.

Linch-Zadel, Lauri. "Wool Batts: From Sheep to Quilt." *Quilter's Newsletter Magazine*. (May, 1986): 34–35 & 49.

Marston, Gwen, and Joe Cunningham. *Sets and Borders*. Paducah, KY: Collector Books, 1987.

Martin, Nancy. *Back to Square One*. Bothell, WA: That Patchwork Place, 1988.

McCloskey, Marsha. *Lessons in Machine Piecing*. Edited by Liz McGehee. Bothell, WA: That Patchwork Place, 1990.

McClun, Diana, and Laura Nownes. *Quilts Galore!* San Francisco: The Quilt Digest Press, 1990.

McClun, Diana, and Laura Nownes. *Quilts! Quilts!! Quilts!!!* San Francisco: The Quilt Digest Press, 1989.

McKelvey, Susan. *Color for Quilters*. Atlanta, GA: Yours Truly, Inc., 1984.

Montano, Judith. *The Crazy Quilt Handbook*. Lafayette, CA: C & T Publishing, 1986.

Nihon Vogue Staff. *Sashiko: Traditional Japanese Quilt Designs*. Tokyo: Nihon Vogue Publishing Company, 1989.

O'Brien, Sandra L., ed. *Great American Quilts 1987*. Birmingham, AL: Oxmoor House, 1987.

Orlofsky, Patsy, and Myron Orlofsky. *Quilts in America*. New York: McGraw-Hill, 1974.

Orlofsky, Patsy. "The Collector's Guide for the Care of Quilts in the Home." *The Quilt Digest* 2 (1984): 58–69.

Osler, Dorothy. *Traditional British Quilts*. London: B. T. Batsford Ltd., 1987.

Patera, Charlotte. *The Appliqué Book*. Des Moines, IA: Meredith Corporation, 1974.

Penders, Mary Coyne. *Color and Cloth*. San Francisco: The Quilt Digest Press, 1989.

Porter, Liz, and Marianne Fons. *Classic Basket Quilts*. Paducah, KY: American Quilter's Society, 1991.

Protecting Your Quilts, An Owner's Guide to Insurance, Care and Restoration, and Appraisal. Paducah, KY: American Quilter's Society, 1990.

Reddick, Mary. "The Batting Story." *Quilter's Newsletter Magazine*. (March, 1986):34–35.

Ritter, Vivian. "Stipple Quilting." *Quilter's Newsletter Magazine*. (September, 1986):46–47.

Rivers, Beverly, and Elizabeth Porter, eds. *Better Homes and Gardens Special Patchwork*. Des Moines, IA: Meredith Corporation, 1989.

Rodgers, Sue H. *Trapunto, The Handbook of Stuffed Quilting*. Wheatridge, CO: Moon Over the Mountain Publishing Company, 1990.

Safford, Carleton L., and Robert Bishop. *America's Quilts and Coverlets*. New York: E.P. Dutton, 1980.

Seward, Linda. *The Complete Book of Patchwork, Quilting and Appliqué*. New York: Prentice Hall Press, 1987.

Sienkiewicz, Elly. *Baltimore Beauties and Beyond, Studies in Classic Album Quilt Appliqué, Vol. 1*. Lafayette, CA: C & T Publishing, 1989.

Acknowledgments

The authors would like to acknowledge and thank the following:

Jan Ankeny, Winterset, Iowa, for making the Take the Night Train quilt.
Kurt and Martha Aschim, Marinette, Wisconsin, for lending us their Mariner's Compass wall quilt.
Eugenia Barnes, Marcellus, New York, for helping us with information on display and care of quilts.
Bernina America, 534 W. Chestnut, Hinsdale, IL 60521 for lending us top-of-the-line sewing machines.
Dorothy Crowdes, Winterset, Iowa, for making the yo-yo table topper.
Jo Diggs, Portland, Maine, for providing the design and instructions for the scenic layered appliqué project.
Luella Fairholm, Winterset, Iowa, for quilting.
Marty Freed, Winterset, Iowa, for making the Little Princess whole-cloth baby quilt.
Helen Young Frost, Tucson, Arizona, for the loan of the antique Ocean Waves quilt.
Lois Gottsch, Omaha, Nebraska, for suggestions for "Beyond Basic Borders and Settings."
Julie Hart, Des Moines, Iowa, for designing and making Julie's Baltimore Basket wall quilt.
Bettina Havig, Columbia, Missouri, and Silver Dollar City, Branson, Missouri, for sharing information on evaluating quilts.
Lelia Neil for long hours spent as our hand model.
Norwood Looms, P.O. Box 167, Freemont, MI 49412, for use of a floor frame and quilting hoop.
Omnigrid, 3227-B 164th SW, Lynnwood, WA 98037, for supplying us with rulers.
Janet Rabe, Ottumwa, Iowa, for quilting.
Kathy Russi, Des Moines, Iowa, for designing and making the Hawaiian Breadfruit quilt.
Toni Smith, Springfield, Missouri, for quilting.
Jan Snelling of The Vermont Patchworks, Box 229, Shrewsbury, VT 05738, for providing the sample tools and supplies for quiltmaking.
Fern Stewart, Des Moines, Iowa, for quilting.
Katie Stoddard for photostyling on pages 14, 16, 19, and 229.
Martha Street, Winterset, Iowa, for making the Sweetheart baby quilt.
Evalee Waltz, Winterset, Iowa, for quilting.
We would also like to thank the Winterset Art Center, where we constructed Americana I and II quilts, as well as the following persons who loaned us quilts: Lloyd and Venita Fons, Daphne Hedges, Kathy Herzberg, and Donald and Ilene Moore.
Special thanks goes to our excellent editor, Sandra O'Brien, and all of the staff at Oxmoor House, and to our families, for their continued support.

Index

About the Authors

Marianne Fons and Liz Porter met in a beginners' quilting class in Winterset, Iowa, in 1976. After the class ended, the students continued to get together and formed the Heritage Quilters, a ten-member club that meets monthly in a member's home. When the club sponsored a quilt show a year or so later, many more local people expressed a desire to learn to quilt. Marianne and Liz, still fledgling quilters themselves, agreed to teach classes—only if they could work as a team to boost each other's confidence.

Over the next few years, the two women taught beginner and intermediate-level classes to hundreds of students, at the same time honing their own sewing and teaching skills. Their collaboration led to the desire to put their English degrees to use writing instruction booklets for quilters. *Classic Quilted Vests* was published in 1982 and sold over 150,000 copies. They wrote *Classic Basket Patterns* in 1984 (republished in 1991 as *Classic Basket Quilts*). *Let's Make Waves* was released in 1988.

Liz Porter and Marianne Fons

In the late 1980s, Liz was a contributing craft book editor with Better Homes and Gardens Books and worked on several projects such as *New Patchwork and Quilting*, *Creative American Quilting*, *1988 Christmas Crafts*, *1990 Christmas Crafts*, and *Special Patchwork*.

Marianne's quilt, *Lady Liberty Medallion*, was the Iowa state winner in the 1986 Great American Quilt Contest honoring the Statue of Liberty. In 1987, she authored *Fine Feathers, A Quilter's Guide to Customizing Traditional Feather Quilting Designs*. Her *World Peace* quilt won Best Overall Workmanship at the 1988 International Quilt Expo in Austria.

Articles by or about the two women have appeared in *Creative Ideas for Living*, *Threads*, *The Quilt Digest*, *Quilter's Newsletter Magazine*, *Midwest Living*, *Crafts*, and *McCall's Country Quilting*. They are contributing editors for *American Quilter* (the quarterly publication of the American Quilter's Society). Both have served on the board of their state's quilting guild—Liz as president and Marianne as newsletter editor—and hold life memberships in that organization.

They served on the steering committee of the Iowa Quilts Research Project, from 1987 to 1990, an effort that registered some 3,000 pre-1925 quilts in their state. In 1991, Liz became a certified quilt appraiser. Marianne has served as the secretary of the American International Quilt Association and as a member of the advisory board of the Virginia Quilt Museum.

Well-known for their fine-quality teaching, Marianne and Liz travel throughout the United States, both as a team and individually, presenting lectures and workshops to quilt guilds, and at quilt shops and symposiums.